PLANET INTERNET

PLANET INTERNET

Windcrest®/ McGraw-Hill

New York San Francisco Washington, D.C. Auckland Bogotá Caracas Lisbon London
Madrid Mexico City Milan Montreal New Delhi San Juan Singapore Sydney Tokyo Toronto

STEVE RIMMER

This book is printed on 50% recycled paper (20% post-consumer, 30% pre-consumer).

Product or brand names used in this book may be trade names or trademarks. Where we believe that there may be proprietary claims to such trade names or trademarks, the name has been used with an initial capital or it has been capitalized in the style used by the name claimant. Regardless of the capitalization used, all such names have been used in an editorial manner without any intent to convey endorsement of or other affiliation with the name claimant. Neither the author nor the publisher intends to express any judgment as to the validity or legal status of any such proprietary claims.

© 1995 by Windcrest.
Published by Windcrest, an imprint of McGraw-Hill, Inc.
The name "Windcrest" is a registered trademark of McGraw-Hill, Inc.

Printed in the United States of America. All rights reserved. The publisher takes no responsibility for the use of any of the materials or methods described in this book, nor for the products thereof.

pbk 1 2 3 4 5 6 7 8 9 DOW/DOW 9 9 8 7 6 5 4
hc   1 2 3 4 5 6 7 8 9 DOW/DOW 9 9 8 7 6 5 4

Library of Congress Cataloging-in-Publication Data

Rimmer, Steve.
    Planet Internet/by Steve Rimmer.
      p.   cm.
    Includes index.
    ISBN 0-07-053014-9   ISBN 0-07-053015-7 (pbk.)
   1. Internet (Computer network)   I. Title.
TK5105.875.I57R46   1994
004.6'7—dc20   94-27583
                CIP

Acquisitions editor: Brad J. Schepp
Editorial team: John C. Baker, Book editor
                Robert E. Ostrander, Executive editor
                Joann Woy, Indexer
Designer: Jaclyn J. Boone
Production team: Katherine G. Brown, Director
                 Brian Allison, Computer art coordinator
                 Linda M. Cramer, Proofreader
                 Wanda S. Ditch, Desktop operator
                 Jan Fisher, Desktop operator
                 Ruth Gunnett, Computer artist
                 Linda L. King, Proofreader
                 Rose McFarland, Desktop operator
                 Stephanie Myers, Computer artist
                 Janice Stottlemyer, Computer artist
                 Toya Warner, Computer artist
                 Brenda Wilhide, Computer artist
Cover copywriter: Cathy Mentzer

*For David and Nancy
and something to spread on toasted paper*

About the author*

Steve Rimmer—not his real name—lives on a 90' restored sailing yacht named *Sea Witch* with his wife Megan—not her real name either—and a Bengal tiger named Fluffy. He spends much of the year in the south Pacific searching for lost seventeenth-century Portuguese trading vessels, a favorite hobby. He speaks 11 languages, not counting Etruscan. At various times, he has worked as a mercenary in the Belgian Congo, a pilot, a nuclear physicist, two separate brain surgeons, a mendicant flute player with a small philharmonic orchestra, the god of a tribe of hyperintelligent penguins, and an employee of the CIA. He has written over 300 books on subjects ranging from sexual dysfunction in leguminous vegetables caused by traumatic early crop rotation to a detailed analysis of telephone styling as it applies to cultural longevity. The latter work earned him a Pulitzer prize, which he declined. His current projects include translating Virgil's *Aeneid* into jive.

*mostly lies

Acknowledgment

A few words are hardly sufficient to describe the contribution of Jackie Boone to this book. She's responsible for its overall design, and for most of the graphics you'll see over the next few hundred pages. The reason that *Planet Internet*'s pages look as if someone has spent hundreds of hours hand crafting every one is because she actually did. Jackie herself appears in several places throughout this book.

Contents

Preface xv
   If you don't like it don't look at it   xvii
   If it's well past midnight...   xviii

Introduction 1
   Citizenship: *something else for sociologists to talk about at parties*   4
   The nature of "things" on the Internet   5
   Newsgroups   6
   A word about pictures   11
   Electronic mail   12
   Anonymous FTP sites   15
   Telnet   19
   Gopher   20
   Finger   21
   The obligatory closing remarks   22
   Author's note   22

A cappella music 23
Acoustic guitar music 23
Acronyms 25
Airlines 26
Alcohol 29
Alternative medicine 30
Anglo-Saxon literature 31
Animation 33
Antiques 34
Arcana arcanorum 35
Archery 37
Audio 40
Babylon 5 43
Bagpipes 44
Bass playing 46
Beer 47
Bicycles 50
Big Book of Mischief 51

Birds   52
Bizarre   53
Body piercing   56
Bonsai   57
Books   59
Books at Wiretap   59
Project Gutenberg   61
British comedy   62
Buy and sell   63
Caffeine   65
Cars   65
Cathouse archives   67
Cats   69
Celtic music   70
Church of the SubGenius   71
Non sequitur   74
CIA World Factbook   75
Classical music   76
Dear Prez   78
Clinton jokes   79
Clipper   80
Coca-Cola   83
Coffee house   85
Coke servers   87
Compact discs   89
Complaints   90
Concerts on the Road   91
Condoms   93
Conspiracies   93
Crafts   95
Crowley   95
Cybersleaze   96
Answers   97
Dead Sea Scrolls   99

Destroy the Earth   100
Devilbunnies   101
Devil's Dictionary   103
Discographies   105
Discordia   105
Dogs   107
Drinks   108
Drugs   109
Early music   111
Electronic Frontier Foundation   113
Electronic newsstand   116
Enya   116
Equestrians   117
Erotic literature   119
Erotic pictures   122
Esperanto   123
Events of the Day   124
Evil   126
Extremists and activists   128
Fanny Hill   131
Flying saucers   132
Food on the Internet   133
G. Gordon Liddy   135
Grateful Dead   136
Guns   137
Heraldry   141
Herbs   142
Home brewing   143
Illuminati   145
The Internet Mall   147
Japan   149
Jazz   152
Juggling   153
Jumping from great heights   154

Laser discs   155
Letterman   157
Lewis Carroll   158
Library of Congress   160
CNS, Inc. gopher service   162
Limericks   163
Lute music   165
Magick   169
McDonald's   172
Monty Python's Flying Circus   174
Movies   175
Scandal rocks toontown   176
Murphy's Laws   178
Oculis Exciditis Porcus Dimidius Facti   181
Origami   182
Pagans   185
Pave the earth   188
Personal ads   190
Photography   194
Pirate radio   196
Political correctness   197
The Prisoner   199
Quotations   201
Raves   205
Red Dwarf   206
Rocky Horror Picture Show   208
Rumors   209
Satanism   213
Satellite television   215
Science fiction   217
Sex talk   220
Society for Creative Anachronism   223
Song lyrics   225
Spam   226

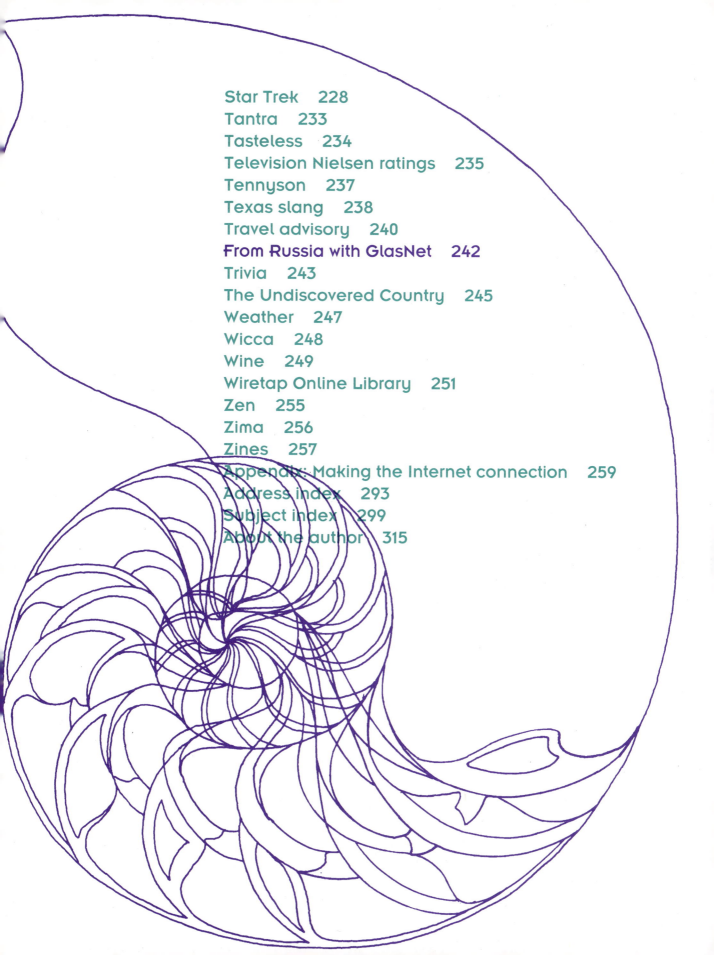

Star Trek 228
Tantra 233
Tasteless 234
Television Nielsen ratings 235
Tennyson 237
Texas slang 238
Travel advisory 240
From Russia with GlasNet 242
Trivia 243
The Undiscovered Country 245
Weather 247
Wicca 248
Wine 249
Wiretap Online Library 251
Zen 255
Zima 256
Zines 257
Appendix: Making the Internet connection 259
Address index 293
Subject index 299
About the author 315

Preface

Imagine walking into a library so huge that it's impossible to see to the ends of the rows of books due to the curvature of the earth. The total number of volumes in such a place would be uncountable. If your object in being there was simply to find something interesting to read, you might well spend the rest of your life at the task without getting past the letter A.

The most scholarly approach to this fantastic library would be to work your way through as many books as possible until you happened upon what you were looking for. Aside from leaving you dead and your quest most likely unfulfilled, this would most certainly work. A far less scholarly approach would be to find people who seemed to be reasonably intelligent and ask them for their opinion of where some interesting books might be found. You'd want to ask them in a very faint whisper, of course, this being a library.

Were you to live long enough, searching through all the books in the library would unquestionably avail you of the most interesting books in the place. Asking the opinion of a total stranger probably would not, although you'd get to find something approaching the books that you were after with enough of your lifetime left to actually read them.

This is one of those instances in which it's better to compromise and be alive than to seek perfection and die trying. The universe is full of such things, which is perhaps why camels, four-cylinder engines, and liberals exist.

The Internet is a library of sorts and perhaps one of dimensions not all that far removed from the hypothetical library that I've been discussing. As of this writing it has over thirty million users, growing at a rate of well over a million per month. It's relatively easy to access, but once you're through the doors, as it were, finding what you want can be singularly daunting. At least a library would probably have directions taped to the ends of the book shelves.

Originally set up to do academic and military research, the Internet has broadened to encompass virtually every sphere of human endeavor, from making wine to designing buildings to having it off behind seedy bars in the parts of town that people usually wash their hands after mentioning. Aside from being a research tool of global dimensions and a communication medium that will carry western civilization proudly into the twenty-first century—and all the other things the more serious guides to the Internet say of it—the Internet is a fabulous place to go and have a good time.

That's what this book is about. While most users of the Internet eventually find some of its more entertaining features, this book will take you directly to them. It also will provide you with enough background for the more esoteric or exotic Net resources to help you decide whether you want to spend a few hours learning more about them.

Actually, it will take you directly to some of them. *Planet Internet* is not an exhaustive survey of the entertaining bits of the Internet; it would have come with wheels attached to it if it were. Rather, it's my opinion of what constitutes the most interesting things to do on the Net. It probably won't turn out to entirely match your opinion on these matters, but it will give you a leg up on surfing the Net while you still are young enough to enjoy doing so.

The most fundamental thing to keep in mind about the Internet is that no book, including this one, really can describe it for you. It has to be experienced. In fact, it has to be experienced daily if you're really to become a part of the Internet, because it all changes so fast. Consider that if one percent of the users of the Internet were to post a message this morning that might be of interest to you, you'd have upwards of 300,000 articles to read today.

The Internet doesn't work quite this way, of course, or no one would ever get anything done on it.

Before you can use this book or any other Internet guide, you'll require access to the Net and some understanding of the software that mediates between you and it. The Introduction of this book will help in this respect, but one of the salient characteristics of the Internet is that your interface to it need not look anything like mine. Before you can use the Internet, you must learn to use your Internet software.

Beginning to work with any new piece of software is a bit daunting. Beginning to work with something the size of the Internet might seem all the more so. You might want to keep in mind that, while the Internet is large, it actually is made up of a manageable number of relatively simple entities that occur multiple times. Secondly, most Internet access software has been written to be easy to use and reasonably user-friendly.

Learning to use the Internet—at least to the degree that you can access its basic elements and generally know what's going on—is arguably less involved than learning to use MS-DOS, Microsoft Windows, or the Macintosh Finder.

P
R
E
F
A
C
E

If you don't like it don't look at it

The Internet is a computer model of the real world. By comparison, television and most of the other conventional media are a computer model of Disney World.

As will be discussed in detail in the Introduction—and as will certainly become apparent as soon as you start reading through the listings that form the bulk of *Planet Internet*—there are no restrictions as to what can be said or distributed over the Internet. Far from there being no formal code of behavior on the Net, at least as it pertains to the contents of things appearing there, even genuine legal statutes that might pertain to the country that you live in are all but impossible to enforce over the Internet.

The result of this unprecedented degree of liberty is that the responsibility for protecting yourself from things that you might not want to read or see reverts from the hands of "the government" or "society" to whatever hands are on your keyboard. If you follow the arms that they're attached to and find they're yours, you'll know who's in charge of your destiny on the Internet.

If you connect to the Internet, you are tacitly accepting responsibility for everything that happens next.

In a world in which almost everything is rated, regulated, and monitored, the freedom of the Net will be refreshing to most of its users. However, this sort of freedom has seen material appear on the Internet that some users might find objectionable. This includes a lot of very explicit sex—erotic documents, erotic graphics, and more recently, erotic digitized sounds—extreme political views, unconventional religions, ideas about race and sexual preference that you might find a bit unpalatable, and so on.

For most of us, dealing with books, movies, videos, albums, or Internet resources that are offensive can be handled by the rule "If you don't like it, don't look at it." Find the command for your computer that clears the screen and use it if something really nasty shows up. Some people don't see things this way; the Internet might not be a very good choice if you consider yourself one of them.

It's been suggested that, if you have children, you should make very certain you never let them anywhere near a computer with access to the Internet. I'm not sure I'd agree with this. Disney World probably is a very nice place, but they can't live there forever. You might want to endeavor to be around when they use the Net, however.

You also might want to endeavor to be around when they read this book.

If it's well past midnight . . .

Planet Internet will provide you with a guide to the recreational facilities of the Internet. These vary, and not everything here will prove recreational to all users of the Net. Some of the resources to be discussed really are pretty serious, unless you apply them to less than serious uses. If you like to read, for example, you'll find the Library of Congress Internet server to be vastly entertaining—no matter how dry and stuffy it might seem in theory.

Alternately, if recreation for you involves writing haiku poetry about exotic building materials, you'll find somewhere on the Net to explore that pastime as well.

I hope you enjoy your time on the Net and that you still manage to get some work done as well over the next few weeks. The Internet can become vastly more interesting than whatever it is you're being paid to do. Be warned: if you suddenly look up from your monitor and find it's well past midnight, you've been on the Net a bit too long.

As a final note, a lot of what appears in this book isn't what anyone would call politically correct. Some of it has been quoted directly from the Internet, which probably explains why it's the way it is. At least, it will once you've spent a few hours using the Net. The rest is my own political incorrectness, of which I'm fairly proud. When it's no longer permissible to stand in polite company and wish death upon cats, confusion upon those liberals who aren't already confused, and bright yellow paint upon Gucci shoes, it's probably about time we all had chips implanted in our heads.

Our differences are what make us worth talking to. Nowhere is this more apparent than on the trackless miles of virtual space that is the Internet.

Steve Rimmer
alchemy@accesspt.north.net

Introduction

The notion of computer networks seems to have become a subconscious part of our culture over the previous decade or so. Perhaps they became commonplace with the advent of bank machines. Personal computers need not be quite as personal as they once were.

The Internet is the biggest computer network in the known universe. As of this writing, it embodies over 30 million users, growing at a rate of over one million per month. It also is the most unusual cultural entity ever to emerge from the collective consciousness of human beings. It's analogous to nothing else that has ever existed. Unlike every other group effort that human beings have organized—from hunting parties on the Serengeti twenty thousand years ago to congressional subcommittees—the Internet has no leaders, no central authority, and no overt rules.

To use the Internet—or perhaps more correctly, to become a citizen of the Internet—it's important to understand what it really is. Most discussions of the Internet begin by touching on what it's not. This one won't be all that different. Human beings like to define the unfamiliar by analogies to things that they presently understand. This is likely to be misleading in the case of the Internet, because it appears much more like conventional networks than it really is.

Let's begin with a bit of what the Internet isn't.

As I write this, if I were to walk down the hall, I'd be able to see the blinking modem lights of the Alchemy Mindworks support bulletin board system. This is a dial-up computer network—albeit a very small one—that people who use Alchemy Mindworks' software can access to get updates, patches, and online help. Most software companies have something similar.

A bulletin board system is an archetypal model for a computer network. It has a defined function, finite resources, and a system operator who specifies and enforces the network's rules. In some cases, it also has a specific commercial interest; some bulletin boards want money to grant you access to their facilities.

If someone were to call our bulletin board and leave public messages advertising erotic pre-Colombian art or asking after a missing cat, they would be deleted by the system operator, as these messages would violate the published rules of the network.

There are a number of larger dialup networks, such as CompuServe, that have multiple purposes. While it's not structured this way physically, CompuServe can be thought of as a network of special-purpose bulletin boards. Most of them have commercial sponsors or are sponsored by CompuServe itself to interest people in spending time—and hence connect time charges—in CompuServe's various forums.

Having logged into CompuServe, you might GO ALDUS to get help with using your PageMaker software or GO NEWAGE to discuss how best to celebrate the summer solstice.

CompuServe has defined rules—for example, "don't upload copyrighted material" and "pay your bill or you will be denied access." It has a central administration in Columbus, Ohio, to enforce its rules, manage the finances of CompuServe, and administer the network in general.

CompuServe works like a big electronic country. It has a government, citizens, laws, a source of revenue, and so on. Like most Western governments, CompuServe's largest concern is CompuServe. It wants to keep you, its subscriber, happy; however, more than this, it wants to make sure it collects its connect charges. In fairness, one can hardly blame it for this; CompuServe is a business.

Imagine a leaderless country, or better still, a leaderless planet. Imagine a huge alien spacecraft appearing one afternoon, beaming up all the politicians and vanishing, never to be heard from again. Before you consider the consequences of this singular event, just enjoy the thought for a moment.

Without a central authority, everyone would become responsible for his or her own actions and requirements. With no arbitrary laws and no one to enforce them if there were any, the only limits on peoples' actions would be their own individual consciences and the pressure of public displeasure or public censure.

This isn't a terribly workable model in the real world, because public censure won't stop someone who decides to steal your car. It really works only if there's some sort of technological restriction prohibiting extreme action or if everyone in the community is reasonably well behaved or can be held accountable for their actions.

This is the sort of stuff sociologists talk about at parties, which is to some extent why so few of them get invited out.

The Internet is something of a leaderless planet, although unlike our model of a real leaderless planet, it's a highly functional society. It works because its participants embody a mixture of accountability to their peers, consciences, and technological restrictions on extreme actions.

The Internet is based on a communications "backbone" originally set up by the United States Department of Defense back in 1969. In its simplest terms, this is a place to connect computers so that they can talk to each other. It assumes very little of the computers in question and is an almost mindless entity. Unlike CompuServe, for example, which provides its users with prompts and messages and a complete graphical user interface for a slight additional fee, the Internet backbone is really a sort of dedicated telephone system for computers.

You might compare this to the conventional voice telephone system that you're used to. In a sense, it's pretty mindless as well. It will connect you with other users of the system, but it assumes that you will know what numbers to dial and that you'll take responsibility for speaking in a language that's understandable by whomever you call.

The proto-Internet originally was used by the American military. After a while, it came to encompass academic institutions that were doing research for the military as well. It turned out to be well suited to academics, who like an environment with lots of information floating around among anyone who's interested in it.

In the mid-1980s, the National Science Foundation Network used the pre-Internet hardware to connect to five supercomputers. By the early 1990s, all sorts of academic, commercial, and individual interests were connecting hardware to the Internet's communication backbone.

Communicating with the Internet is a computer thing, unlike communicating with CompuServe. While the latter is done using computers, CompuServe addresses the outside world using human-readable commands, messages, and prompts. For practical purposes, the Internet moves things around using an elaborate protocol that makes sense only to computers. Computers organize the electronic information from the Net into electronic mail, newsgroups, and such so that people can make sense of them.

A computer connected to the Internet can put "things" on the Net and read "things" from the Net. We won't worry too much about what "things" are just at the moment. The computer, not the Net, is responsible for what it puts on and reads from the Net. The Net can thus remain mindless; its only responsibility is to make sure that things put on it eventually get to the other computers connected to it.

Assuming that the Net itself has no inherent intelligence, you'll notice that nowhere in the foregoing model is there anyone with the authority to say what sort of "things" the net will handle. This isn't an omission caused by a simplified explanation either; it's how the Internet works. Actually, it's how the Internet must work, just as it's how the telephone company must work. With 30 million users, any thoughts of enforcing global content rules on the Internet become laughable.

Citizenship:
something else for sociologists to talk about at parties

There usually is about a month every summer when Alchemy Mindworks more or less shuts down, such that everyone involved can get some vacation time in and recharge their brains. During this period, the aforementioned support bulletin board gets left to its own devices to some extent. Aside from having someone call it now and again to answer pressing questions, the system rules usually don't get enforced. Invariably, people violate them. Messages appear advertising erotic pre-Colombian art, listing other bulletin boards, asking questions about software we've never heard of, and so on.

The curious thing about this is that many of the users of the bulletin board take just as much umbrage at this misuse of the hardware as the system operator would, were one around. The bulletin board has a finite amount of access time. People who misuse it waste this time, making the system more difficult to get onto for people who want to use it for its intended purpose. Leaving inappropriate messages on it makes it harder to find the mail that you actually are looking for. It's not uncommon for the system operator to return from his vacation to find that miscreants on the bulletin board have been told off by its users in far harsher language than he would have employed.

The Internet also is a finite resource, if a much larger one. It works by the same unwritten rule, however. It's called the rule of *bandwidth*. No matter how sophisticated your access to the Net is or how fast you can read, there will be a finite limit to the number of "things" that you can deal with in the time that you have available. People who misuse the Internet waste its bandwidth and make the use of it less effective for the rest of its citizens.

Internet miscreants can be banned from access to the network only in very extreme cases, and only then if the owner of the computer through which they access the Net chooses to delete their accounts. However, it's remarkable how effective public censure on the Net can be. The elemental function of the Internet is one or another form of conversation. There's very little point in using the Internet if no one wants to talk to you.

The rules of the Internet often are referred to as *netiquette*. This is a good description of them, as it implies that they're more of a matter of courtesy and common sense than some arbitrary and ineffable set of laws. If you don't do anything on the Net that would be inappropriate amongst a gathering of your friends—and allowing that your friends aren't

anarchists who meet on alternate Fridays to discuss bomb-craft and the ultimate destruction of civilization as we know it—you'll probably get along fine on the Net.

I'll discuss some of the finer points of netiquette later in this Introduction.

The important thing to keep in mind about using the Internet is that you're not buying a service, as would be the case for CompuServe or for the Alchemy Mindworks bulletin board. You're participating in a community. If everyone on the Internet undertakes not to abuse the system, it will keep working.

The nature of "things" on the Internet

For users of the Internet, the mechanism by which things move around the Net—the underlying protocols of the network hardware itself—can largely be ignored. It's useful to understand how the Net behaves in general terms, so you'll know why your e-mail might not get where it's going instantaneously, for example—I'll get into this in detail presently—but you needn't be able to make complete sentences out of the unpronounceable acronyms of the lower levels of the Internet just to use its facilities.

Let's begin with a brief introduction to some of the characters of the Internet. These are the resources that you're most likely to get involved with. Specific examples of them form the body of this book. These are, for practical purposes, the "things" of the Internet.

Here's something very important to keep in mind about the Internet. What comes out of the wire that connects your computer to the Internet is a protocol—a lot of computer-readable binary hieroglyphics—rather than a complete user interface. The Internet-specific software on your computer will make this into something that you can work with. If you're using dial-up Internet access through a third-party Internet provider, the software resides on their computer.

Different Internet access software will present its users with radically different user interfaces. In theory, all these applications do essentially the same things, but they'll do them in different ways. You might access the Internet through a complex graphical user interface on a Macintosh computer, a very simple text-based interface over a dial-up system, and so on.

The appendix describes how to access the Internet via several of the major Internet providers, including CompuServe, Delphi, and America Online. Specific instructions will vary enormously based on exactly how you're accessing the Net. Before you can use this book, you'll have to learn how to use your specific Internet software.

Having said this, keep in mind that most access packages are designed to be very simple to use; the Internet may be vast, but it's not particularly hard to work with.

Newsgroups

As with many aspects of technology, newsgroups began as something quite different than what they presently are. While their function evolved, their name remained. It's no longer particularly descriptive of the function they serve, but it persists none the less.

Newsgroups in general are referred to as Usenet.

A newsgroup is a place to go and exchange messages with other users of the Internet. Messages in a newsgroup are called *postings*. Newsgroups are specific to particular topics. If you wanted to deal with "Star Trek," book reviews, laser discs, antique Jaguars, or any of countless other topics, you would seek out the appropriate newsgroup and "subscribe" to it.

Once again, the word "subscribe" is a holdover from an earlier time, and perhaps doesn't describe the function in question very well.

You can think of a newsgroup as being the message section of a more conventional computer bulletin board. You can leave messages—postings—in a newsgroup, and other subscribers to the newsgroup will be able to reply to them. You can reply to their replies. Postings in a newsgroup are *threaded*, which means that if you read a posting with replies—and perhaps replies to its replies, and so on—you'll be able to follow the thread of replies until it runs out.

Here's a bit of a look behind the scenes of how the Internet really works. There are thousands of sites on the Internet, each one supporting the thousands of available newsgroups—almost three thousand, as of this writing. You might well ask how your reply to a posting in one particular newsgroup finds its way to where it's supposed to go. Actually, it doesn't. Each site maintains all the current newsgroup files, which are updated periodically with new postings and replies. This is important to keep in mind. It means that your replies to postings in a newsgroup will not be immediately accessible by other subscribers to the group.

As with other aspects of the Internet, there is no central repository of newsgroup contents to which your postings are instantly transmitted and from which other users interactively access Usenet files—just a great deal of cooperation.

Postings remain current in a newsgroup for a while, then fall off the end of the posting queue. Many newsgroups undertake to archive their old postings at FTP sites. We'll discuss FTP sites later in this introduction. The nature of archived postings and other elements of a newsgroup will vary with the group itself.

Many newsgroups maintain a list of frequently asked questions, or FAQ. If you're new to a newsgroup, you might inquire whether it maintains an FAQ. Reading the FAQ of a newsgroup is an element of netiquette, as it will help you get up to speed about the basic elements of the group without wasting bandwidth by posting a lot of frequently asked questions.

While it's convenient to think of newsgroups as being something like computer bulletin boards, it's important to keep in mind one very important difference between the two: newsgroups are exclusively public forums. Everything you post to a newsgroup becomes readable by anyone who cares to do so. If you post something embarrassing, vulgar, or mindless, everyone will get to see it. Thereafter, it will be archived and preserved for posterity. Think before you post.

"I Was a Knucklehead,"

Contributors to newsgroups frequently get really worked up about issues in their newsgroups. Very often, you'll find some pretty heated replies to postings in newsgroups. These are referred to as *flames*. Some postings might seem to deserve to be flamed, and some matters incite a considerable degree of justifiable passion. However, ill-conceived flames usually sound like some hothead with more fingers than brain cells, rather than a brilliant, incendiary riposte. Before you flame someone else's posting, read someone else's flames.

While it hasn't been discussed as yet, the Internet supports electronic mail. If what you have to say isn't suitable for public scrutiny, it belongs in an e-mail message, not in a newsgroup posting.

As an aside, there's a newsgroup called *alt.flame*, should you find that you really just like spouting off without thinking.

Newsgroups are organized using dotted hierarchical notation, something that turns up in other aspects of the Internet. Here are the basic classifications of the most mainstream newsgroups:

alt	Newsgroups about various topics
bionet	Newsgroups about biological sciences
bit	Bitnet newsgroups
biz	Newsgroups where commercial information is posted
clari	ClariNet newsgroups
comp	Newsgroups about computers
courts	Legal newsgroups
eunet	European newsgroups
info	Newsgroups gatewayed from mailing lists
misc	Miscellaneous newsgroups
news	Newsgroups about Usenet
rec	Recreational newsgroups
relcom	Newsgroups from the former Soviet union
sci	Scientific newsgroups
soc	Newsgroups about culture and social sciences
talk	Newsgroups for talking

There are a few things worth knowing about the newsgroups on this list. To begin with, the *alt* and *rec* newsgroups are where most of the things of interest to readers of this book will take place. The *clari* newsgroups are distributed by a commercial entity, Clarion, and must be paid for by the sites that carry them. For this reason, you might find that your access to the Internet doesn't include access to these groups. The *clari* newsgroups deal largely with actual news.

Each Internet site that supports Usenet newsgroups is empowered to carry—or not carry—specific newsgroups. In most cases, you'll find that you have access to all the available newsgroups. Don't be too surprised if a few peculiar cases are missing, however. Some Internet providers are uncomfortable carrying a few of the more extreme *alt.sex* newsgroups, for example. As I write this, it's illegal for Canadian Internet sites to carry the *alt.fan.karla-homolka* newsgroup, as this pertains to a murder trial upon which the Canadian courts have imposed a publication ban.

At a minimum, newsgroup names consist of one of the foregoing prefixes and a descriptive name. As such, there are newsgroups like *alt.exotic-music* and *rec.antiques*. Some newsgroups are subsets of more general topics and have more specific names. You'll find *alt.sex* for general postings about sex, but also *alt.sex.bondage*, *alt.sex.movies*, *alt.sex.pictures*, and quite a few other *alt.sex* newsgroups that I won't get into here.

Newsgroups are an extremely fluid quantity. New groups are created periodically, and old ones fall out of use. You can retrieve the current list of active newsgroups from the FTP site *ftp.uu.net:/networking/news/config/*. If you're uncertain what an FTP site is, read on.

Note that because of the continually changing nature of newsgroups, there is the possibility that some of the newsgroups listed in this book might have changed names or vanished entirely by the time you read this. That's the nature of the Internet.

Here's another bit of newsgroup lore. People who browse around in newsgroups but don't post anything are called *lurkers*. This sounds a bit disreputable. Once again, this probably isn't a very well-chosen term. There's nothing wrong with lurking in newsgroups. If you're new to a newsgroup, or new to the Net in general, constrain yourself to lurking for a while to get a feel for the flavor of a newsgroup.

Some newsgroups are pretty easy to understand. For example, if you subscribe to *alt.music.a-cappella*, you'll find a discussion of unaccompanied singing. Should you be interested and somewhat knowledgeable about such things, you probably will be able to ask intelligent questions and post informed messages almost immediately.

Some newsgroups are a bit more ineffable than they might seem. For example, the newsgroup *alt.music.enya* deals with music by the Irish new age musician Enya. It's a very engaging newsgroup, but it's important to realize that it's inhabited almost exclusively by Enya's fans. Posting a message that is critical of her latest album will get you roundly flamed.

Finally, some newsgroups are almost like little secret societies. You will need a great deal of prior knowledge or a lot of lurking before you'll be able to participate intelligently in these groups. For example, the *alt.devilbunnies* newsgroup deals with the nature and practices of devilbunnies. You might be a bit unclear as to exactly what a devilbunny is. Most of us are.

As another example, *alt.illuminati* is a newsgroup based on the novels of Robert Anton Wilson. You wouldn't be able to make much sense of it if you hadn't read at least a few of his books.

Newsgroups in this book are designated by the following notation:

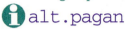alt.pagan

One of the unusual sorts of postings to be found in newsgroups are binary files—usually scanned pictures or sounds—that have been uuencoded. The uuencoding process turns the data in a binary file into readable ASCII text, suitable for use in a posting. A corresponding uudecoder will turn the text back into a binary file. This is what the first part of a uuencoded picture typically looks like:

```
From access.digex.net!not-for-mail Wed May 25 10:04:37 1994
Path: access.digex.net!not-for-mail
From: ldgrim@access.digex.net (Larry Grim)
Newsgroups: alt.binaries.pictures.erotica.orientals
Subject: - jlov0097.jpg (1/1) {Asian female}
Followup-To: alt.binaries.pictures.erotica.d
Date: 15 May 1994 17:24:32 -0400
Organization: Express Access Online Communications,
Greenbelt, MD USA
Lines: 1567
Distribution: world
Message-ID: <2r63ug$d1p@access3.digex.net>
NNTP-Posting-Host: access3.digex.net
X-Posting-Software: xmitBin v1.9 by D. Jim Howard (deej@cadence.com)

BEGIN -- CUT HERE -- Cut Here -- cut here -- jlov0097.jpg 1/1
M_]C_X  02D9)1@ ! 0$ E@"6  #__@ 
R2&%N9&UA9&4&4@4V]F='=A<F4($EN
M8RX@26UA9V54<:&06QC:&5M>2!V,2XV+C<%D-C,*"*_]L A  (!@8'!00
M"@''"0@("0(D+"<0P+"HP&R U.#0T-3$S-S$\\$S^!0+1D=2$Q.2$B
M,,CPM'0S,3$S\"(P;$Q+`&UL;FQ@<&QL;6QL;6QL;&QL;&
M,,,`(4,``C0``$````$!`@("``````(#```$#`PP&AHH`````
M M_\0!0(04!1@$BD4!`0$!!0^$A00$^_P`!/00(0%($!$$!
M                $"$/0<""('"``@=$!""ZA
M  ``)*B`1$`!$`(&I`2@$`# 0 !$($`@@S```D!OY8?Gd3&Q9(
M!H<180<Qc80g80A3MM]$"\qy87$!!A:S\=28G\"DN-4V-S@Y
```

Should it not be obvious from the header at the top of the file, this is some sort of erotic graphic—even if it isn't all that exciting in its present form. For reasons that will be discussed in greater detail in the section of this book that deals with "Erotic pictures," most such files are sent as uuencoded newsgroup postings, rather than as binary image files.

Because there is a finite maximum size for the individual blocks of text posted to a newsgroup, large files often are broken up into multiple sequential postings.

If the foregoing file were the only posting for the picture in question, you would unpack it by opening it with a text editor and deleting everything from the top of the file down to and including the line that starts *BEGIN*. The remaining data can be uudecoded to the original file, in this case a JPEG graphic.

If the foregoing file were one of two or more postings comprising a single destination binary file or picture, you'd have to undertake a bit more action with your text editor. Having cleaned up the top of the file, move down to the bottom of the file and delete everything beginning with the line that starts *END*. Having done so, read the next file in the sequence in and clean up its header so the uuencoded data from the second file comes immediately after the end of the first file. Repeat this process for as many source uuencoded files as exist for the picture in question. When you're done, you'll have a file suitable for running through a uudecoder.

You can find a uudecoder program for your computer by doing an Archie search for the word *uudecode*. Ask your network administrator or Internet provider how to use Archie.

There are a few catches to this process. Some uudecoders check the data that they're decoding to make sure that none of those mysterious little characters has become altered. Some don't. If you uudecode a damaged file, or a file that has been reassembled incorrectly with your text editor, the resulting binary file will be incorrect. In the case of a picture, this usually will mean that the picture won't unpack. Be careful with the uuencoded text.

Note that you must use a real text editor, not a word processor in its document mode, to edit uuencoded text. It usually will have to be able to handle large files, especially if you'll be reassembling uuencoded binary files and pictures from several source text files.

Retrieving and recreating uuencoded files takes a bit of practice to fully understand, but it's easily mastered.

A word about pictures

Once you have correctly reconstructed uuencoded pictures back into their original image files, you'll require a way to look at them. The most common image file formats in use for pictures that are to be uuencoded are GIF and JPEG, as these produce relatively little uuencoded text. Somewhat ubiquitous formats, viewers for these files exist for most of the popular hardware platforms and operating systems.

If you're using a PC system, you might want to have a look at the image file software produced by my company, Alchemy Mindworks. It's called Graphic Workshop. As of this writing, it's available in MS-DOS and Windows implementations. Current shareware evaluation versions of it can be downloaded from *uunorth.north.net:/pub/alchemy*.

The second thing you should keep in mind about pictures on the Internet is that, while they're sort of free, they're not necessarily free of copyright restrictions. If you download a picture—either one that has been uuencoded and posted in a newsgroup or one that's available from an FTP site or a Gopher server, to be discussed in a moment—it actually might have been scanned from an image that has some copyright restrictions associated with it. There's pretty well no way of knowing if this is true of a specific image.

If you download a picture that you like and use it for Windows wallpaper on your computer or just add it to your image file collection, your potential risk of legal action is somewhat less than that of the earth suddenly leaving its orbit, jumping to light speed, and wandering aimlessly across the universe in search of adventure. If you use such a picture for a commercial application, on the other hand, you might find yourself confronted by a pack of rabid lawyers.

The third thing that you should keep in mind about pictures on the Internet, as alluded to a few moments ago, is that some of them are "adult" graphics. For the most part, these are confined to clearly labelled erotic picture newsgroups, and as such, no one who downloads such material from the Net should be shocked or outraged by its content, unless they just enjoy shock and outrage in general. A few bare breasts and the occasional somewhat kinky orgy do turn up at otherwise respectable FTP sites, however.

To be sure, the freedom of the Internet does require that you take responsibility for dealing with whatever turns up on your monitor as a result. If you really can't handle graphics with sexual content, either don't download any graphics from the Net or be really certain you know what you're taking.

As an aside, pursuant to the issue of copyright for downloaded pictures, as of this writing, the only instance in which anyone has really gotten nasty over the matter of scanned commercial photographs turning up where people can download them has been in the case of the publishers of several adult magazines.

Electronic mail

Electronic mail works like regular mail to some extent, except that it's a lot faster, infinitely cheaper, and is unlikely to present the recipient

of your mail with something that looks more like a road kill than a letter due to a mishap at the post office. The speed of electronic mail makes letter writing a far more interactive process than it ever was back when letters existed solely on paper.

Electronic mail, or *e-mail*, involves moving small bits of text around the Internet. Electronic mail messages originate in an editor, a simple word processor for writing letters, and are read by mail reader software. The two functions actually are integrated in most cases, such that you can read your mail and immediately respond to it.

Unlike complex word processing documents, electronic mail messages are simple text. You can't include italics, big headlines, or graphics in a conventional electronic mail message. Electronic mail uses the most elemental form of computer communications—pure text—as it's something that can be handled on any computer, no matter who made it and what sort of mail software it's running.

By convention, there are a number of things that you can do to the text in an electronic mail message to add emphasis to your words. Specifically:

- Typing words in UPPERCASE is considered to be SHOUTING. It's acceptable where verbal shouting would be acceptable, such as to draw attention to the beginning of a message, and less so for text that appears in the body of a message.
- Words that would have been set in *italics* if electronic mail supported them usually are written with asterisks before and after them, as in "The Honda Civic is a *really* ugly car."
- Likewise, words that would have been set in **bold face** usually are enclosed in underscores.

Because electronic mail essentially is sent between yourself and one other person, you're free to use any text effects that will make sense to the intended recipients of your messages. For example, some of the messages that I receive on the Net are from people who use the Ventura Publisher desktop publishing software. They use Ventura coding for special effects. Italicized text is written as "this is what <I> italics <D> look like to Ventura." Really dedicated Ventura people often add special characters in Ventura notation as well. I confess that I have to look these up.

Electronic mail is sent to addresses, rather than to individuals. Here's my e-mail address:

alchemy@accesspt.north.net

My account on the Internet server that I use is called *alchemy*, which is the name of my company. The *accesspt* bit is the name of the Internet server that I use to access the Net. The *north* bit is an abbreviation of the name of the company that owns the server.

The Internet is particularly good at moving small text objects around, and electronic mail is reliable and reasonably fast. It's impor-

tant to keep in mind, however, that not all Internet servers are connected to the Net by blazingly fast hardware and not all servers are available all the time. Finally, not everyone reads their mail the moment that it shows up; Internet users who access the Net through a dial-up server might not check their mail for days. Don't expect a reply to your mail instantaneously.

One of the issues that comes up in conversation from time to time about Internet electronic mail is its privacy, or lack thereof. If you send electronic mail to someone else on the Net, it will present itself only to the designated recipient. This does not make it private, however. Many other parties might have access to your mail if they were sufficiently determined to do so.

There are certain protections inherent in Internet mail, the most obvious one being that there's a staggering amount of it. Someone wanting to spy on your mail would have to undertake to read a stunning volume of text. Having said this, consider that there are probably people using the Net who have little else to occupy their time with. Be especially careful to avoid including such things as credit card numbers in electronic mail.

You should also keep in mind the legal implications of not particularly private mail. If you post a message in a newsgroup claiming that one of your local elected officials sells illegal drugs to farm animals, you might well be accused of libel should this allega-tion not turn out to be true. If you were to write the same thing in a private paper letter and send it to someone you know, you probably could not be accused of libel. While electronic mail is analogous to conventional paper mail, its questionable privacy makes the analogy less than complete. Posting this sort of thing as electronic mail on the Internet is not the same as writing it down and mailing it.

As I touched on in the previous section of this Introduction, one important application of electronic mail is as an alternative to posting things in newsgroups if what you want to post is semiprivate, likely to offend other users of the newsgroup in question, or is rabidly laced with flames. In some cases, there is a legal distinction between saying "he sells illegal drugs to farm animals" and "you sell illegal drugs to farm animals." This is a fairly amorphous issue at the moment and one that eventually might make any number of lawyers unbelievably rich. Some common sense and perhaps a bit of restraint will help keep them from becoming unbelievably rich at your expense.

Another application of electronic mail, as will appear throughout the listings of this book, is as a medium over which to receive mailing list postings. An Internet mailing list is information that is electronically mass-mailed to every Internet mail address on a particular list. Most mailing lists are free—all you need to do is e-mail their administrators with a request to be included on the list in question.

Mailing lists are indicated in this book using the following notation:

bagpipes@cs.dartmouth.edu
bagpipes-request@cs.dartmouth.edu

In this case, the first item is the electronic mail address to which items for the mailing list are to be sent. The second is the electronic mail address to which you should address your request to have your name added to the mailing list.

Finally, keep in mind that as the Internet evolves, its electronic mail facilities will become more and more intertwined with those of other networks. For example, it's possible to send and receive electronic mail between the Internet and users of CompuServe. You might find some fairly unusual message headers attached to mail that you receive.

While electronic mail is always handled as simple text, there are cases in which the text will appear in a form that your mail reading software might not be able to display. For example, mail can be sent from the Japanese NiftyServe network to users of the Internet, but many Internet mail packages won't read it. These messages can be downloaded, at which point they'll turn out to be simple text. This is one of the wrinkles that turns up from time to time in a system as far reaching as the Internet.

Anonymous FTP sites

Thus far, the Internet "things" we've dealt with have been reasonably user-friendly. They've been elements that software running on your computer or on that of your Internet provider presents in a comfortable, familiar way. Accessing FTP sites over the Net requires that you get personal with some of the hardware that makes Internet sites work.

The acronym FTP stands for *file transfer protocol*. An FTP site is a repository of files that you can transfer to your computer. The mechanism of an FTP site isn't necessarily hard to use; it will most likely be singularly unfamiliar, however.

FTP sites are listed in this book using the following notation:

ftp.uwp.edu

Note that the FTP sites listed in this book typically specify a file to look for or a subdirectory to look in. I'll deal with subdirectories in detail in a moment. Here's an example of this notation:

cathouse.org:/pub/cathouse/

Subdirectory names always end in a slash. The previous line, then, defines a subdirectory at the FTP site *cathouse.org* that typically will contain multiple files that you might want to look at—or possibly, as in this case, more subdirectories. As an aside, *cathouse.org* is a real FTP site.

Alternately, you'll find many FTP sites listed in this book that indicate specific files. Here's one of them:

`ramses.cs.cornell.edu:/pub/elster/perot/clinton.humor`

Note that the last item on the line does not end with a slash.

There are all sorts of files available over the Internet. These include documents, pictures, digitized sounds, executable software, and manifest specialized bits of data. I'll get into the exact nature of what you can find at FTP sites and how to work with it in a moment.

The computer that runs an Internet FTP server uses an operating system called Unix. If you're male, you might have a sense of why Unix is so named after you've used it for a while. Unix purports to be the world's most powerful computer operating system and the most difficult thing in the known universe to get along with. Learning Unix in detail is a lifetime's undertaking. Fortunately, you'll require only a minute understanding of Unix to work with FTP sites.

For practical purposes, the FTP mechanism allows you to run someone else's computer over the Internet. You'll have only limited access to its resources, but this is sufficient to locate files and fetch them to your system. The user interface involved is a command line, rather than a mouse and icons. The commands that you'll have to type at this command line are drawn from Unix.

If you're familiar with the MS-DOS operating system, you'll find the behavior of Unix to be distantly familiar.

There are relatively few Unix commands that you'll need to work with an FTP site. Here's an overview of them:

- ls—List the files in the current directory
- page—Display the contents of a text file using the paging software on your local computer or server
- cd—Change directories
- get—Transfer a file to your local computer or server
- quit—Close the connection with the current FTP site

Unlike MS-DOS, filenames on a Unix system can be extremely long. They can contain multiple periods and several characters that are not legal in filenames under other operating systems. Note that Unix commands and filenames are case sensitive. The command *ls* and the command *LS* are not identical; the latter would typically not be recognized.

The disk structure of an FTP site will be familiar to most users of personal computers—that is, as a set of hierarchical subdirectories. The owner of the site is free to set up the directories in any way he or she sees fit, but most FTP sites maintain a subdirectory called /pub, for "public," that contains all of the files that you will be allowed to access. If you attempt to access a file or a subdirectory to which public access has not been granted, the system will say "Access denied."

Note that the forward slash is used to indicate a directory path under Unix, unlike under MS-DOS, which uses the backslash.

To change to the /pub directory, you would type:

cd /pub

As you look through the directories of an FTP site, you'll typically move further down the system's directory tree. Typing cd .. will move you back up the tree by one level, and typing cd / will move you back to the root directory.

The command prompt will display your current directory path.

To find out what files exist in the current directory of the FTP site that you're connected to, type ls. This is analogous to the MS-DOS DIR command.

On many FTP systems, each directory will include a simple text file called README or INDEX to provide you with capsule descriptions of the contents of the directory in question. You can view these files with the page command. For example, type:

page README

The software that handles the page command actually resides on your system, not on that of the FTP site. As such, the commands for browsing through a document being paged will vary.

Having found a file that you'd like to have, you can fetch it to your local computer with the get command. For example, to download the file PLANET.TXT from an FTP site to your system, you would type:

get PLANET.TXT

Once again, keep in mind that filenames are case sensitive under Unix.

Having finished your browsing at one FTP site, you can terminate your connection with the quit command. You also can terminate your connection with the current FTP site and attempt to open a connection with a new one by using the open command. For example, here's how you'd open a connection to the FTP site *ftp.spies.com* (this is a real FTP site, by the way; most of them have fairly peculiar names):

    open ftp.spies.com

There are a few things that can go wrong in your use of FTP sites. The first is that an FTP site might refuse your attempt to connect to it, usually because it has reached its capacity of users. In some cases, you'll be informed of other FTP sites that carry the same files. Try connecting to one of them instead. Alternately, try back later. Most FTP sites are part of larger computer systems, rather than running on hardware dedicated to managing the FTP's files. You'll probably find them easier to access after business hours. Keep in mind that this means after the business hours in the local time where the FTP site is located.

Also, some FTP sites don't get along completely seamlessly with external commands such as page. On occasion, you might find your connection broken if you exit the page command prematurely.

The speed at which files move across the Internet will be determined by the physical hardware connecting a particular FTP site to the Net and by the amount of traffic on the Net at the moment that you get a file. In some cases, transferring even files of modest size can take a while.

The most elemental sort of file that you'll encounter at FTP sites will be text files. These should be readable on all computers. There's one very small catch in using text files from the Internet on some systems. The end of a line in a Unix text file is marked by a carriage return. If you're using a computer running MS-DOS, most of your applications will want text files with lines that end in carriage return and line feed pairs and might not behave themselves properly if the line feeds are missing. Your network administrator or Internet provider should be able to help you overcome this problem.

In many cases, you'll find that files at FTP sites have been archived. An archive compresses files to make them smaller—to allow them to be stored using less hard drive space and to be transferred more rapidly—and to keep multiple files together. There are several sorts of archiving systems in popular use:

- ZIP—The ZIP archive standard is popular among PC systems.
- ARC—The ARC archive standard used to be popular on PC systems, until it was abandoned due to legal problems. Older archives still turn up as ARC files.
- SIT—The SIT, or StuffIt, archive standard is used on Macintosh systems.

- TAR.Z—TAR.Z archives are popular in Unix environments.
- GZIP—GZIP is popular in Unix environments.

While these archive standards initially appeared on the systems that I indicated, compatible unarchiving utilities have been written for them to run on most other platforms. As such, for example, you can download a ZIP file and unpack it even if you're using a Macintosh system.

There are a few things to keep in mind about this. Most computer operating systems have differing filenaming conventions. In unpacking a Unix TAR archive on a PC system, for example, the unarchiving software might have to modify the filenames that come out of the archive.

If you download executable software, it must have been written for the computer that you'll ultimately be running it on. Unpacking application software out of a Macintosh archive onto a PC system won't avail you of a useful program.

Your network administrator or Internet provider should be able to help you find appropriate unarchiving software for your system. Alternately, use the Archie resources of the Net to look for the appropriate tools.

Telnet

The Telnet function allows you to connect to a remote computer and use its functions to some extent. The extent will be determined by the owner of the computer. As its name might imply, Telnet usually involves linking to a remote system through a telephone line.

In most cases, the Telnet sites that will turn up in this book are interactive systems that will allow you to do online shopping, database searches, and so on. Unlike other functions of the Internet—FTP sites, gopher servers, and so on—the user interface of a system accessed through Telnet is entirely up to the owner of the system. Every system accessed through Telnet will typically be different and might take some getting used to.

Not all Telnet systems want to talk with you. While the ones listed in this book are all publicly accessible computers, many systems that connect to the Internet through Telnet are private and will require a password or logon code. You can try *anonymous* or *guest* for these if you think you've encountered a public access Telnet system. If this doesn't get you through the gate, you're probably not welcome.

As an example of a function accessible through Telnet, you can order books from a bookshop called Book Stacks Unlimited over the Internet. This service is discussed in detail later in this book. When you Telnet to *books.com*, you will be presented with a set of text menus that will allow you to query Book Stacks' database, place orders, and so on.

All the publicly accessible Telnet systems that will turn up in this book are menu-driven and about as user-friendly as things get on the Internet. Keep in mind that most of them actually are commercial enterprises who want your business. They have a vested interest in making things easy for you, and they'll want to know if you encounter any difficulties.

When you connect to a system over Telnet, watch for an e-mail address in the opening message and write it down if one appears. If you have trouble using the service later on, you'll have someone to contact about what went wrong.

Gopher

Gopher is a piece of software that allows you to access a large selection of resources on the Internet in a somewhat more user-friendly manner than is possible through anonymous FTP transfers. You can think of Gopher as being a menu-driven interface to FTP sites, although in practice this analogy is somewhat flawed. Because of the way it works, Gopher doesn't allow you to access everything that you can get at by connecting to FTP sites directly. Not all FTP sites are registered with Gopher, and as a rule not all the files at an FTP site that is registered with Gopher will appear in Gopher's menus.

Having said this, it's worth noting also that some services available through Gopher don't turn up as FTP sites, or at least, not in any form that you'd want to use them. Gopher makes things like getting files and searching resources vastly easier.

More than this, however, you might access a site on the Internet using Gopher by selecting *Wiretap Online Library*, for example, rather than *ftp.spies.com*. Gopher is user-friendly, and talks to you in English, rather than in netspeak.

Gopher actually is a large database of Internet sites maintained at the University of Minnesota. It grows almost daily, with new facilities being added periodically. In addition to allowing you to fetch files from FTP sites, Gopher has a growing number of commercial facilities, interfaces to government archives and resources, searchable references, and so on.

Note that the Gopher site at the University of Minnesota has a large but finite capacity. It's possible that Gopher might be inaccessible or might be very sluggish to work with during periods of peak activity.

Gopher sites are listed in this book using the following notation:

```
Wiretap Online Library | Articles
| Aeronautics and Space | Airport
3-Letter Abbreviations
```

In most cases, the menus required to reach a specific Gopher resource will be nested. The foregoing example is a complete path to a file that is accessible through Gopher. To locate the file in question, begin by selecting the Wiretap Online Library gopher. While Gopher interfaces vary, you typically can do this either by selecting Wiretap Online Library from the list of available Gopher sites or by searching for it, or for part of it. Searching for *Wiretap*, in this case, should do it. With thousands of Gopher sites available around the world, picking a site from the list is possible, but hardly all that efficient.

Having selected the Wiretap Online Library gopher, you would be presented with a list of first-level menus, one of which would be called Articles/. Select this item, and a second-level menu list will appear. One of the items will be Aeronautics and Space/. Select this, and a third-level menu will appear. The file in this case is entitled Airport 3 Letter Abbreviations.

As with FTP sites, items in a Gopher menu that end in a slash indicate that they lead to a dependent sub-menu. Items without slashes are files.

Some Gopher items end in a question mark, like this:

4. Library of Congress <?>

These entries connect to searchable databases. If you select one, a prompt will appear to allow you to enter a key word to search for.

Finger

The Finger function really is meant to locate users on the Internet, although this is not how it will turn up in this book. A secondary function of Finger has evolved as some sites on the Net have created dummy users. If you Finger such a dummy user, some software will run and send you back whatever it's been designed to do.

Fingerable entities on the Internet are indicated by the following notation in this book:

```
copi@oddjob.uchicago.edu
```

If you Finger this address, a page of interesting trivia relating to the current day of the year will appear on your monitor.

Of course, there are those who will complain that any discussion of fingering users on the Net is obscene and sexist. It's unclear whether the original creator of the Finger software had this in mind when it was named, but one hopes so.

The obligatory closing remarks

The thing that makes computers so much more useful than toasters is that a computer can be adapted to become whatever tool that you require. By running appropriate software, it can be a financial management tool, a drawing tool, a writing tool, or a time-wasting tool, among many other things.

Likewise, the thing that makes the Internet a much more useful resource than the Alchemy Mindworks bulletin board or CompuServe is that it's capable of being almost anything. Not restricted to either a single function or to things that will necessarily generate revenue, it's an expression of all who use it. That probably sounds a bit too Zenlike to properly describe the Internet.

Beyond its staggering capacity and limitless resources, the Internet is an interesting place to enjoy yourself. Like some enormous computer game, just when you think you've seen everything there is to see, a new facet of the Net will open up before you, and the adventure will begin again.

The adventure awaits you now . . .

Author's note

The graphics used in *Planet Internet* reflect the sorts of images available from sources on the Internet. Some are sexual, as the Internet itself is pretty sexual. Female readers of this book might note that the nudes in this book are mostly female. This does not reflect any bias on the part of the author or publisher of *Planet Internet*, but rather is indicative of the images to be found on the Net at the time of this writing.

A cappella music

ℹ alt.music.a-cappella

The phrase *a cappella* is Italian. In a classical sense it means "as of the chapel," that is, in the style of church music. For the rest of us, it means singing without instrumental accompaniment. It's comforting to know that bellowing in the shower has a proper name.

A cappella music properly encompasses a variety of forms, by no means all of which are liturgical. The *alt.music.a-cappella* newsgroup is a thoughtful, lively forum for both singers and people who just like the sound of no guitars whatsoever. It's a place to find out about upcoming performances—most of them in southern California as I write this—and little known recordings of unaccompanied voices. As I was wandering through *alt.music.a-cappella*, I found a review of what sounded like an agreeably eclectic compact disc of a cappella music. It included several choral works and a rendition of Queen's "Bohemian Rhapsody"—something to look out for. (At least until the loud bit with the guitars toward the end, Queen's version of "Bohemian Rhapsody" is *a cappella* as well.)

Aside from being extraordinarily well mannered—especially for the Internet—the *alt.music.a-cappella* newsgroup is genuinely interesting, even if your interest in unaccompanied singing is somewhat peripheral. If you're growing shellshocked by the excesses of popular music, it's worth a quick lurk to see what lies beyond synthesizers, percussion machines, and walls of backup vocalists.

Acoustic guitar music

📁 ftp.nevada.edu:/pub/guitar

📁 casbah.acns.nwu.edu:/pub/acoustic-guitar

ℹ rec.music.makers.guitar

ℹ rec.music.makers.tab

ℹ rec.music.makers.acoustic

The guitar is a somewhat evolutionary instrument, having developed from the Renaissance lute and the cittern. The lute was a classical performance instrument, and the cittern was a somewhat more base instrument suitable for banging out a few sea chanties when the boys were into the home brew again. Perhaps in keeping with its origin, the guitar can be either or both—and countless things besides.

It's interesting to note that, in academic circles, the nylon or gut string guitar is regarded as a serious performance instrument; lutes had gut strings. Steel string guitars, like metal stringed citterns a few hundred years ago, are decried as folk instruments and hardly worthy of a serious musician. One suspects that, in such circles, radio and compact discs are regarded as passing curiosities as well.

Because of its somewhat schizophrenic nature—a popular instrument with classical allusions nipping at its heels—contemporary guitar music often is an interesting fusion of techniques. Performers such as John Renbourn and Jon Anderson arguably owe as much to renaissance lutanists as they do to earlier masters of electric guitar and other "popular" genres. One need not listen to Yes very carefully to hear fragments of what might be Bach or Scarlatti.

Perhaps the most appealing element of playing guitar is that it has a moderately kind learning curve. It's possible to play one at least to the extent that it doesn't kill nearby small animals with a few weeks of serious practice. By comparison, most brass instruments require months to achieve enough lip to make noises that don't sound like imminent plumbing problems. Nascent violin players should begin their study of the instrument with the construction of a soundproof room.

Fingerstyle guitar playing seems to be enjoying a renaissance of its own at the moment. In a sense it represents the real flowering of acoustic guitar technique, allowing the instrument its true expressive potential. Alternately, if you prefer a less eclectic explanation, it's the most impressive thing that you can do with an acoustic guitar that doesn't involve igniting it.

There are several resources on the Internet that will be of interest to advanced acoustic guitarists. Perhaps the richest of them is *ftp.nevada.edu:/pub/guitar*. You'll find an impressive library of transcribed guitar tablature for popular music there. Tablature is another bit of lute lore to have survived the ages, by the way. While conventional sheet music really is written for keyboard instruments, tablature allows guitar music to be written in a form that makes direct sense to someone playing a guitar. The music to the right is the tablature for Ian Anderson's song "Nursie," as found at *ftp.nevada.edu*.

If you're used to sight reading conventional sheet music, the peculiar text-based tablature of the net might take a bit of getting used to. Once you get a feel for it, however, you'll wonder why guitarists have suffered with playing from piano scores for so long.

A slightly different source of acoustic guitar music can be found at *casbah.acns.nwu.edu:/pub/acoustic-guitar*. It offers neither as rich a variety of transcribed music, nor does it embrace the enjoyably challenging quite as much. However, the transcribed selections are liberally annotated and typically are presented as tablature where needed followed by lyrics and conventional chord names. Among other things, there are a fair number of obscure tunes from Jerry Garcia's solo albums there.

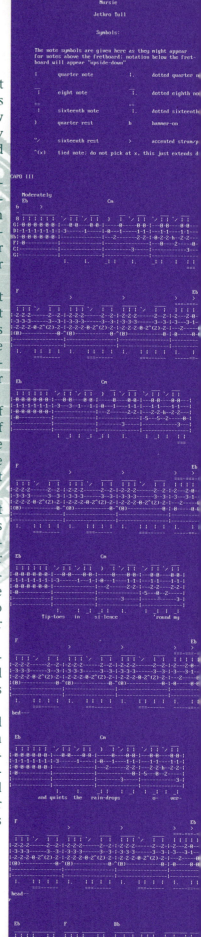

Acronyms

 csn.org:/pub/misc/glossary.acronyms

One of the things that makes English a very much more interesting language than, say, Latin is that English is constantly evolving. A mongrel language with bits of practically every other tongue on earth within itself, English is fluidly adaptable to all occasions. If a word doesn't exist in current English for a particular occasion, licensed users of the language are free to make one up. Licenses to speak English are easy to come by, too. Fortunately for the rest of us, the English didn't think to copyright their invention until it was far too late.

Some other languages have very awkward or convoluted paths for creating new words. Have a look at something technical written in German, for example. New words in German are frequently created by concatenating existing words. Specialized German words often run to several dozen letters each. They're a typesetter's nightmare, among other things.

We do much the same thing in English, actually, although English borrows the concept of acronyms from the Mediterranean languages. An *acronym* is a word created from the first letters of each of the words in a longer phrase. After a time, many acronyms become accepted as genuine bits of English.

In the mean time—before our colloquial acronyms make it as accepted words—they seem to breed in dark places, fusing themselves into newer and still more ineffable words. Specialized professions seem to bring with them specialized acronyms. Frequently the same acronym will mean wholly different things in different contexts.

Consider that in computer circles, the acronym VGA is a "video graphics array." It also can mean "venous gas aneurysm." Most people probably would rather have a video graphics array—at least until the warranty expires.

Excerpt from glossary.acronyms

BB	Bases on Balls
BB	Best of Breed
BB	Bunnies and Burrows
BBA	Bachelor of Business Administration
BBB	Better Business Bureau
BBC	British Broadcasting Corporation
BBL	Barrel
BBN	Bolt, Beranek, and Newman, Inc. [Corporate name]
BC	Battlecars
BC	Before Christ
BC	British Columbia
BC/BS	Blue Cross/Blue Shield

BCD	Bad Conduct Discharge
BCD	Binary Coded Decimal
BCDIC	Binary Coded Decimal Interchange Code
BCE	Before the Common Era (substitute for BC)
BCNU	Be Seeing You [Net Jargon]
BCP	Byte Controlled Protocols
BCPL	Basic Combined Programming Language
BCS	Bachelor of Commercial Science
BCS	Binary Compatibility Standard
BCS	Boston Computer Society
BCS	British Computer Society
BD	Bachelor of Divinity
BD	Bank Draft
BD	Bills Discounted
BD&D	Basic Dungeons & Dragons

Airlines

 `rec.travel.air`

 `ftp.spies.com:/Library/Article/Aero/airport.lis`

 `Wiretap Online Library | Articles | Aeronautics and Space | Airport 3-Letter Abbreviations`

The day after the manuscript for *Planet Internet* gets borne away by Federal Express, beginning its journey down to Windcrest/McGraw-Hill in Pennsylvania, I'm going to be borne away on an L-1011 to the hills of Wales. The hills of Wales have few equals; they almost justify the flight. Almost.

Some people dread flying because of the heights. I dread it because of the food.

Airline travel is a peculiar institution. Airports frequently exude the atmosphere of a high-tech version of a Moroccan bazaar in which everything costs three times what it's worth. A well-chosen airline can make even a protracted flight bearable. A poorly chosen one will have you praying for engine trouble and an unscheduled landing within 15 minutes of leaving the ground.

Like so many other aspects of technology, choosing an airline embodies a monumental catch-22. You can't know what an airline is like until you're strapped in and largely at the mercy of the cabin crew. By then, it's much too late to change your mind.

One way to sneak around this apparent impasse is to seek the advice of people who travel a lot. You can find all sorts of them in the *rec.travel.air* newsgroup. If you're planning a trip, the frequent fliers therein will advise you on a choice of airlines, tell you lurid tales of airports that you might do well to stay away from, and will very often help you find a better deal on ticket prices than your travel agent probably will. Some of the regulars of *rec.travel.air* seem either to only disembark long enough to connect to the Net, or else to do so from the clouds by skyphone.

One of the things that makes *rec.travel.air* such a worthwhile resource for travelers is that you need not base your decisions on a single opinion. Post a question about any element of air travel and you'll be awash in a sea of pundits. Consider the excerpt for this section. I should note that this is a sampling of the replies to the initial post; it lurched along for dozens of postings in this vein.

Another interesting resource for air travelers is the list of three-letter airport abbreviations available from the Wiretap Online Library. Some time ago, my guitar went astray on its way back from Manchester. In fairness, the airline did get it back—six weeks later, in a large plastic bag, and they did pay for it after a suitable amount of haggling and harsh language. Prior to someone dropping a 747 on it, it went clear around the world. Using the *airport.lis* file, I was able to retrace its journey from the profusion of adhesive labels holding what was left of the case together:

MAN	Manchester, Great Britain
YYC	Calgary, Alberta, Canada
SIN	Singapore
MNL	Manila, Philippines
ORY	Paris - Orly, France
MAN	Manchester, Great Britain
YTO	Toronto, Ontario, Canada

No record survives of when it was turned into a toothpick sculpture.

 ### Excerpt from `rec.travel.air`

I am planning to fly with my family from San Francisco to Santiago, Chile. I can fly there on US airlines (United and American) but can get lower fares on the Chilean or Costa Rican airlines (LAN and Lasca). These little airlines make me nervous however...

Lan Chile is not a "little" airline. It operates a modern fleet of Boeing 767s from North America to Santiago. American might be taking you there on Boeing 727s or DC-10s for example, which could be ten or twenty years older than the Chilean planes...

You have a chip on your shoulder the size of the USA... LAN Chile (and Ladeco) are indeed good airlines... I bet that their service is probably better...

I meant they are not little in the "these little airlines" sense which connotes a DC-3 chicken flying operation or something. Bigger is not better. I would rather fly a carrier with five Boeing 767s then one with a huge fleet of several hundred aircraft of varying age.

Just look at the civil aviation accidents in the U.S. compared to Canada and Europe (Western).

The US airlines (majors) didn't have a fatal accident in 1993. The same cannot be said of the foreign airlines. I would compare the fleet maintenance of American, Delta, or United to any airline in the world.

Death risk per one million departures:
(from FF Magazine, March 1994)

North America	0.53
Western Europe	0.80
Australia/NZ	1.09
Latin America	4.87
Asia exc. ex-USSR	2.97

I never said that the American airlines were unsafe, I was just a bit concerned by the original poster's allusion to the fact that the Chilean carrier Lan Chile and Costa Rican carrier Lacsa were "frightening" to him because of their size and their not being America... I would feel perfectly safe on an American carrier as I would on most others, but don't European and Canadian airlines (for example) spend more on maintenance?

Air France no doubt spends a ton on safety, but even so I'd be worried about flying with employees that engage in such unsafe practices as running onto runways and rioting on the tarmac...

The figures quoted must be wrong if they refer to international departures since QANTAS has never had a fatality and Air New Zealand has lost one passenger-carrying plane on a tourist, non-scheduled flight to Antarctica.

The best rule of thumb is to pick a nice major airline with a good safety record. American ranks in the top ten, as well as Delta and Southwest...no passenger fatalities on the major airlines last year...

Alcohol

 `ftp.spies.com:/Library/Untech/alcohol.mak`

 Wiretap Online Library ¦ Questionables ¦ How To Make Alcohol

There's a good chance that you'll find more useful information about making your own alcohol in documents discussed elsewhere in this book, under "Home Brewing" and "Wine." The *alcohol.mak* file provided by the Wiretap Online Library has the ring of truth about it, as if its author had been testing a bit too much of his own brew.

Within certain broad and extensively inebriated limits, you can make all the beer and wine that you like for your own consumption. The same is not true for distilled beverages, which most governments tax so heavily as to be unwilling to allow anyone else to horn in on their revenue. As such, depending on where you're reading this from, the techniques described in *alcohol.mak* probably will prove to be illegal.

They also will prove to be only semicoherent at best, although this should not be considered a condemnation of this unique document. Written by someone with considerable experience at brewing up moonshine under difficult circumstances, it's an homage to a longstanding American tradition.

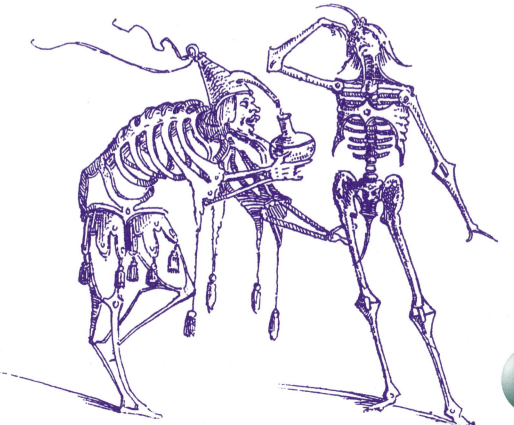

✂ Excerpt from `alcohol.mak`

First you must obtain (steal) a holding tank. I recommend those six gallon Alhambra water jugs which are often left on porches and in driveways for refills. Just take it off the porch at 3:00 AM and run it home. Now, put it where you are going to put your still. They need to be kept together. Hide your still even if you don't have parents... This is illegal by federal law, and you could get busted pretty well. Make your still so it is collapsible and you can fit it all into a small box. Hide the box in your room. When you are going to use the still, take it out and hide it behind some bushes where a passing state trooper, snoopy neighbor, or fed busting you for pirated games won't see it. Keep the Alhambra jug where the still is going to be, cause they are way too big to hide anywhere.

Alternative medicine

ⓘ `misc.health.alternative`

There are those who'll tell you that conventional medicine only ceased to use tarot cards and leeches because they became unfashionable and that, when it gets down to details, most doctors can't deal with anything more complicated than a serious case of dandruff. You can find a lot of them in the *misc.health.alternative* newsgroup.

Alternative medicine is curiously attractive in that it presupposes that just about everything short of death and liberal tendencies can be cured, if only one is sufficiently aware of the natural world to know how to go about it. Unfortunately, most alternative medicine has not been the recipient of quite the level of scientific research that conventional remedies have, with the result that there's a potential degree of confusion over which aspects of alternative medicine are medicine and which are snake oil. Snake oil was alternative medicine once as well.

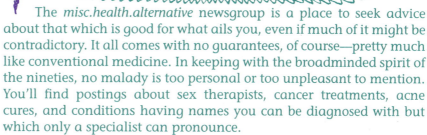

The *misc.health.alternative* newsgroup is a place to seek advice about that which is good for what ails you, even if much of it might be contradictory. It all comes with no guarantees, of course—pretty much like conventional medicine. In keeping with the broadminded spirit of the nineties, no malady is too personal or too unpleasant to mention. You'll find postings about sex therapists, cancer treatments, acne cures, and conditions having names you can be diagnosed with but which only a specialist can pronounce.

If you find yourself in ill health and you don't like what your doctor is saying—or perhaps if you just don't like what he's charging—you should consider spending some time lurking about in *misc.health.alternative*. Having said this, keep in mind that while netiquette specifies that newsgroups are not to contain commercial postings, libel, or excessive profanity, there's nothing preventing them from including a certain amount of science fiction.

Anglo-Saxon literature

 ftp.uu.net:/doc/literary/obi/Anglo-Saxon/

The phrase "Anglo-Saxon" has come to serve as a substitute for the phrase "vulgar words that shouldn't be used in polite company," perhaps suggesting that the people to whom it refers were largely barbarians. To be sure, they didn't drive Jags and weren't much for tofu salads, but the Angles and the Saxons created a sophisticated culture back when the last vestiges of the Roman empire were slipping inexorably into darkness.

The Angle and Saxon people dominated the southern portion of Britain about 1500 years ago, after the last of the Roman legions withdrew. Quite a few British place names recall them. Essex, for example, originally was east Saxony. The celtic tongue spoken by the Angles, *aenlisc*, was the forbearer of English.

Anglo-Saxon English was largely a spoken language, and many of the traditions and culture of Britain at this time perished with the coming of the Norman invasion in 1066. One of the most renowned of the Anglo-Saxon tales to have survived is a ninth-century bardic poem that recites the legend of Beowulf. Both structurally complex and literarily sophisticated, it speaks of a culture more advanced than that of the Normans who supplanted it.

The Wiretap Online Library includes the complete text of Beowulf, translated from the original old English by Francis B. Gummere in 1910. A lot more elemental than Shakespeare and nowhere near as pretentious, it's a good read even after a millennium.

If the Anglo-Saxons themselves were a pretty hearty lot, scholars of Anglo-Saxon literature periodically require peeling off the wall. Once you've read Beowulf itself, you really owe it to yourself to check out *not.beowulf*, which is available at the same FTP site. It's quite a bit shorter and rather easier to read. Any ninth-century bard who'd tried this one on would have found himself strung up by his own harp strings.

Finally, keep an eye out for the electronic Beowulf. Not quite the contradiction in terms it might seem to be, it's a sophisticated project to restore the original manuscript of Beowulf and make it available in an electronic form. It involves using ultraviolet photography and fiber-optic backlighting to reveal previously hidden sections of the work. As of this writing, more than 150 sections of the manuscript have been photographed.

Ultimately, toward the end of this decade, a complex reference with hyperlinks and commentaries on the Beowulf manuscript is planned. The editor of the project is Professor Kevin Kiernan from the Department of English at the University of Kentucky (*kiernan@beowulf.engl.uky.edu*).

Excerpt from Beowulf

LO, praise of the prowess of people-kings
of spear-armed Danes, in days long sped,
we have heard, and what honor the athelings
*   won!*
Oft Scyld the Scefing from squadroned foes,
from many a tribe, the mead-bench tore,
awing the earls. Since erst he lay
friendless, a foundling, fate repaid him:
for he waxed under welkin, in wealth he throve,
till before him the folk, both far and near,
who house by the whale-path, heard his mandate,
gave him gifts: a good king he!

✂ **Excerpt from** `not.beowulf`

Monster Grendel's tastes are plainish.
Breakfast? Just a couple Danish.
King of Danes is frantic, very.
Wait! Here comes the Malmo ferry
Bring Beowulf, his neighbor,
Mighty swinger with a saber!
Hrothgar's warriors hail the Swede,
Knocking back a lot of mead;
Then, when night engulfs the Hall
And the Monster makes his call,
Beowulf, with body-slam
Wrenches off his arm, Shazam!

Animation

ⓘ `rec.arts.animation`
ⓘ `rec.arts.anime`
ⓘ `rec.arts.anime.info`
ⓘ `rec.arts.anime.marketplace`
ⓘ `rec.arts.anime.stories`
🧘 `ftp.tcp.com:/pub/anime/Images/`
🐧 National Chung Cheung University ¦ miscellanies ¦ Japanese Anim Picture

Animation is one of the most expressive of the graphic arts and one of the most complex. It offers the potential for almost unlimited imagination—it can render on film anything that can be envisioned—but the level of work required to create even modest animation has strategically limited what has been done with it.

In addition, it has made the prospect of cutting corners in creating animated films attractive. Much of early animation looks so impressive because of the craftsmanship that went into creating it. This is a quality of animation that has been lost to a large extent, turning up only in a few fairly high-budget projects of late.

As the list of newsgroups and other resources at the beginning of this section might imply, there's considerable interest in animation about the net. The *rec.arts.animation* newsgroup is a general discussion of animation, covering everything from major releases by Disney down to this season's cartoons on Saturday morning. It offers an eclectic discussion of animation, embodying the views of both cartoon watchers and to some extent cartoon makers.

The *rec.arts.anime* newsgroups deal specifically with "japanimation," that is, animation being created in Japan. Much japanimation has a unique plastic quality about it, with very fluid movements and unworldly images. If you haven't encountered any of it moving, you might want to browse the FTP or gopher sites listed at the beginning of this section for a few still images captured from Japanese animated films.

Antiques

rec.antiques

There's a distinction between antiques and old stuff that should have been thrown out 200 years ago and unaccountably was not. This distinction, admittedly, is less clear than it might be in some circumstances; a warm summer afternoon when the air is thick with tourists is such a circumstance.

More than simply being old, an antique should be an example of the finest work of its age. At any period in history, one can find both master craftsmen and hacks. It's comforting to think that posterity preserves the work of the former and recycles that of the latter, although the reality often is very quite different.

The *rec.antiques* newsgroup is a lively microcosm of the antiques trade. You'll find people inquiring about the value of the cracked neo-Victorian Torquay toothpick holder that's been in the family for generations—typically, less than the value of the toothpicks contained therein—and serious antique dealers exchanging bits of esoterica. Unlike many newsgroups, things frequently are bought and sold through *rec.antiques*.

One of the most interesting aspects of *rec.antiques* is the occasional advice about how to date objects, spot fakes, and generally make some sense of the intricacies of the past. The excerpt in this section, dealing with scrimshaw, is typical of this. Should you not have encountered the term before, scrimshaw is ornate carving done by sailors during the last century. It usually is found on bone, whale teeth, or walrus ivory.

Excerpt from rec.antiques

I recently acquired—at auction—some purportedly genuine scrimshaw. There are five pieces in all, three whale teeth and two walrus tusks. Or at least that's what they look like. How can I tell tooth from tusk from plastic? And if it's genuine material, is there a valid test to differentiate new from old? And finally, how can one

distinguish between recently carved and 150 years old? All the auctioneer would say was "These pieces have been in storage since 1972."

Plastic fluoresces under ultraviolet light; bone doesn't.

These things were made by 19th century European whalers working in the arctic. To tell genuine from modern fakes, either fiberglass or whale tooth needs some experience of handling the real thing. The scenes were of nautical or even pornographic themes. Christies in London are having a sale this week of a very important scrimshaw collection, prices range from 200-10,000 pounds. A hot needle test is OK to test a piece in an unobtrusive place, but won't tell you the age of the tooth.

Oh, I'm getting a bad feeling about this. I tried the hot-nail test last night: plastic. Anyone interested in buying some really attractive replica scrimshaw pieces?

Arcana arcanorum

 `ftp.spies.com:/Library/Documents/arcana.doc`

The Arcana is a curious little document of somewhat recent origin, purporting to have been written by "the prophet Aloysius;" no mention of who he actually might be is contained in the file.

The Arcana is a sort of low-budget oracle. It purports to allow you to perform divination without the expense of a pack of tarot cards or the effort of painting runes on stones. The selection of tarot cards or the casting of runes, says the author of this document, when done in modest quantities, appears to be random but actually is the intelligence of the universe communicating with us. As such, it hardly matters what you use to select random elements from. A pack of playing cards is easy to come by.

How useful you find the Arcana will be determined by how much faith you put in the foregoing premise and in divination in general. There's a certain comfort in the thought of an intelligent universe and perhaps more so in the thought that the universe is sufficiently egalitarian as not to care what means you use to communicate with it.

It seems worth noting that the Bicycle Playing Card Company produces both poker decks and tarot cards. If the former are easier to come by, the latter are a good deal more attractive.

Excerpt from `arcana.doc`

ARCANA ARCANORUM came about on one summer's day when I was lazily pondering (as I often do) about the Universe. Surely, there must be some truth to the Tarot and similar methods of divination: they have been around for millennia; this proves that there must be something to them. I am a mathematician by trade, and it occurred to me that the divining power lies not in the Cards themselves, but in the fabric of space-time.

Statistical laws imply that a deck, properly shuffled, will yield the same chance of a given Card being drawn. The key to this axiom is that this is true—but it is a law of averages; if you draw a Card from a deck ten thousand times, you'll find that each Card has roughly the same chances of being drawn. Equilibrium is the key; the key to Equilibrium is number. The key to Divination, I found, is in the Cards that are chosen at first. The Universe is forced to average the selection of a Card out with large numbers of drawings; but for small numbers, the Universe has a method to communicate with us, the sentient beings inside Her womb, waiting to be born.

It dawned on me then that the deck of Cards (Tarot, Thoth, etc.) —nay, even the method of Divination—is irrelevant. Whether you are throwing sticks on the ground, picking Cards from an ornately-decorated deck, or casting rune-inscribed dried clay markers, the effects are the same. The power to divine is in the person, not in the divining instrument.

Thus came my Illumination: Why use a deck of Tarot Cards? Why cast runes? Why throw sticks and consult a chart? If it is true that the Diviner is important and not the medium, then it is unimportant which medium actually is used, and all things will return to Equilibrium, as they always have and always will.

Hence ARCANA ARCANORUM, the Playing-Card Tarot, was born. If medium is not the message after all, then why not use a very simple, easy-to-understand, easily-obtained, inexpensive one? That is, the average deck of playing Cards that can be bought in any store.

Archery

 alt.archery

Depending on where you live and how tight your grocery budget is, you might regard bow sports as anything from a bit of diversion to a source of protein. I tend toward the former; there's nothing like an afternoon spent with several dozen arrows keeping the cardboard box population in check.

Archery has a long and noble history, although very little of its past need have much bearing on the craft as it's practiced today. Contemporary bows are brilliant examples of high technology doing something that used to be brutish and primitive. A modern compound bow will multiply by several times the strength of whoever pulls it. Alloy arrows don't warp or split like their wooden forebearers. Bow sights and other targeting innovations make it possible to shoot predictably. You can get fiber-optic sights for a bow to allow you to target it accurately in the dark.

The days of a length of cord tied between a bent twig are, thankfully, long past.

There's something singularly elemental about archery—even if all you're shooting at are paper targets. Assuming that your bow didn't come from K-Mart, the only thing between you and the target before you is your own skill. Archery is largely intuition, with a bit of extra muscle tissue in your left arm.

The sophistication of contemporary bows and such does make the sport of archery considerably more complex than it once was. There are numerous very good bow designs available, all sorts of different weights of arrows, and pointy bits for the ends of them. Not just any bent twig will do.

If you currently shoot or are thinking that the sigh of a bowstring might be a bit more satisfying than the rumble of a treadmill machine after a long, hard day in that corner office, the *alt.archery* newsgroup is an exemplary resource. It offers the opportunity to bend the ears of a good number of serious archers. You can avoid having the first bow that you buy be a decorative but otherwise useless wall ornament, or you can debate the finer points of bow sports with people who actually engage in them.

Compare this to the proprietors of most of the shops that sell archery supplies—and footballs, and tennis rackets, and jogging shoes, and treadmill machines.

Excerpt from `alt.archery`

Many years ago... I was into target archery. I've not shot for a long time, but I am now thinking of getting... a crossbow. I have a number of questions...

I wish to obtain a crossbow for the following reasons:

- target shooting (not hunting)

- to appease my general interest in crossbows

- lastly, and probably most controversially, self defense. I live in a bad neighborhood—home breakins and assaults and murders happen with disturbing frequency. I wish to be able to defend my home, loved ones, and own life, if need be, and I do not wish to own a firearm. I am aware that a bow is not ideal for this purpose... but it is better than nothing, which is what I have now.

Thus, I am looking for information on:

- Crossbows appropriate for the above uses, and sources for them.

- Is there any reasons whatsoever to obtain a compound crossbow?

- I don't know much about crossbows — what should I know?

- What is the price range for a good quality crossbow suitable for my intended purposes?

- Can one generally use crossbows at archery ranges?

- What is the accuracy of a crossbow compared to a standard bow?

- Are crossbows unstrung after use like a target bow, or left strung like a compound bow?

- What are typical draw weights?

- Drawing down a long bow with nocked arrow is trivial, but it is not obvious to me how this is done with a crossbow. How does the trigger mechanism work? How do you not fire it once it is drawn?

- Is the purchase of crossbows regulated as firearms are?

If you don't want a firearm, I would advise a small baseball bat or an ax/sledge hammer handle or possible avoidance/running.

Compounds do not have to have a let-off, and compound crossbows don't, as far as I know. I do know that there are quite a few hunting type crossbows out there that are compound. Not sure of the ratio of recurves to compounds.

Same safety applies as with firearms/bows. For care, I would refer you to the instructions from the manufacturer of the crossbow that you buy. Different crossbows need different levels of care (one thing that comes to mind is some crossbows need to have the part of the stock the string slides across waxed, and others don't).

[Archery ranges] should be ok. Crossbows bolts don't penetrate any better than compound bows, but some people just don't like them.

The only thing that I know of that makes a crossbow more accurate is that you don't have to hold the weight back while aiming.

For the hunting style, typically 100 pounds minimum [draw weight].

If you draw it, you fire it with the heavier weight bows. It is too difficult to try and decock a 150 pound draw bow with one hand while using the other to pull the trigger to release the string.

If you really are dead set against a firearm, you should still leave your crossbow in the closet. The next best thing to a firearm is a big can of that red-pepper spray and a baseball bat. The pepper spray is quick to bring into action, is good for multiple shots, and will stop a lot of criminals. It won't kill them, but killing them really isn't important, keeping them from killing you is. If you really want to kill them, hose 'em down with the pepper spray and then beat 'em to death with the bat. This will look much better for you when you go to court for killing an intruder (assuming you live to). Juries don't take well to exotic killing machines like crossbows.

Sporting goods mail order houses like Cabelas and Gander Mountain sell crossbows. Their catalogs can be ordered from ads in many sporting magazines, like Outdoor Life, Field and Stream, etc. Occasionally, the paramilitary supply catalogs like U.S. Cavalry and Brigade Quartermasters will offer crossbows but the selection tends to be limited, and features only the high priced 'Rambo' types.

Most of the crossbows I have seen lately are compound. They are a little easier to draw, and they shoot a little faster than the recurves. Holding the draw weight isn't a factor, but engaging the trigger mechanism seems to be a little easier with the reduced full-draw weight of the compounds.

They look something like a firearm, and a very nasty one at that. For this reason, they are subject to the same inane laws as firearms in

many jurisdictions, check your local laws. California, for example, is currently considering a new 'assault weapon' ban, and said law counts crossbows. Yeah, I know, when's the last time somebody held up a 7-11 at bow point? But I haven't heard of any mass bayonetings lately either, and they banned them too. Check *rec.guns* for further info.

[The cost is] two to five hundred dollars, plus accessories.

Audio

 `rec.audio`

 `rec.audio.high-end`

Lo, ye veterans of the turntable wars, proponents of tube sound, owners of platinum-plated speaker connectors, and hangers on upon the retinue of infinite baffle speakers, if you like nothing better than to debate the merits of audio technology, the *rec.audio* and *rec.audio.high-end* newsgroups will provide you with almost as much enjoyment as your sound system. Bubbling with topics that range from mildly esoteric to wholly demonic, they offer advice to newcomers and platonic dialogs as to the true nature of sound to the enlightened.

Serious audio—that which doesn't come from Sears—is a somewhat bewildering topic. There are a number of manufacturers of unconventional sound equipment, some of which seems to require an engineering degree to properly appreciate. Typically very expensive, these are not the sorts of things that you'd want to buy only to find out that you've mortgaged the cat for a lemon.

To further complicate the issue—at least for the true audio perfectionist—the relative merits of various amplifier, speaker, and other component technologies often are diminishingly subtle. Not wishing to have the speaker inquisition camped out in our front pasture with a writ for heresy bearing my name, I won't suggest that these differences are inaudible, but one arguably requires better than average ears to fully appreciate them. The *rec.audio* newsgroups will let you compare notes with other sets of ears.

In fairness, you probably will find the postings in *rec.audio* to be amusing even if your sound system came with folding headphones and a belt clip. Among the topics that are being bashed out as I write this are:

- Could the Russians turn a few dollars by making really good vacuum tubes on the supply runs to the Mir space station? The consensus is that they probably couldn't, as "natural"

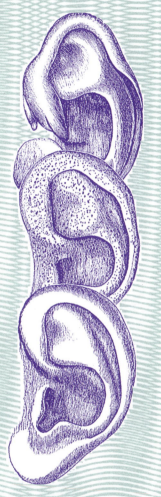

vacuum isn't nearly as clean as the artificial vacuum usually found in tubes, even if you use really good imported vacuum brought in fresh every morning by Federal Express.
- Is there any future in plasma speakers? Should the technology have thus far eluded you, plasma speakers work by passing an electric current through an acetylene flame to generate sound. Conventional wisdom says that the Russians have more chance of making a killing with vacuum tubes.
- Does Dolby surround sound actually sound any different than sound from two sets of stereo speakers? Everyone who listened to surround sound in a stereo shop and bought it said it did and everyone who listened to surround sound in a stereo shop and turned it down said it didn't.
- Can headphones "mess with your head"? This discussion digressed into things like listening to music through headphones and a subwoofer, such that you could feel it as well.
- Would there be any interest in a class action lawsuit against the audio magazines that recommended that people daub green magic marker ink on their compact discs a few years back? Little enthusiasm was exhibited for this, perhaps on the assumption that people who didn't do it don't care and people who did are too embarrassed to admit it.

Quite a few more mundane—and more brand-specific—topics also were discussed.

If you're thinking about upgrading your stereo or if you can talk decibels and oversampling with the best of them, you'll find these two newsgroups invaluable.

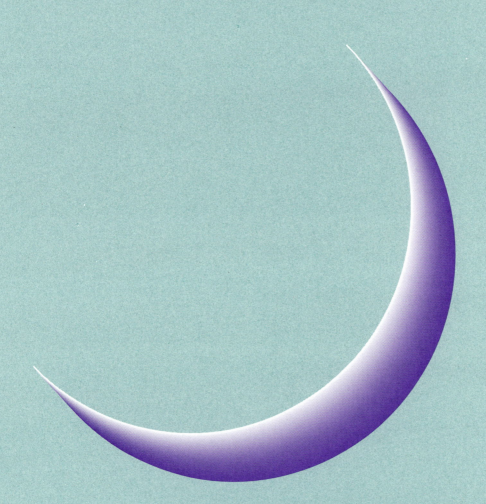

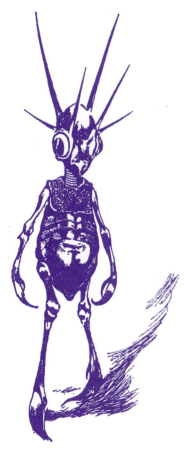

Babylon 5

 `alt.tv.babylon-5`

It was the dawn of the third age of mankind . . . . it also was the dawn of one of the more riotous newsgroups on the Internet. Opinions vary about the "Babylon 5" television series—it's regarded as everything from a pale clone of "Star Trek" to science fiction at its most imaginative. You'll find both extremes and everything in between expounded upon at length in *alt.tv.babylon- 5*. Perhaps this in itself is a comment on the worth of the series; nobody would get anywhere near this worked up about it if it were mediocre.

The *alt.tv.babylon-5* newsgroup is a place to exchange views about "Babylon 5" episodes, to discuss the technical details and minutia of the show, to go head-to-head with vile aliens and other lesser species who really don't like it, and to trade bits of inside information about recent and upcoming installments. A singularly lively newsgroup, *alt.tv.babylon-5* seems very much like some of the more unruly levels of the Babylon 5 space station itself—thick with laughter, shouts, the taste of blood, and the aromas of exotic drinks from unvisited worlds. At least, it is if you have a bit of imagination.

Be warned, however—while the subjects of the postings in *alt.tv.babylon-5* are frequently of things alien to these shores, the language is all in English. It's frequently pretty coarse English, too—both the fans and detractors of "Babylon 5" are a vocal lot, and the flames in *alt.tv.babylon-5* frequently reach stellar proportions. Sidearms are not checked at the door.

The "Babylon 5" episodes can be found uplinked on satellite television at G4-21 on Friday mornings at 10:00 AM EST as of this writing—as well as on local broadcast stations everywhere. See the section of this book dealing with "Satellite television."

43

Bagpipes

 cs.dartmouth.edu:/pub/bagpipes

Dartmouth Colleg cs:dartmouth.edu
¦ Bagpipe Archives

bagpipes@cs.dartmouth.edu

bagpipes-request@cs.dartmouth.edu

The pipes are one of those remarkable instruments that can sound like the voice of the heavens in the right hands or like a hundred barn cats in heat in the wrong ones. While one usually thinks of the great highland pipes of Scotland when this instrument turns up, there are several sorts of pipes currently in use. The smaller uilleann pipes are a common feature of Irish music. They play in a more convenient key and won't deafen anyone standing within 50 feet.

I should note that I've had the good fortune to live next door to a highly accomplished piper, and I've had the opportunity to acquire all sorts of pipe lore without having to suffer through hours of chanter screeching and other phenomena common to novice pipers.

Pipes of one sort or another have been around since classical times, although the arrangement of pipes and a mechanism to blow them—a bag or a bellows—is somewhat more recent.

Pipers appear to be quite active on the Net. The aforementioned references include several frequently asked questions, documents, and a mailing list. In the latter, you'll encounter discussions of acquiring and maintaining pipes, the proper attire for formal playing—a sporran by itself is not sufficient—how to locate reeds and other essential elements of pipers' hardware, and so on.

There's even a set of T_EX macros to assist in typesetting pipe music.

Excerpt from the Bagpipe Mailing List

What do you do to keep your pipes running in the winter? One friend of mine in Edmonton just puts them away for the winter, but maybe there's a better way. Any interesting tips, pointers, suggestions?

Well, a tip that I heard from a local Toronto piper which I have not yet tried is to put a guitar humidifier in the bellows. These snake-like foam rubber things are used by a lot of stringed instrument

players to keep their instruments working through the winter, so it may well work with the pipes too. I suspect that it is less of a problem with the highland pipes because in that case the humidity of one's breath would keep the reeds just moist enough. However, I bet that the continuous drying out and rehydrating of the bag would be pretty rough in cold dry climates.

Sigh—I put my uilleann and northumbrian pipes away in the winter and the summer too. They start sounding good (or more to the point, I spend less time fussing with them than playing) in early spring and stop working by mid June—then in the fall the same cycle happens again. I used to have the time and energy to keep them going all year round—one definitely needs winter and summer reeds.

The most exciting thing that has happened to me recently has been plastic—I got a plastic highland practice chanter with plastic reed. It always works, and I can carry it around in freezing weather or play it in the rain, and it doesn't take five minutes to put on or off when I have to go chase my kid. It has a nice tone if I use a lot of breath support, too. Now if it only had more notes....

Let me pass on something which Christy O'Leary said he did to keep the pipes going on tours with the Boys of the Lough, in hot dry regions, when he has to contend with hot stage lights as well as the climate. He says he just takes a humidifier with him — the same kind

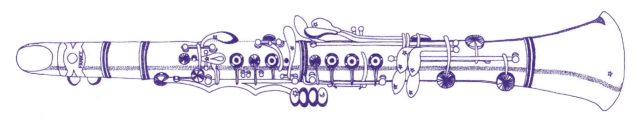

of thing you put in a child's room — and put it on stage, just under the bellows, and turn it on. He said it worked fine.

About once a month, I run a clarinet cleaner through my drones, blow stick and up into my chanter with light clarinet oil ... I'm trying to add a bit of oil into the wood to replenish the natural ones as they diminish, to reduce the tendency of the moisture to so rapidly be absorbed and depleted.

Bass playing

- rec.music.makers.bass
- alt.guitar.bass

There are traditionally two sorts of stringed bass instruments, these being the upright bass and the bass guitar. Paradoxically, while they're frequently treated as being species of the same instrument, they harken from two very different evolutionary strata of instrument design. The upright bass is a huge viol, while the bass guitar evolved from conventional guitars.

The diminishing popularity of the upright bass, despite its superb sound and acoustic dynamics, might stem in some small part from its dimensions—and perhaps its cost. Not the sort of fiddle you'll get under your chin without considerable difficulty, an upright bass doesn't lend itself to a life on the road.

Electric bass guitars are somewhat simpler instruments than electric six-string guitars, but they have aspects of subtlety and nuance none the less. Some of this might be perceptible only to bass players, of course. Rarely regarded as a foreground instrument, the refinements of bass guitar design and bass playing often are less than obvious.

Despite the apparently simple operation of a bass guitar—bang the strings and sound happens—there's a considerable range of playing techniques for bass. With the application of string popping, different picking techniques, and so on, the instrument can do quite a lot more than make booming noises.

Perhaps more so than a conventional electric guitar, refined bass guitars are subtle and personal things. It's singularly difficult to choose a bass that really suits you in 15 minutes at the back of a music shop. Having benefit of conversation with other bass players is invaluable.

The *rec.music.makers.bass* and *alt.guitar.bass* newsgroups offer a forum to discuss the purchase of your first bass—or perhaps your tenth—to trade playing techniques, to discuss instrument modifications and maintenance, and generally to enjoy the company of other bass players. It's also a handy place to come to learn the wisdom of lifelong bass artists. For example, when the tubes start glowing bright blue it's time to turn down the volume.

Beer

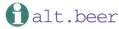 alt.beer

There actually are two aspects of beer popularly discussed on the Internet, these being brewing and consumption. You'll find a separate section dealing with the former under "Home brewing" elsewhere in this book. The *alt.beer* newsgroup offers a place to talk about drinking beer.

Beer is a timeless beverage. The ancient Egyptians had it, and possibly several middle eastern cultures before them. It has been refined through millennia, enjoyed by kings and commoners—although the kings rarely admit to it—and has become the foundation for one of the few truly stable growth industries in the western world. Whereas people might not have enough money to feed themselves, shoe their children, or pay their taxes, they'll always find a few coins for a drink.

In some countries, all of these are largely the same thing, of course. The taxes levied on beer can be thought of as a contribution to the government coffers that help pay for shoes and food and politicians' trips to Jamaica.

The *alt.beer* newsgroup is a place to discuss the merits of various brands of beer. This is not a newsgroup for people who just drink the usual suds at the pub down the block. Beer is an art form, and there is more subtlety and refinement in a glass of beer than in all the great paintings of history. At least, there is if you really get into the matter.

If you frequent *alt.beer*, you'll become aware of great beers around the world, the criteria for a perfect pint, and numerous issues of beer drinking that absolutely never turn up in the brief snatches of conversation permitted in beer commercials.

Excerpt from `alt.beer`

Note: This is a collection of responses to the question, "What is the world's worst beer?"

Anybody taste Billy (Carter) Beer? Don't know who brewed it (if that's the word) but I've still got several cans of the stuff, hoping that someday it will have value as political memorabilia. I sure have no urge to pop a top.

RJ's Ginseng Beer, brewed by the Stevens Point Brewing Company in Wisconsin. It was the ill-conceived brainchild of the Chicago-based company that bought out the brewery in September of 1992. Fortunately it did not live long.

Carlsberg Elephant Beer is definitely an acquired taste. Urk!

Victoria Bitter, from Australia, is quite awful. I am from Australia, by the way. I just can't stand the old VB.

Speaking of the worst... what ever happened to Red, White, and Blue? That was far worse than... Billy Beer.

Stoney's Beer from the hills of Pennsylvania around Bloomsburg. Even the charm of 16 ounce longnecks can't redeem this swill.

I'm not sure if anyone has already mentioned this one, but my friends and I tried a god-awful poor excuse for a beer called "Harley-Davidson Beer." It came complete with the cycle logo and all. No one could finish their cans. It was that bad! Someone must have purposely created the worst beer possible just to see how many people would buy it for the name/novelty. Anyway, this beer takes the cake for undrinkability... a warning to all!

Worst beer I ever tasted in England was, without a doubt, Fremlins bitter. I think it's brewed locally in Kent. It definitely tasted like it had some sort of petrol-based substance in it, like kerosene (although I can't be sure as I've never had the comparative pleasure of drinking kerosene).

Some time ago my father and I embarked upon a "bad beer" binge. I guess it was to remind ourselves that we should be thankful for the wonderful beers we have. The one that springs to my mind like a shot was called "Liebotschoner(sic) Cream Ale". It was... in a word — putrid. Can't say as though I didn't expect it since it only cost about US$4 a case. It would definitely get my vote for being outlawed let alone worst beer.

A couple of weeks ago I tried Mickey's Big Mouth for the first time. We were stuck in a bar for half an hour and it was $4 for a pitcher. I'm not very familiar with American malt liquors, but I'll take this is a fairly accurate example of the style. It tasted like ordinary mega-brew (not much taste) with the addition of extra alcohol and corn. In fact the flavor was *extremely* grainy. Quite disgusting.

The worst beer I've tasted to date was called "Golden Promise Organic Beer." What "organic" means in the context of beer I don't know, but it was from Scotland so I was expecting a heck of a lot more from it. Maybe that's why I remember it being so bad.

Has anyone from the Philadelphia area ever had Piels or Piels Light? A few years ago, a case of 16 ounce returnables would run you about 7 dollars. Rancid yak sweat in a bottle, but cheap.

Piels is terrible. Coors Light actually has some resemblance of taste when compared to Piels. I never had the guts to try Piels light.

Utica Club. Hands down. I think the secret is in the water. Just writing the name gives me a headache.

The world's worst beer is (arguably) Singapore's "Raffles Light." A truly awful, incredibly bad beer, even by the standards of light beer.

DB Draught is pretty gruesome.

The worst beer I can recall having tried was Steeler, a local beer in Hamilton, Ontario brewed by Amstel. Rumor had it that Steeler was just Amstel brewed with Hamilton's less-than-perfect tap water. Having consumed Hamilton's tap water, it certainly sounds plausible.

I had that stuff once while visiting in the Hamilton area. Not the worst I'd ever had (that would be Pearl Light), but it was nothing to get excited about.

We have two... contenders for the worst beer ever brewed, well maybe not brewed, but whatever. Boulevard, a Kansas City treat. Truly bad.

PLEASE!!

Colt 45 Ice. Probably one of the worst beers ever. It kind of tasted and smelled like a dead skunk, only without the redeeming qualities.

I recall a beer called Jacob's Best which was pretty bad... I don't think it even worked for slugs.

There are any number of Wisconsin breweries that put out a generic lager that tastes like rotted newspaper. Among these beers are: Regal Brau, Hi Brau, Wisconsin Club, Rex, Huber... but the worst is Brunig's.

Bicycles

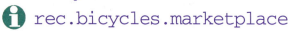
rec.bicycles.marketplace

There are people who would not regard one of those machines from K-Mart with two wheels and handlebars as being a bicycle. In the rarefied world of leading-edge bicycle technology, it's possible to have long and truly relevant discussions about issues such as seat posts and spoke implementations. The better bicycle designs take into account matters such as suspension, rider geometry, chain path, and all sorts of other factors that the people at K-Mart have clearly never given a moment's thought to.

If you're serious about your bicycle, you will no doubt find many kindred souls in *rec.bicycles.marketplace*. It's something of a dual-purpose newsgroup, as it includes both eclectic discussions of all manner of bicycle technology and numerous advertisements from individuals selling bicycles or related bits.

The *rec.bicycles.marketplace* is a very serious newsgroup. If you're looking for advice about bicycles, you'll find it here, typically without any pale attempts at Net humor or ill-considered flaming. Keep in mind, however, that the advice that you receive might be a bit over your head. If the perfect bicycle were to turn out to be available only from a manufacturer located halfway up Mount Everest, one suspects that the regulars in *rec.bicycles.marketplace* would be hiring on Sherpas even as you read this.

Big Book of Mischief

 `ftp.spies.com:\Library\Untech\tbbom13.txt`

 `Wiretap Online Library | Questionables | The Big Book of Mischief v1.3`

Don't try this at home. *The Big Book of Mischief* is a long treatise about how to make explosives, pick locks, and generally do things likely to endear you to people lobbying for tougher anti-crime legislation. Actually, very few of the techniques discussed there are all that reliable, and their presentation is a bit incoherent at times. The recipes for devising homemade explosives are particularly nasty and not at all unlikely to cause useful portions of your anatomy to become detached from the rest of you if you experiment with them.

A rough overview of the discussion of explosives in this document suggests that most of them will indeed explode. Very few of them will do so predictably, to wit, after you've removed yourself to a safe distance.

The discussions of lock picking are inconsiderately vague, and genuinely incorrect in a few places. One suspects that the authors of several motion picture screenplays, who have their characters open locks with a bent paperclip, have used *The Big Book of Mischief* as reference.

Other inventions, such as pop-can explosives and tennis ball cannons, will only cause devastation for their intended recipients if you can convince their intended recipients to make them and subsequently set them off.

Despite its having few practical applications for all but the most self-destructive miscreants, *The Big Book of Mischief* is an engaging read. You might want to consider it as a repository for all the half truths and folk wisdom of society's darker side. It also is a disturbing insight into how destructive various common household chemicals can be if they get together unexpectedly.

Birds

rtfm.mit.edu:/pub/usenet/
news.answers/pets-birds-faq/

Of all the creatures populating the earth, birds are perhaps the most attractive. Aside from looking pretty—except for the buzzards—they embody one of the innermost aspirations of humans, the freedom of flight. They are as much unlike human beings as anything can be without going into politics.

Small domesticated birds make engaging pets, or at least, they can. As with any pet, there's a lot more to keeping birds than simply buying the requisite hardware and feeding them regularly. Birds are complex creatures. Choosing a bird that's appropriate to your lifestyle, for example, can mean the difference between bringing a diverting companion into your home and letting a maniacal demon loose in your living room.

For example, many people who have an interest in exotic birds wind up owning some species of parrot. There are a number of lesser parrots available, such as lovebirds, for those who imagine themselves too clever to spring for the deluxe model. The articulate qualities of parrots are engaging for about a week, but most parrots don't know when to shut up. Having your parrot offer to perform convoluted sexual acts with your guests—however well meaning the offer might be—is certain to cause you some measure of embarrassment.

There's a lot to know about choosing and caring for birds. The files at the FTP site listed at the beginning of this section will prove to be of enormous assistance. They'll help you choose a bird that will not make you want to spit roast it shortly after bringing it home, and give you pointers about food, cages, medical problems, and other nuances of bird ownership.

While the publisher of this book would no doubt frown on my expanding the acronym which forms the name of this FTP site, you might want to look it up in the acronyms list mentioned elsewhere in this book if it proves unfamiliar. There are few aspects of pet care to which it's more applicable than to the domestication of birds.

Bizarre

 talk.bizarre

Rational thought can be something of a labor, especially toward the end of the week. Sometimes we all just want to cut a hole into an alternate universe, hop through the reality matrix, and vanish into illogic. It's hard on your Reeboks, but it will certainly improve your day.

In centuries gone by, people in this frame of mind might be encountered in the village square babbling incoherently and subsequently would find themselves involved in major career shifts. There's not much of a dental plan available for the town idiot. Things have gotten a lot better in recent years; you can go exercise your ability to be off the wall on the Net. If you're really good at it, people might even applaud. You won't hear them, of course.

If you're really bad, they'll flame you, but this is arguably better than being required to stagger from mud hut to mud hut drooling and begging for scraps of food.

The *talk.bizarre* newsgroup is arguably the most unusual of the undirected groups. Its only requirement seems to be that postings to it must be very, very strange. A quick stroll through it as I wrote this turned up haiku poetry to the memory of Richard Nixon—not all of it wholly Zenlike—plans for mutant Barbie dolls, long and detailed complaints about users of the America Online network . . . and the following fairly lucid explanation of what *talk.bizarre* is really all about.

 Excerpt from talk.bizarre

This is the group where police sirens can be dimly heard in the distance.

This is the group where children should be neither seen nor heard, but felt.

This is the group where colors can be expressed in cartesian coordinates.

This is the group where you must check your Topsiders at the door.

*This is the group where the Keywords line *must* be left blank, or else.*

This is the group where the ghouls roam the arctic wasteland, seeking blood.

This is the group where your appendix is no longer a vestigial organ.

This is the group where you can get souvlaki 24 hours a day, free of charge.

This is the group where your status is measured by your skill at logging.

This is the group where microbes are regarded as our reincarnated ancestors.

*This is the group where the real Kraft mayonnaise simply *cannot* be creamier.*

This is the group where "Sacco and Vanzetti" are three four-letter words.

This is the group where you can be cured of most kinds of spinal disorders.

This is the group where Etruscan couples can meet and discuss current events.

This is the group where a smile is your passport, but the papers are forged.

This is the group where marsh gas is an irritating and persistent menace.

This is the group where you may be deified if you know the theme to Studs.

This is the group where we bear no love for those accursed Catalan knights.

This is the group where you may bathe your soul in harmful ultraviolet rays.

This is the group where you pass an eternity before being sent to alt.angst.

This is the group where almost everybody uses Percodan on a regular basis.

Perhaps the implication in this is that anyone who doesn't understand it probably won't understand *talk.bizarre* either.

B
I
Z
A
R
R
E

The amusement value of the *talk.bizarre* actually is somewhat variable. It seems to range between sophomoric ranting with no real direction to long threads of pithy remarks and clever observations. One has the sense that a lot of the instigators of the postings have their own names at the tops of their lists of favorite authors.

The primary requirements for seeking out the interesting bits of *talk.bizarre* are a fairly broadminded sense of humor—the ability to laugh heartily at grass stains and clouds will be an asset—a fair bit of time to kill, and no meaningful aversion to harsh language. This is the ideal newsgroup for people who like the tenor of *alt.flame* but prefer a somewhat more intellectual environment.

Body Piercing

 rec.arts.bodyart

Pierced ears are very common in western cultures, and pierced noses not unheard of. However, you can pierce all sorts of other parts of your body, and many devotees of body art do. Popular targets include your nipples, navel, penis, labia, and buttocks.

Check the current position of your hands. If they've unconsciously moved to protect any of the aforementioned areas of your body, you probably don't want to read any further.

The *rec.arts.bodyart* newsgroup is a gathering place for people who like to punch holes in themselves, as well as for those interested in tattoos. It typically includes discussions of where to pierce, what to pierce it with, and the possible results of doing so.

As with more conventional pierced ears, pierced nipples and other areas have a metal object more or less permanently inserted in them to prevent the openings in question from closing up. You can make a fashion statement with the things thrust through you, and quite a lot of discussion of unconventional jewelry floats around in *rec.arts.bodyart* as well.

Much of the interest in piercing seems to be sexual. Nipple rings also are said to be particularly useful in bondage games.

There is a serious side to body piercing, of course, in that, if it isn't done properly, the pierced area can become badly infected. The regulars at *rec.arts.bodypart* will tell you how to get pierced and how to avoid complications. You'll find frequent postings comparing the techniques, facilities, and prices of professional piercing in various large cities.

Finally, you'll find numerous postings describing in exquisite detail what it feels like to be pierced, to walk around with bits of metal dangling from you, to make love with a pierced partner and, perhaps more amusing still than not warning someone about being pierced before she goes down on you, trying to get through an airport metal detector with several large metal rings in your jeans.

Unlike many of the *alt.sex* newsgroups discussed elsewhere in this book, there doesn't seem to be a predominance of male participants in *rec.arts.bodyarts*. It also is an unusually civilized and articulate newsgroup. There are few other sources of information about this somewhat esoteric practice that are as complete and informative.

It just might make you feel a bit creepy to read it.

Bonsai

alt.bonsai

A hundred feet beyond the back of our house is a forest of jack pines that seems to stretch into the heavens and goes back for miles. There's an immeasurable serenity in communing with trees. For one thing, none of them have phones.

The immeasurable serenity of communing with trees is a bit more difficult to achieve if you live in an apartment. For this and all sorts of other reasons, you might want to investigate the practice of growing bonsai plants. A *bonsai* is a tree or shrub grown in a small vessel and typically stunted to keep it dwarfed.

Bonsai plants date back to sixth century Japan. The earliest written record of them is found in a scroll from the Karamkura period, between 1192 and 1333 A.D.

Most conventional trees can be grown as bonsais. The more classic bonsai varieties include Japanese Black Pine, five-needle pine, Sargents Juniper, and Japanese maples. Bonsai techniques allow both the stems and the foliage of a tree to be dwarfed.

The *alt.bonsai* newsgroup is a place to discuss growing bonsai trees with other bonsai gardeners. It frequently includes postings about unusual species to plant, sources for seeds and tools, and bits of useful bonsai lore. It's an accessible source of information about bonsai gardening, with almost no flaming—not surprising, I suppose, for a group of people concerned with trees.

Excerpt from `alt.bonsai`

I am interested in locating Mimosa pudica (Mimosa) and Acacia (bull's horn acacia or others) seeds or trees. Also, has anyone had experience with these trees as bonsai in the mid-Atlantic area? I had a mimosa tree in Mexico City. It was a fat grower and even produced nice pinkish-white flowers that looked like delicate tufts of feathers. Mimosa and Acacia are mentioned in the Brooklyn Botanical Gardens book on indoor bonsai. Thanks for the help. I will share the results.

I have about fifteen Acacia species growing as seedlings. I am fond of legumes, and probably have a couple dozen legume species in all. I got many of my seeds from Carter Seeds... They stock about 40 Acacia species. Being a wholesaler, their smallest seed package (from US $5 to 15) is one ounce and contains from hundreds to thousands of seeds.

I have a lot left over, and I've been meaning to offer them on the Net. Might as well make this the time. To those who e-mail me their mail address in the next two weeks, I will send a share of my legume seed stock.

Species are Acacia contricta, cyanophylla (X), farnesiana, floribunda (X), greggii, horrida, melanoxylon (X), pendula, podalyriaefolia (X), rubida, stenophylla (X). ['X' denotes species that produce phyllodes—flattened leafstalks—instead of leaves, which I think will make for not-so-good bonsai.] Also, I have some Cercidium floridum (blue palo verde) and Prosopsis pubescens (screwbean mesquite) seeds; from what I've read here, these Southwest US desert species put out long tap roots and are probably not suitable for bonsai.

Some of the Acacias have more potential than others. Before I knew what they were, I got the species that produce phyllodes as they mature, and they look hopeless (but I continue to grow them for their novelty value). I asked a couple Aussies about these typically Australian species and both said nobody they know of does Acacias there. After one year, the other species are looking cute the way only legumes can.

The Simon & Schuster book has one entry of Acacia sp. They are not specific about species. Looks kind of nice, whatever it is.

I haven't seen much in the literature on Acacia. Someone wrote to me that in South Africa, they do a local species in an umbrella style, typical of their appearance on the veldt. One subscriber wrote of having some indoor Acacia farnesiana, and I have a couple dozen in their third year, and they seem to have potential.

Legitimate bonsai legumes I have are Pithecellobium Flexicaule (Texas ebony), Calliandra haematocyphylla (red powderpuff), Robinia pseudocacia (black locust), Akebia quinata (akebia), Ceratonia siliqua (carob), Albizia julibrissin (silk tree), and Jacaranda mimosifolia (jacaranda). I also am growing A. baileyana, decurrens, and xanthophloea; Gleditsia triacanthos (honey locust); Leucaena gigantica; and some mystery legumes that I collected locally, and haven't classified.

I had a Mimosa pudica (sensitive plant) many years ago. I remember it flowering and even producing viable seeds. That was before I was into bonsai. I don't think they get very big; do their trunks ever get thick?

Books

 `books.com (Book Stacks Unlimited)`

While there are several ways to actually order books over the Internet, the house favorite is unquestionably Book Stacks Unlimited, which is available through Telnet at the address listed at the beginning of this section. The *books.com* site offers an extensive database of titles; it's not restricted to technical books. You can search the index by author, subject, title, and so on. Having found the books that you're after, you can place an order by plastic.

I was pleased to note that Book Stacks Unlimited carries all my books, for example—even my fiction. This is clearly a book shop of taste and discrimination.

Books at Wiretap

 `ftp.spies.com:/Library/`
`Wiretap Online Library | Electronic Books at Wiretap`

The Wiretap Online Library offers a pretty extensive selection of copyright-free books and other documents as text files. Many of these are volumes that would be difficult to find as conventional books. At present, mass market books seem to require mention of the private lives of the British royal family, alleged wrongdoings by President Clinton, or a sure-fire way to lose weight if they're to make it into print. The Wiretap Online Library clearly has no such restrictions. As of this writing, it offers almost 200 titles.

Here's a brief selection of what you'll find there. This list is decidedly abbreviated. You'll find multiple works by many of the authors listed here, and quite a few authors not listed here at all:

Albert Hoffman: *Problem Child*
Ambrose Bierce: *The Devil's Dictionary*
Anthony Trollope: *Ayala's Angel*
Artephius: *The Secret Book* (Alchemy)
Baroness Orczy: *The Scarlet Pimpernel*
Beowulf (F.B. Gummere Translation)
Bram Stoker: *Dracula*
Chaos Industries: *The Big Book of Mischief*, v1.3
Charles Darwin: *The Voyage of the Beagle*
Charles Dickens: *The Cricket on the Hearth*
David Hume: *An Enquiry Concerning Human Understanding*
Descartes: *Discourse on Reason*
Doyle: *Hound of the Baskervilles*
Edgar Rice Burroughs: *Tarzan and the Jewels of Opar*
Francis Bacon: *The New Atlantis*
Geoffrey Chaucer: *Canterbury Tales*
H. Ryder Haggard: *King Solomon's Mines*
H.G. Wells: *The Invisible Man*
Herman Melville: *Moby Dick*
Horatio Alger Jr: *Cast Upon the Breakers*
Jack London: *The Call of the Wild*
John Buchan: *The Thirty-Nine Steps*
John Cleland: *Fanny Hill*
John Gay: *The Beggar's Opera*
John Milton: *Paradise Lost*
Joseph Conrad: *Heart of Darkness*
Jules Verne: *Around the World in 80 Days*
L. Frank Baum: *The Wonderful Wizard of Oz*
Lewis Carroll: *Alice's Adventures in Wonderland*
Louis Leclerc: *Does America Say "Yes" to Japan*
Louisa May Alcott: *Little Women*
Lucy Montgomery: *Anne of Green Gables*
Malaclypse the Younger: *Principia Discordia*
Mark Twain: *Tom Sawyer Abroad*
Marx and Engels: *Communist Manifesto*
Mary W. Shelley: *Frankenstein*

BOOKS AT WIRETAP

Nathaniel Hawthorne: *The Scarlet Letter*
Paul Tsongas: *A Call To Economic Arms*
Plato: *The Republic* (Jowett Translation)
Quran
Rabindranath Tagore: *Gitanjali (Song Offerings)*
Robert Louis Stevenson: *Dr. Jekyll and Mr. Hyde*
Rudyard Kipling: *The Jungle Book*
Shakespeare: *Complete Works*
Sophocles: *Oedipus Trilogy*
Thomas Hardy: *Far from the Madding Crowd*
Virgil: *Aeneid* (Dryden Translation)
W. Somerset Maugham: *Of Human Bondage*
Walter Scott: *Ivanhoe*

Some of the foregoing books, especially the fiction titles, are a very interesting read. Many, such as *The Jungle Book*, *Frankenstein*, *Ivanhoe*, and *King Solomon's Mines* have become famous as movies, quite eclipsing the novels that gave them birth. The novels typically are more entertaining than the films.

Project Gutenberg

Unlike politicians and imported cars, books don't deteriorate with age. While it's common to consider authors of a hundred years ago as being crusty old pedants suitable only for use in propping up wobbly desks, the likes of Jonathan Swift and Edgar Rice Burroughs were pretty leading-edge in their days. They also wrote quite a lot better than many contemporary authors — incomplete sentences, dangling participles, and poorly mixed metaphors aren't common features of classic literature. ¶ If your most recent trip to Waldenbooks left you wondering if there's much future to the written word, you might want to investigate the Project Gutenberg archives. Organized by (hart@vmd.cso.uiuc.edu) Professor Michael Hart, Project Gutenberg is working toward the day when virtually all uncopyrighted books and other documents will be freely available as electronic text. According to Michael Hart, "The Goal of Project Gutenberg is to give away one trillion e-text files by December 31, 2001. This is ten thousand titles each to one hundred million readers." ¶ The documents released by Project Gutenberg are plain ASCII files — they can be read and printed out with anything from the DOS EDIT command to Microsoft Word for Windows. About four new electronic text books or other documents appear each month. ¶ You can find both literature and reference works in the archives of Project Gutenberg. Among the former are *Peter Pan*, *Alice in Wonderland*, *Anne of Green Gables*, *Paradise Lost and Regained*, *Moby Dick*, *Tarzan of the Apes*, most of Shakespeare's plays and sonnets, the *Canterbury Tales*, *Oedipus*, *Pride and Prejudice*, the *Wizard of Oz*, *Wuthering Heights*, and *Frankenstein*. Among the latter are *Roget's Thesaurus*, the *CIA World Factbook*, the NAFTA treaty, *Zen and the Art of the Internet*, and the *Koran*. ¶ Perhaps the largest drawback to these works is that most of us experienced them in high school back when — most high school English teachers could make *Fanny Hill* dull and pedantic. Project Gutenberg offers a way to read many of the hottest books of the last millennium without having to go to a bookshop. You needn't even tell anyone what you're reading if you don't want to. ¶ Indiana Jones owes quite a bit to H. Rider Haggard — he wrote the Allan Quartermain stories. *Frankenstein*, the novel, is a much more interesting story than any of the dozens of movies of the same name. The dirty bits in Chaucer are a lot raunchier than the dirty bits in most contemporary writing. H.G. Wells wrote exceedingly interesting science fiction — in fact, he invented it. ¶ There are numerous FTP sites and gopher archives which offer the Project Gutenberg files. From my humble experience, the most interesting is *info.umd.edu:/info/ReadingRoom*.

British comedy

alt.comedy.british
dixie.aiss.uiuc.edu:/pub/
cathouse/humor/british.humour/

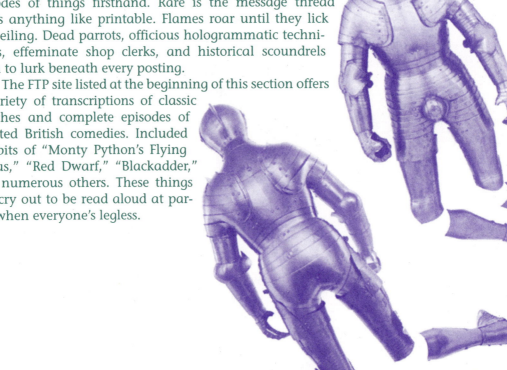

British comedy ranges from the inexcusably silly to the lethally incisive. It has a quality that television in the colonies never quite manages to duplicate. Typically a denizen of public broadcasting—there are just too many unmentionable words and innuendoes in British comedy for the nervous dispositions of the American networks—the "britcoms" are an engagingly esoteric alternative to television that requires a laugh track so you'll know it's funny.

The best of the British comedies are unique creations, often engendering fairly rabid followings. You might want to have a look at the sections of this book dealing with "Monty Python's Flying Circus" and "Red Dwarf" for examples of these.

The *alt.comedy.british* newsgroup offers a rowdy pub-down-the-corner atmosphere to trade favorite quotes, gossip, rumors, queries, and frequently censored rude bits from popular British comedy. It's inhabited by both North American users—who are limited to whatever makes it across the pond—and British viewers who've had the advantage of seeing the latest episodes of things firsthand. Rare is the message thread that's anything like printable. Flames roar until they lick the ceiling. Dead parrots, officious hologrammatic technicians, effeminate shop clerks, and historical scoundrels seem to lurk beneath every posting.

The FTP site listed at the beginning of this section offers a variety of transcriptions of classic sketches and complete episodes of selected British comedies. Included are bits of "Monty Python's Flying Circus," "Red Dwarf," "Blackadder," and numerous others. These things just cry out to be read aloud at parties when everyone's legless.

Buy and sell

ⓘ misc.forsale

While stinking of greed and the lust for vast wealth—admittedly in pretty small quantities—the *misc.forsale* newsgroup offers a singular function on the Internet. While commercial activities are largely frowned upon on the Net, you can peddle just about anything you like in *misc.forsale*. There are two catches to this:

- You'd best not do it on a commercial basis.
- Plan to deliver exactly what you promise.

As with all other newsgroups, miscreants in *misc.forsale* are liable to flaming that will make most major oil field infernos seem like mere brush fires by comparison.

Few of the users of *misc.forsale* seem wont to abuse it. It presents itself as a very orderly set of advertisements for everything that you could ever want. A quick scan of the contents of *misc.forsale* might offer you a few cars, a fair bit of computer equipment, several offers of high-end sound hardware, lots of compact discs, a few family pets—cats can be shipped freeze-dried for a slight additional fee—and all sorts of one-of-a-kind exotic items certain to tease the jaded junk collector into brief paroxysms of excitement.

Unlike newspaper classified ads, which tend to be pretty thick with baby clothes and antique particle-board furniture, the advertisements in *misc.forsale* are interesting to read even if you don't have any interest in buying what they offer. For example, here's something you won't find in most newspapers:

CASH paid for any old books concerning occult/magick and other unusual subjects. Please email me.

If your tastes don't run to the completed works of Aleister Crowley, this might look nice in your living room:

Yamaha upright piano for sale. Excellent condition. Tuned once a year. Buyer must move. Make an offer.

I don't particularly like upright pianos myself, but I was taken by the next ad:

Registered Welsh Ponies FOR SALE

GlanNant Strawberry Fields : 12.2 h chestnut roan mare. Born 1985. (Plum Creeks Ace / GlanNant Primrose Lane) Good hunter pony.

Wollen Hills Feisty : 12.1 h dapple gray mare. Born 1988. (GlanNant Ballad / Findeln Cricket) Flashy, sweet, nice hunter. Needs exp. rider.

> *Salterbrook Merry Tricks : 13.0 h dark gray mare. Born 1989. (GlanNant Bard / Findeln Cricket) Beautiful big stride. Needs exp. rider.*
>
> *Morton's Southern Dreams : 12.2 h chestnut mare. Born 1991. (Quorn Dream Weaver / GlanNant Sunshine) Has been ground driven and ridden W,T,C. Jumps nicely on lungeline. Very friendly.*
>
> *GlanNant Image : 12.1 h dark gray colt. Born 4/23/93. (GlanNant Country Roads [12.1 h] / GlanNant Idyll [13.2 h]) Beautiful mover. Very friendly. Has been handled often.*
>
> *Also Available : STUD SERVICE*

I wonder how you'd mail a Welsh pony. I'm pretty certain stamps won't stick to their noses, and you can't get one in a Federal Express package. Perhaps this next offering:

> *King size waterbed. Waveless, new mattress, new heater, new mattress pad, new seamless liner, oak Captains pedestal frame, 8 drawers, two cabinets, one long storage space right down the middle. Paid mega bucks for this bed. Asking $250.00 or best offer. We are located in southern California.*

Waterbeds have never been as popular in Canada as they are in the southern parts of the States. If the furnace decides that its warranty has expired out here, one would like to be able to retire to a warm bed without the prospect of encountering icebergs there.

The *misc.forsale* newsgroup is a great place to go virtual window shopping. You might even find something that you want. Keep in mind, however, that there are no regulatory agencies policing transactions carried out over the Internet. If the shadowy character who offers you a fantastic deal on a collection of mint condition Studebaker rearview mirrors takes your money and runs, he's gone.

Caffeine

alt.drugs.caffeine

Almost everyone uses drugs—even the ones who show up on the television news now and again standing proudly atop a mountain of seized cocaine. One of the most commonly used drugs is $C_8H_{10}N_4O_2$, caffeine. Caffeine is a stimulant found in coffee and Coca-Cola.

Keep in mind that most of those guys who seize cocaine for a living couldn't start the day without their particular drugs. Most of the rest of us couldn't either.

The effects of caffeine on its users is a matter of considerable debate. The debate rages in the *alt.drugs.caffeine* newsgroup. This newsgroup is somewhat more scholarly than most.

Cars

rec.autos

I love cars. Perhaps I should qualify that: I love certain select cars. Occasionally when one of my cars is in the shop, I have to rent a car at the place around the corner from the garage. They rent Nissan Sentras for the most part. This is enough to convince people who feel that they love cars in general to qualify their affection somewhat.

One of the singular characteristics of cars is that, in an otherwise largely electronic world, they're intricate mechanical devices. Perhaps this is one of their attractions. However, being based on quite a few side effects and outright perversions of several physical laws, there are all sorts of things that can go wrong with a car.

There also are innumerable areas of consideration in automotive design, maintenance, customization, and even automotive politics suitable for a lengthy diatribe. The *rec.autos* newsgroup offers a place to talk cars. It features reviews of new cars, frequently from various participants who have owned or at least test-driven them. This is invaluable if you're considering buying a car, as it frequently will allow you to benefit from the experiences of those who have gone before you. For example, as I write this Chrysler has just released its Neon. The *rec.autos* newsgroup has a lot to say about it at the moment, both bad and good.

Unlike magazine reviews written by professional journalists, car reviews in *rec.autos* are written by the rest of us, authors with no axes to grind.

The *rec.autos* newsgroup also is a worthwhile forum for things like tracking down hard to find parts or getting help with obscure problems. If you want to know why your '88 Fiero revs too fast on acceleration, this is the place to ask. (It's the throttle cable binding in its housing, by the way.)

 ### Excerpt from `rec.autos`

American cars — Why should I buy one?

Since the Ford Probe is built in America, by Americans, I would suspect that for all intents and purposes it is an American car.

Since the Chrysler LHs are built in Canada, by Canadians, I would suspect that for all intents and purposes they're Canadian cars.

It don't work that way...

I consider my Canadian-built Civic a Canadian car... not! Canadian auto engineers did not do *any* work on *any* Civic. Honda is not a Canadian or an American company. Japanese got the profit.

The U.S. Government uses percent content of American-made parts to determine the nationality of a car, I believe. Accords, for example, were American cars by that metric. I presume this holds for the current Accords as well since Honda has been upping the U.S. content of its U.S.-made cars.

Where are the Probe parts made? Where are LH parts made?

Probe: Mostly Ford parts for body, interior. Mostly Mazda parts for engine, transmission.

LH: Almost all Chrysler traditional suppliers in US. Assembled in Canada. Chrysler gets profit. Hence, mostly Americans benefit.

What I cannot understand whenever I hear these arguments is what difference it makes. U.S. car companies employ workers overseas, and overseas companies employ U.S. workers, so it's not a simple matter of "If it's a U.S. company, U.S. workers work" and vice versa. And as for the companies themselves, I don't give a hang how much money any of them make or where the profits go. Why should I? Am *I* any better off if a U.S. car company posts a banner year?

More jobs won't necessarily be created, for the reasons I cite above, so I don't care. "What's good for G.M. is good for America" is no longer true in this global economy, and there's no other reason I should care if the parent company is Japanese, German, Italian, Norwegian, Polish, or from the good 'ol U.S. of A.

Cathouse archives

 cathouse.org:/pub/cathouse/

Welcome to the cathouse.org archives. It's my goal to build them into the best waste-of-time archives on the Internet. Let me know what you think will improve them. (Sorry, the correct answer is not GIFS!!!)

Jason R. Heimbaugh, jrh@uiuc.edu

So begins an exploration of the Cathouse archives, one of the most engaging of the text resources on the Net. Beyond being, as its curator describes it, a "waste-of-time archive," it's just seething with files of interest or of some genuine use. I'm not certain whether the suggestion that some of the residents of Cathouse might actually be useful would offend Jason Heimbaugh.

You can kill hours at Cathouse without trying. It offers thousands of files on a variety of topics. The basic categories of files as of this writing are:

- Humor
- Lyrics
- Movies
- Rush Limbaugh
- Television
- Urban legends

Diving into the /lyrics directory, for example, you'll find a pretty extensive list of performers. Here's what it contains at the moment:

AC/DC
Aerosmith
Alabama
Allman Brothers Band
Arlo Guthrie
Black Crowes
Blue Oyster Cult
Blues Brothers
Bob Dylan
Boston
Charlie Daniels Band
Commander Cody
Credence Clearwater Revival
Dire Straits
Don Maclean
Eagles
Eric Clapton
Genesis
George Thorogood
Golden Earring

Guns 'n Roses	REO Speedwagon
J.J. Cale	Rolling Stones
Jethro Tull	Rush
Jimmy Buffett	Sam Kennison
Joe Walsh	Scorpions
Kentucky Headhunters	Spinal Tap
Kip Adotta	Steppenwolf
Led Zeppelin	Steve Earle
Lynyrd Skynyrd	Steve Miller Band
Marshall Tucker Band	Styx
Melissa Etheridge	The Who
Molly Hatchet	Tom Lehrer
Monty Python	Tom Petty
Motley Crue	Top 100 Country Songs
Muppets	Ugly Kid Joe
Patty Loveless	Van Halen
Phil Collins	Violent Femmes
Pink Floyd	Weird Al Yankovich
Pirates of the Mississippi	Whitesnake
Police	ZZ Top

I don't think any of these artists are represented with lyrics to every tune they've written or performed, but there's a tremendous wealth of songs therein.

The /humor directory is better still. Here's a selection of the current categories:

Animals	Murphy's laws
Authors	Netwit
Better	Politically correct
Bob Christ	Quotes
British Humor	Religion
Christmas	School
Computer	Sex
Dave Barry	Simon
Death	Sports
Flying	Standup
Geography	Synonyms
Jobs	Television
Life	Test
Monty Python	Women

The humorous articles can range from short jokes to extensive tracts on matters of great import, such as political correctness and animals. Dead cats in trees seem to be popular—a sentiment I can certainly agree with.

Don't connect to the Cathouse archives if you're in a hurry. The temptation to look at just one more file is a major schedule killer.

Cats

rec.pets.cats
rtfm.mit.edu:/pub/usenet/news.answers/cats-faq/

Cats strike me as being an intermediate sort of pet, midway between a dog, which will demand attention and give you its fanatical loyalty, and a garter snake, which you can keep in the fridge when you can't be bothered with it. Actually, you can keep cats in the fridge too, although only if you're prepared to contend with a lot of animal rights groups stationing SWAT teams across from your house.

I confess to having totally missed the appeal of cats as pets, although I can appreciate that some people like them. My favorite treatise on the care and well-being of domestic felines was Skip Morton's immortal *101 Uses for a Dead Cat*.

We enjoy the questionable services of a number of wild rural cats, who occasionally will attempt to ingratiate themselves with the lady of the house by leaving us dead mice. A dead mouse, or large portions of one, is clearly the perfect gift for someone who has everything.

All this notwithstanding, cats are living creatures, and if you intend to own one—as much as anyone really owns a cat—you should undertake to see to its well-being. Unfortunately, most of the parties prepared to offer you advice about taking care of your cat want to sell you something to assist you in doing so. You might well ask whether you require cat food that costs more than human food, for example. The *rec.pets.cats* newsgroup is arguably a much better place to seek an answer to such a question than would be the side of a tin of cat food or any 800 numbers printed on them.

The *rec.pets.cats* newsgroup is frequented by people who like cats and expend a fair bit of energy looking after them. You can just share cat tales there, or you can actively seek advice and information. The *rec.pets.cats* newsgroup describes itself as follows:

> Rec.pets.cats is a newsgroup devoted to domestic feline issues. The group has been characterized as friendly and helpful. Flame wars are limited to two, possibly three, topics: cats on vegetarian diets, declawing cats, and sometimes whether to keep cats indoors only or allow them outdoors as well. New readers are advised against starting these topics up ....

Unlike dogs, cats have the impression that they're capable of seeing to their own needs because about 5000 years ago along the banks of the Nile this was more or less true. In a more common urban environment, a domestic cat might run up against a lot of things its instincts haven't prepared it for. A great deal of the art of cat care is in finding a comfortable marriage between what a cat thinks it wants to do and what reality holds in store for it if it does.

The FTP site at *rtfm.mit.edu* mentioned at the beginning of this section offers a very useful and frequently asked questions document about cat care compiled by members of *rec.pets.cats*. It includes discussions of choosing a cat, feeding it, how to deal with a cat and other pets, veterinary considerations, the dangers of household plants, and so on. If you own a cat or are thinking about adding one to your life, both you and your cat will be much happier life forms if you check it out.

Celtic music

 `rec.music.celtic`

Celtic music includes traditional music from Ireland, Scotland, England, Wales, and Brittany. Far from merely being old tunes that can be used without fear of copyright violation, Celtic music is a vibrant, living art form. There are several record labels—or perhaps more correctly compact disc labels these days—that release new Celtic discs, and there are dozens of practitioners of the art.

One of the people that I play with also would have me note that Celtic music is not the tunes that play incessantly on Saint Patrick's day, which he likes to refer to as "paddy pub music."

Unlike mainstream popular music, contemporary Celtic music isn't driven by the market forces of the Billboard Top 10 lists and other overtly commercial institutions. The music still is played by musicians, rather than producers. The result often is a diverse blend of styles and influences, crackling with energy. If you've never had a serious listen to Altan, Cherish the Ladies, Martin Carthy, Silly Wizard, Maddy Prior, or Fairport Convention —the list probably could run for several more feet of type—you'll probably be blown away by the first disc that you hear.

Also unlike popular music, which has a ruthlessly efficient marketing machine, Celtic music just sort of happens. There are a number of relatively large Celtic labels and countless other tiny ones. Concerts by Celtic performers are likely to be small affairs; the acoustics are enviable but the publicity often could be better. It's heartbreaking to discover that the band that you've wanted to hear for a year and a half was in town two weeks earlier, unbeknownst to you, and now are playing several hundred miles to the south.

The *rec.music.celtic* is a newsgroup to trade bits of the lore and esoterica of Celtic music. You find mention of impending concerts and of new discs. It seems that everyone who posts messages in *rec.music.celtic* knows of at least a few obscure Celtic artists on disc. Whether you've been listening to the sounds of pipes and fiddles for years or would like an approachable introduction to them, you'll find no finer place to spend a few hours.

The beer's free. It's virtual, but you can drink all you like.

Church of the SubGenius

 alt.slack

The Church of the SubGenius is another of the many inside jokes of the Internet, fully comprehensible only to the enlightened. If you feel like lurking somewhere truly strange, however, it can be vastly entertaining for the rest of us. Loosely woven around the prophesies and teachings of its head messiah and pontiff Bob Dobbs, the Church of the SubGenius as manifested in the *alt.slack* newsgroup is a drunken stagger between eclectic topics, utter nonsense, incoherent ravings, and pithy remarks.

One acolyte of the church offered this description of what *alt.slack* is all about—hotly contested in subsequent postings, of course:

> Slack is about the ability to produce, without effort, money, sex, and general material welfare... As for what we're fighting for, we're fighting for a quasiorgasmic paradise of sex, money, and pleasure. What we're fighting against is the space bankers and the Con. As for egotistical... well, if you can find someone more egotistical than "Bob," follow him instead.

If you don't quite understand that explanation, you might like this one better:

> Well, for one thing, Slack is what you get from The Church of the SubGenius and it's a religion, Bob-damn it! You have to pay for it though — at least you have to buy the Book of the SubGenius or else you won't know what you really think. How can you tell your Short Duration Personal Saviors from your False Profits without buying a vowel from "Bob"?

Further commentary is offered as:

> Anyone who has ever eaten a "Gummi Worm" is damned. If they liked the taste, all their friends are damned too. Real SubGenii wouldn't go near anything gummi... Anyone with a blank bumper sticker on their car is not damned... Anyone who smokes goofy flavors of tobacco (like Maple-Rum) in their pipe laughably lacks slack and is damned. Real SubGeniuses smoke real tobacco, either in a pipe or mentally! Not tutti-fruity-minty junk.

The response to this posting was perhaps the most incisive, and perhaps best exemplifies the SubGenius philosophy:

> Ahem...

beable beable beable beable beable beable beable beable
beable beable beable beable beable beable beable beable
beable beable beable beable beable beable beable beable
beable beable beable beable beable beable beable beable
beable beable beable beable beable beable beable beable
beable beable beable beable beable beable beable beable
beable beable beable beable beable beable beable beable
beable beable beable beable beable beable beable beable
beable beable beable beable beable beable beable beable
beable beable beable beable beable beable beable beable
beable beable beable beable beable beable beable beable
beable beable beable beable beable beable beable beable
beable

Thank you.

That's a direct quote, I should add.

Not everything in *alt.slack* is totally spiritual, mind. There also is a great deal of useful insight into the human condition. My personal favorite as I wrote this was a long thread entitled "Fun with Jehovahs." It begins:

A few principles to remember:

1) These are essentially decent (but woefully misguided and, in all probability, none too bright) people out to Spread The Word Of The Lord. Physical assault is right out of the question; even squirting water on them is right out...

2) If you're feeling masochistic, you may wish to attempt to reason with them and try to refute their arguments. This is easily as productive a use of time as pissing up a rope. They have their faith; their faith is strong; therefore, they are right and you are wrong. Don't bother.

3) As with other organisms, JWs react in a Pavlovian manner to external stimuli. If you're polite to them (even to the extent of saying "Not interested, thank you" and firmly shutting the door), they have experienced a pleasant encounter with a fellow human being and, who knows, a future recruit. If, on the other hand, you walk up to the front door stark naked and invite them to a black mass in the basement, fondling your genitals all the while, chances are they will react with disgust and not bother you any more.

4) A continuation of 1): As a rule, JWs tend not to be the charismatic savior type. Once you've scared them off once, they tend not to return. In a way, this is disappointing, as I haven't had a chance to vent my spleen at a Jesoid in public since... 1988.

With this in mind, here's a list of suggestions on dealing with JWs. With imagination, you can come up with more, I'm sure... All of these gambits assume you've been wakened from a sound sleep on a

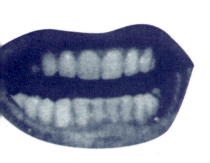

Sunday morning, are somewhat unready to deal with strangers on short notice, have some means of ascertaining that you are in fact dealing with door-to-door religious fanatics and have prepared to one extent or another.

1) The Paramilitary method... A good variation would have you coming to the front door munching on a large piece of meat impaled on a "Rambo" style knife. For extra effect, offer them some. The Paramilitary method can either be played screaming style or in a low, intense, "I just flew back from the Ho Chi Minh trail and *boy*, are my *arms tired*!!" sort of voice. Think Jack Nicholson.

2) Out-rant them. Have a copy of the Book of the SubGenius handy. Read selected passages from the Economicon. Point out some of the more bizarre art and claim to have witnessed the Fighting Jesus tear himself off the cross and start beating the Romans over the head with it.

3) Open the front door bearing a boom box on your shoulder. For best effect, you should play Devo, "My Way" by Sid Vicious or "Go To Hell" by Alice Cooper.

4) Invite them to an orgy (variation on 3), above. Same wardrobe.

5) While physical assault is out, verbal abuse is perfectly acceptable. Dog them down the block shouting that they support Nazi terror in the Vatican, that a JW daycare center was shut down under suspicion of child abuse, that they're in league with both Lyndon Larouche and the Queen of England to flood Kennebunkport, Newport and Cape Cod with illicit heroin, Thorazine and adrenochrome...use your imagination.

6) Using a pay phone and a false (but plausible) name (say, John R. Dobbs), call 911 and tell the operator there are people ringing doorbells and trying windows, doors and locked cars. The boys in blue will do the rest, particularly if you sound desperate.

Like most other fanatics, JWs tend to regard adversity as spiritual exercise. I say, let's help them exercise their spirituality to the fullest and *beyond*.

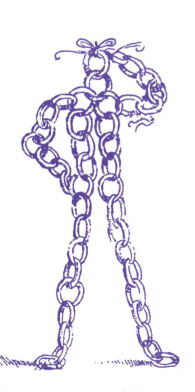

Non sequitur

Some Internet newsgroups have rather ineffable purposes. As discussed elsewhere in this book, you can spend months lurking in *alt.devilbunnies* or *alt.slack* without ever finding out what really is going on. Posting a question asking the obvious questions will more than likely avail you of an explanation far more confusing that the normal postings of the newsgroup involved.

By the way, the acronym *alt* stands for "anarchists, lunatics, and terrorists." This might have been sufficiently obvious not to require mentioning if you've experienced some of the more unusual *alt* newsgroups.

The prize for the most fundamentally strange and meaningless *alt* group probably deserves to be awarded to the *alt.alt.alt.alt.alt* newsgroup. Its postings deal, for the most part, with the possible meanings of its name. Regarded as everything from an inscription by long-forgotten alien visitors to a sort of combination mantra and bad haiku poem, *alt.alt.alt.alt.alt* is the subject of intense debate and philosophical argument.

As the penultimate time-waster—second only to waiting for a committee of liberals to agree on a name for itself—*alt.alt.alt.alt.alt* is an engaging place to talk about nothing with the best of them. Few newsgroups offer the possibility of a less substantial topic.

CIA World Factbook

 Internet Wiretap | Electronic Books | CIA World Factbook

Some acronyms are more evocative than others. One need merely mention the CIA to call forth images of spies, covert operations, clandestine meetings, and guns made out of soda straws. While the ebb of the Cold War has made the CIA less interesting to documentary film makers and screenplay authors, it still is a force to be reckoned with if you happen to be planning to set up a small nuclear power or a drug cartel.

Aside from spying on people, the CIA expends vast resources in information gathering. Some of its most effective work is accomplished not by sneaking into other countries and knocking off insane dictators with fancy hardware, but rather in knowing more about everyone else's business than they do. The CIA does incredible amounts of research into somewhat mundane things, like the amount of annual rainfall in northern India or the percentage of the population of Bolivia that owns television sets.

The CIA World Factbook is a distillation of much of the research carried out by the CIA over the years. Despite its title, you won't find bomb plans, unlisted phone numbers for Saddam Hussein, or the locations of any secret tunnels. It has buckets of statistical information about most of the nations on earth, however. It includes data about climate, global and national politics, population, economic issues, and so on.

Whether you're thinking of setting up a branch office in lands far away or if you're just curious about the average household income in the Netherland Antilles, you'll find the CIA World Factbook invaluable.

Classical music

 rec.music.classical

Classical music is popularly regarded as melodic fiddle-scratching written by dead guys who didn't have the sense to work out a copyright arrangement back in the late Middle Ages and, as such, are now useful for low-cost compact discs. People who listen to classical music likewise are often thought of as being dead too, except that no one's gotten around to mentioning it. Occasionally, a dead classical musician might turn up in the movies and enjoy a brief renaissance.

Actually, all of these statements are arguably true if you shop for classical discs at Sears but are somewhat far removed from the reality of classical composition and performance. Classical musicians were regarded as being classical only long after they died.

Many of them were pretty interesting characters while they were alive. For example, Antonio Vivaldi, who wrote "The Four Seasons," among many other works, was a priest who divided his time between teaching violin at a Venetian orphanage for girls and keeping several mistresses happy. He could have inspired a mini-series worth of documentaries today.

Much of the body of work regarded as being classical is exciting, moving stuff. While little of it lends itself to being edited down to fit in three and a half minutes for use on the AM radio and none of it works well with rap lyrics, it represents the best of several centuries of composition.

One of the unfortunate aspects of classical music is that it often is very difficult to know how to introduce one's self to it. Transcending the compact discs at Sears requires some idea of which discs to buy. Asking the kid behind the counter at your local record shop probably won't help, even if she's willing to take the Walkman off her head long enough to listen to you.

The *rec.music.classical* newsgroup is a great place to inquire about classical performance and recording, whether you're thoroughly immersed in musicology or merely getting the soles of your feet wet. You'll find announcements of new compact disc releases, discussions about nuances of classical performance, and endless threads about classical trivia. The one in the excerpt that follows is arguably representative. It serves to illustrate that classical music is anything but dead.

 Excerpt from rec.music.classical

Time for another mindless thread! I wonder which pieces have struck you, when you first heard them, as absolutely appalling!

My major contender for this honor would be Respighi's Roman Festivals. This is not to say that I don't enjoy this piece. I would like to know which is a real brain-frying version of it. I have the Ozawa and BSO on DGG, but I think there are better ones…

My favorite "Festivals" is on Chesky. It was once in a Reader's Digest set and is conducted by Massimo Freccia. Makes Toscanini's highly (and, to me, unaccountably) praised version sound like a Sunday afternoon nap.

I feel tempted to say Tchaikovsky symphonies. I can no longer listen to the finale of his fifth seriously. It is surprising how poorly he understood even the basics of orchestration.

Hey! Now I've got! Yes! This must be *the* most absolutely appalling piece of music that has *ever* been written! I don't know if it was intended to be a serious one. It is - ta-dah! - "Comoedia (de?) Fine Temporum" (or was it "Temporum Fine"?) by Carl Orff. I really hope Orff intended it to be a joke. But even then, it is a rather poor joke.

I think Berg string quartets would rank up there. I had to listen to them for a class. I realize they are very technically demanding, but I think I could fake a better sounding quartet in that style.

Probably not *absolutely* appalling because it's still Schubert, but for me the "Tragic" symphony has an appropriate moniker.

Elgar's Second Symphony. What a load of loud and pointless strutting about.

Which only demonstrates that you fail to understand the piece. It can be viewed as a requiem for the elegant Edwardian age which was just ending, or the end of Empire, but 'strutting about'? Never!

Funny that someone mentioned a Reader's Digest collection. A friend of mine in college had a Reader's Digest collection, possibly the same one. One record was devoted to music of the twentieth century. There was a piece entitled Voices of Ancient Children or Ancient voices of Children by either John Cage or some other loser. What a piece of utter, totally unredeemable rubbish… In one section, it sounds like someone dragging boxes across the floor. In another section, it sounded like a woman having some strange sexual experience. Overall, this is the most absolutely appalling excuse for music that I have ever heard.

If we are talking about recordings, I own a winner: this is a Telarc CD containing both Beethoven's Wellington's Victory and the insufferable tone poem Hunnenschlacht by Franz Liszt. It is performed by Kunzel-Cincinnati S.O. If you ever have unwanted guests, I suggest you pop *this in the CD player and go for a stroll... when you come back, your guests will have disappeared.*

Well, as long as we're allowed to bash Beethoven — the first movement of the fifth. Every time I hear it (which is entirely too often) it sounds worse.

Most music by minimalist composers. Minimalist music is the only "serious" music that, upon first hearing, I feel I fully understand and yet intensely dislike.

Symphony Fantastique by Berlioz. Only the fourth movement has any redeeming qualities, and having to sit through the third to get to the fourth sort of cancels anything the fourth has to offer.

Anything by Mauro Giuliani (1781-1829). Give me Stockhausen, Crumb or Carter any day, but spare me those ding-a-ling guitar concertos of Giuliani. I bet even Roger Lustig can't find merit in such froth.

Dear Prez

President Clinton has an e-mail address. Perhaps predictably, it's *President@Whitehouse.Gov*.

Actually, this is only partially true. While the address goes along with the fancy chair and Air Force One, photographs of the oval office don't illustrate a terminal connected to the Internet on the President's desk. Bill Clinton doesn't read his e-mail.

If you send electronic mail to *President@Whitehouse.Gov*, you'll receive an automatic form letter back in reply.

According to the Whitehouse, electronic mail sent to *President@Whitehouse.Gov* does get read, ostensibly by a team of volunteers who screen all the incoming letters. Some are said to be summarized for the President's eyes, although it's uncertain whether he ever gets around to looking at them. Individual replies are never sent.

Ultimately, e-mail messages are said to be printed out and added to the paper mail that is received by the White House. Comments about specific issues are tallied. If you include your post office mailing address with your message, you'll receive some official presidential propaganda concerning the issue that you've written about.

It's worth noting that the incoming mail is screened for both threatening messages and cranks. In light of the latter, be advised that beginning your message "Dear Bubba," "Dear Mr. Bill," or "Dear Slick Willie" will get it shredded pretty early on.

Clinton jokes

 `ramses.cs.cornell.edu:/pub/elster/perot/clinton.humor`

I'm not certain if it's politically correct for me to laugh at jokes about Bill Clinton, living north of the border as I do. Canadians have their own political jokes. Sadly, they keep getting themselves re-elected.

The canonical list of Clinton jokes at the FTP site mentioned at the beginning of this section is certain to please everyone who didn't vote for the current president, and their numbers seem to be growing. Whether you merely lunge for the mute button every time Bill or Hillary appears on the screen or if you have "Clinton and Gore, gone in four" tattooed prominently on your dog, you'll find comfort in this list.

I should point out that almost none of these jokes are suitable for polite company.

 Excerpt from `clinton.humor`

BILL CLINTON STATUE COMMITTEE
1040 Buffoon Street
Little Rock, AR 72205

Dear Friend,

We have the distinguished honor of being on the committee for raising five million dollars for placing a statue of Bill Clinton in the Hall of Fame in Washington D.C. This committee was in a quandary as to where to place the statue. It was not wise to place it beside the statue of George Washington, who never told a lie, nor beside senator Joe McCarthy, who never told the truth, since Bill Clinton could never tell the difference. We finally decided to place it beside the statue of Christopher Columbus, the greatest democrat of all. He left not knowing where he was going, did not know where he was, returned not knowing where he had been, and did it all on borrowed money.

Over 5,000 years ago, Moses said to the children of Israel, "Pick up your shovels, mount your asses and camels, and I will lead you to the promised land!" Nearly 5,000 years later, Roosevelt said, "Lay down your shovels, sit on your asses, and light up a Camel, this *is* the promised land!" Now, Bill Clinton is going to steal your shovels, kick your asses, raise the price of Camels, and mortgage the promised land.

If you are one of the fortunate few who has anything left after taxes, we expect a generous contribution to this worthwhile project.

Fraternally,
The Bill Clinton Statue Committee

Clipper

alt.privacy.clipper

Clipper is an issue that has gone unnoticed on CNN, rarely makes any of the sorts of newspapers that most people would be prepared to have delivered to their homes, and typically is dodged by government spokespeople if it comes up at a press conference. It's fantastically sneaky, very high tech, and profoundly disturbing. The discussions that appear in the *alt.privacy.clipper* newsgroup sound like something that might have surrounded the drafting of the Declaration of Independence. Actually, the similarity might be more profound than it initially seems.

Clipper is a technology being sponsored by the American government as a system to allow encrypted secure telephone conversations and other "common carrier" traffic to be implemented with a standard set of hardware. The Clipper "chip" would allow a central government agency, probably the NSA, to maintain the encryption keys, such that, while anyone could access the technology, no one could actually access the information that it was being used to transmit without authorization.

Well, almost no one could. The NSA would by default have access to the contents of Clipper-encrypted information. It also would have the facility to monitor the frequency of encrypted Clipper traffic, such that anyone using Clipper to place a lot of encrypted phone calls could be identified.

Clipper is a somewhat ill-defined issue that changes subtly with time. It can be regarded as a fundamental assault on privacy by the government, and one that might ultimately affect anybody with a telephone on his or her desk. While it sounds like an uneasy fusion of paranoia and "Star Trek" at times, the *alt.privacy.clipper* newsgroup is an essential read for anyone who takes privacy issues seriously.

It also is a fantastic place to go to exercise your argumentative muscles—not since first year university philosophy has anything so didactic in the art of logic appeared in such an interesting and contemporary form.

Excerpt from alt.privacy.clipper

As for the problems involved in implementing key escrow, they fall into two categories: (1) problems stemming from legal access to escrowed keys and (2) problems stemming from illegal access to escrowed keys. My statement is that with respect to problem (2) Clipper is as vulnerable as any other widely fielded crypto (U.S. military cryptos, for example) whereas clearly problem (1) is unique to Clipper.

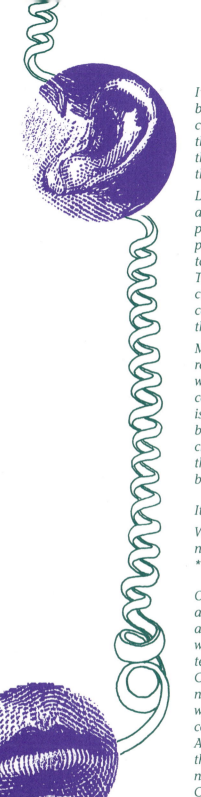

I'm mostly concerned, actually, with problems that fall somewhere between the two: that is, unauthorized access by people who, in some circumstances, would have legal authorization. I'm concerned that the key access mechanisms, as actually implemented (as opposed to the way they're written on paper), may not be adequate to prevent this.

Let's consider a couple of scenarios. One is where someone in high authority (let's say the president, just to be concrete) orders the people at an escrow agency to release the keys. Another is where a police officer, or an FBI agent, says "Look, we've been working together for five years, and you know I wouldn't abuse my authority. This is an emergency, and I didn't have the time to dot the i's and cross the t's. Can't we just do without the formal paperwork?" You can make up your own scenarios for yourself; this is just the sort of thing I'm thinking about.

My question, then: in this sort of situation, would a mid-level clerk refuse? I'm sure that some people would: there are some people who would rather resign than do something improper. I am not, however, confident that every single mid-level clerk in the Federal government is that honorable. I believe that if most people are given the choice between obeying a questionable order and losing their job, they won't choose to lose their job. The habits of obedience to one's boss, and the everyday patterns of working relationships, are often hard to break.

It's really very simple:

Would you trust your neighbor with your credit card details? Probably not. Well, your neighbor could be elected president and then you *will* trust him/her with your Clipper key! Need I say more?

One thing about Clipper. We do need a universal encryption algorithm that makes it possible to send fairly "safe" messages to anybody. This does not eliminate possible high-level abuses, but it will reduce problems in ordinary transactions. For example most telephone and credit card fraud is relatively low tech. Quite simply Clipper can get rid of 99% of the problems (excluding "inside" which no scheme can prevent) associated with people reading and playing with other peoples messages. While it may not stop the FBI or phone company, it will stop a lot of private security and rogue local cops. And if it is universal, it will provide protection to everybody, not just those who happen to have a copy of a particular program. This does not mean that you should not have access to protection beyond Clipper, but I think it can be regarded as a useful first step.

Actually, what would be *really* neat is if someone were to sneak in and wipe out one of the escrow databases. Then *nobody* could decrypt messages!

Well, the government may not be very moral, but they're not that stupid. Presumably each of the keymaster agencies *will* keep multiple copies of the tapes, physically separated, so that even if one building burns down or a copy gets stolen they'll still have backups. You'd basically have to shoot the keymasters as they're walking out of the NSA vault with their briefcases handcuffed to their arms, and if you did that they'd trash the batch of keys they'd just made. Or you could zap them with big magnetic fields and hope they didn't notice.

And if some organized crime group starts trashing multiple backup tapes, we'll probably discover that both keymaster agencies have hired the NSA to provide safekeeping for one of their copies, and who knows if it's really the original or one they regenerated from the set of keys they stole when they made them....

You can't trust the state to act in the best interest of the people. It is not in their vision of things.

I agree that until the malfeasers are exposed, it isn't good, but fear of a monolithic "state" just doesn't play in this country.

Well, I disagree. I, personally, wouldn't trust the IRS, NSA, CIA or any other government agency farther than I can throw a Hum-Vee. The trend toward disarming the citizens of this country in the name of "stopping crime" is also very alarming. Wasn't total registration of firearms one of Hitler's proudest moments?

I'd say that the entire Clipper question boils down to: who do you think is driving this bus? You or J. Edgar?

For many, perhaps. But for me, it's one step subtler than that: even though I believe that, on the whole, it is "We The People" who drive the bus, I think it remains that way only because at least a few of us are constantly watching out against "J. Edgar." The question of whether the current administration might abuse the power of something like Clipper is interesting only in an impeachment hearing (or similar proceedings); the question of whether some possible administration could abuse it is very much in order in this debate.

[*Publisher's note*: Shortly before *Planet Internet* went to press, the Clinton administration, under pressure from Congress, backed down from its support of the Clipper chip.]

Coca-Cola

- alt.food.cocacola
- ftp.spies.com:/Library/Article/Food/newcoke.txt
- wiretap.spies.com | Wiretap Online Library | Articles | Food and Drink | Laszlo Nibble:The New Coke

Some people awaken to the heady aroma of freshly brewed coffee teasing at the periphery of their senses, beckoning them to the promise of a new day. I never acquired a taste for coffee, resembling as it does the aftermath of an oil change that's been put off too long. I start each day with a Coke.

Coca-Cola has a long and noble history. It really was made with cocaine during the previous century, and as you'll find if you investigate the resources discussed in this section, it's only somewhat removed from this today. A few of its other ingredients read like protest signs around a proposed toxic waste disposal site. One wonders at the long term effects of phosphoric acid when taken internally. At least, I do—almost every time I open one.

Unlike *alt.food.mcdonalds*, which is discussed elsewhere in this book, the *alt.food.cocacola* newsgroup offers relatively few food fights and discussions of the darker side of that which we eat and drink. It's largely inhabited by aficionados of soft drinks, and the level of profanity is unusually low for a newsgroup. The detailed trivia about Coke, cola politics, the history of carbonated drinks, and a literal pop culture is frequently amusing to wander through for 15 or 20 minutes.

This is a worthwhile newsgroup to frequent if you'd like to soak up some light esoteric chatter for use at parties.

Besides Coke bar trays, Coke posters, Coke T-shirts, and old 45s of Coke's more successful jingles, there is the Coke one can actually drink. If you're curious about the nature of Coke, you absolutely must seek out the file *newcoke.txt*, mentioned at the beginning of this section. It includes a brief discussion of the politics behind the legendary introduction of "new" Coke, a pretty reasonable approach to making new Coke taste like real Coke, and perhaps most remarkably, a recipe to allow you to brew up a batch of syrup and make your own Coke. I confess I've not tried the latter, but it looks decidedly convincing.

Excerpt from alt.food.cocacola

The Coca Cola Bottling Co. stock name is COKE: it is up 3/8 at 32 1/8. The Coca Cola Company, KO, is unchanged at 41 5/8. Coca Cola Enterprises, CCE, is down 1/4 at 17 3/8. Coca Cola Femsa S A DE CV ADS, KOF is up 3/8 at 31 5/8.

This may be a stupid question, but could someone explain to me the difference between the different areas?

I'll have a go. Someone correct me if I'm off here (what am I saying? This is Usenet — *of course* someone will correct me!):

— The Coca Cola Bottling Co stock name is COKE: it is up 3/8 at 32 1/8 — Owns regional companies that put the product into cans and bottles, and distributes the product to stores and vending machines.

— The Coca Cola Company, KO, is unchanged at 41 5/8 — The parent company that owns all the patents, owns the name "Coca-Cola" and its trademarks, and sells syrup to bottlers and fountains (restaurants) nationally. I believe Coca-Cola Foods is part of this company, and they're the ones responsible for Minute Maid OJ and the forthcoming "Fruitopia" drinks.

— Coca Cola Enterprises, CCE, is down 1/4 at 17 3/8 — Responsible for the licensing of the name "Coca-Cola" to clothing, knick-knacks and other non-food items bearing the Coca-Cola name.

— Coca Cola Femsa S A DE CV ADS, KOF, is up 3/8 at 31 5/8 — Looks like a Mexican or South American affiliate. Maybe it's the company responsible for producing the coca extract?

You know, I've been thinking... It would be great if Coca-Cola came out with a product called Coke Premium (or for those PC people, Premium Coke) This coke would be bottled in *real* six-ounce *glass* bottles, and contain *real* sugar. (Not sucrose, fructose or any other -ose.) Yeah, this would be a more expensive soda, but I would pay the extra money for it.

Sucrose *is* table sugar. That's what you want in the Coke.

Is it not possible to import foreign Coke, or does Coca-Cola put a restriction on it? It sounds to me that in the States, there is a niche market of people who are prepared to pay extra for Coke with sugar in it, so why doesn't some entrepreneur import a load of European Coke to the States? If there was such a demand for it then the guys in Atlanta may start putting sugar back into US Coke.

Check the ingredients: High fructose corn syrup and/or Sucrose. I don't consider that sugar. Sure doesn't taste like sugar.

For the last few months now, here in Toronto and southern Ontario, I've seen bottles of stuff called Coke II. Would any coke-ologists care to enlighten me? Due to diabetes, I'm reduced to drinking just soda water these days (don't like Diet Coke much anymore...) and I've been curious.

Coke II = "New" Coke. If you're a diabetic, you'll want to stay away from this stuff.

I've seen somewhere that there's a book that is dedicated to the history of Coca-Cola. I'd love to get a copy of it.

There are a number of books on the history of Coca-Cola, beginning with the one that all other authors use as a reference, *Asa Griggs Candler* by his son Howard (Asa founded The Coca-Cola Company). Alas, it was a limited edition put out in 1950 by Emory University Press. My company (Alexander Books) is reprinting this work, and it will be out later this year.

Until then, you might try one of the other fine references on Coca-Cola.

I am immodest enough to recommend *The Real Ones*, by Elizabeth Candler Graham (great-great granddaughter of Asa) and myself (Barricade, 1992). You can order it through any fine bookstore.

Another book on Coca-Cola that we hope will be of interest is *Classic Cooking with Coca-Cola* from Alexander Books (1-57090-002- 7). It goes into U.S. release next month!

On the back of my Big 20 diet Coke, right under the listed ingredients, is the apparent warning, "Phenylketonurics: Contains Phenylalanine." What's the deal?

A percentage of people, Phenylketonurics, are incapable of processing the amino acid phenylalanine, which is a major component of Nutrasweet. Consumption of any product with Nutrasweet can cause blindness, seizures and other nasty things.

Coffee house

alt.pub.coffeehouse.amethyst

The *alt.pub.coffeehouse.amethyst* newsgroup is a singular institution and one not to be missed if you find yourself weary of the flames and excesses of much of the Internet. It's a virtual coffee house, and postings to it are intended to simulate the sort of conversations that might take place in a real one. Here's how it describes itself:

Amethyst is a coffeehouse built by knocking down most of the interior walls in an old Victorian house. The decor is done mostly in tasteful purple tones, in keeping with the name. There are many padded armchairs and sofas to sit on, and coffee tables to hold drinks. There is a counter area, covered with shiny modern espresso machines. There is a low stage with an open mike and a resident set of bongo drums and battered upright piano. There are no facilities for playing recorded music. There is a sunroom area formed by large bay windows and an abundance of potted plants in one corner. The back wall is covered with photographs of people who are important in the guests' lives. The other walls are covered in bookshelves containing all manner of works. There is a large kitchen out the back which is open for anyone to cook in, with sharing of meals encouraged. Another door leads to a bathroom. The front door has a small silver bell over it, which tinkles when the door is opened. By the door are coathooks, and a cork bulletin board, hung at a 30-degree angle. On the side of one of the bookshelves is the Quote Board, on which guests can write any quotations they feel like sharing. Upstairs is off-limits, and the residence of Mrs. Shelley, the owner.

The Fictional Characters

Mrs Shelley owns Amethyst. She is strong-willed and vocal on human and social rights. She's willing to debate scientific hubris at any time, and she sometimes retires early to write poetry or stories. If asked, she says her first name is Mary.

Galileo makes darn good coffee, tea, and other beverages, making good use of the ultra-modern espresso machines on the counter. He's quite interested in astronomy, and all sorts of scientific achievements.

Father Darwin is always ready to lend an ear. He likes chatting about religion and biological evolution, and how many things can be true without having to condemn the beliefs of others. And if you have any sins to confess, he's the one to talk to.

None of these folks will deny or confirm that they actually are their historical namesakes, so it's silly to ask, and besides, they couldn't possibly be anyway (right?).

Postings to *alt.pub.coffeehouse.amethyst* are intended to be fragments of conversation written in the third person. In reading through multiple postings, you probably will have the sense of reading a somewhat disjointed, stream-of- consciousness novel left over from a time before yuppies roamed the earth. The following is a fragment of one such conversation. None of these things make particularly lucid sense unless you've read them from the beginning.

And now Voluspa has had enough. She wails and bangs her head on the table, jostling the coffee. "No more! I can't stand any more!" she cries in a mock-tortured voice.

"According to parliamentarian rules, shouldn't we hold a plebiscite before continuance?"

"Now just a dadgum minute here... Nobody, and I mean nobody, tries to hold my *plebiscite. Unhand me varmit, or you ain't gonna be continuancing nothin' nowhere no time soon!"*

"Decaf," the voices in his head whisper. "Switch to decaf."

The *alt.pub.coffeehouse.amethyst* newsgroup, despite its somewhat off-the-wall qualities, is singularly enjoyable. Its participants are periodically unfathomable, and it probably is wise to lurk for a bit before you actually begin to play the game. Nonetheless, once you do finally order up a cup of espresso and join the conversation, it's pretty easy to imagine those Victorian walls and fictional staff members to be just as substantial as you are.
If you are....

Coke servers

 colonsay.dcs.ed.ac.uk:/pub/jhb/silly/cokemachine

There are a number of soft drink machines connected to the Internet so that their owners can see if they require replenishment without having to actually visit them, and their regular customers can see if they still contain pop without having to walk all the way to where they reside. You can inquire about their status as well. This is probably one of the most pointless things you can do on the Net and is vastly diverting for this reason. Most of these machines are located in the United States. One of them—and by far the house favorite—lives in Australia. I find great satisfaction in calling halfway around the world to see if the Coke machine there is out of lemonade.

Here's what the Coke machine in Australia said the day I wrote this section:

> *[mackerel.ucc.gu.uwa.edu.au]*
> *The UCC Coke machine.*
>
> *Slot 0 has sold 4 drinks of type lemonade.*
> *Slot 1 has sold 26 drinks of type lemonade.*
> *Slot 2 has sold 29 drinks of type club.*
> *Slot 3 has sold 9 drinks of type club.*
> *Slot 4 has sold 39 drinks of type coke.*
> *Slot 5 has sold 24 drinks of type coke.*
> *Slot 6 has sold 102 drinks of type coke.*
> *May your pink fish bing into the distance.*

The various finger-able Coke servers have different displays. Here's one of the ones in North America:

> *CSH Drink Finger Information Server, V0.99 Fri Oct 29 16:32:58 EDT 1993*
> *WARNING: This software doesn't contain any bugs!*

MOTD: ——————————————————————————————
Helpful Hints: finger info@drink.csh.rit.edu for 'help' type action.

Tue May 18 14:31:46 EDT 1993

X client support finally added. To check out 'xdrink' do a 'finger displayname:0@drink.csh.rit.edu'. Soon, (if everything goes well (as in, if you give drink.csh.rit.edu permission to use your x server (as in xhost +drink.csh.rit.edu))) xdrink will pop up. Hopefully, the balance will be $0.00 so that you can't drop any drinks, but if it happens not to be, then go ahead and drop something... unfortunately, unless you know where the coke machine is, it will just end up being a free drink for someone who is around when it drops.

Enjoy
CSH Drink Admin

———————————————————————————————————————

Login name: drink   In real life: Drink
Directory: /u2/u0/drink   Shell: /bin/csh
Never logged in.
Plan: Balance: $ 0.00

1) JOLT!!	$ 0.50	Full	(23/44)	
2) JOLT!!	$ 0.50	Full	(23/44)	
3) Mystery Slot?!	$ 0.50	Empty	(0/44)	
4) Diet Stuff	$ 0.50	Full	(18/44)	
5) Coke Classic	$ 0.50	Empty	(0/44)	

Drink	3+ hrs	1-3 hrs	0-1 hrs	Total
:::::	:::::	:::::	:::::	:::::
JOLT!!	23	0	0	23
JOLT!!	23	0	0	23
Mystery Slot?!	0	0	0	0
Diet Stuff	18	0	0	18
Coke Classic	0	0	0	0

Clearly, someone worked really hard on this software. It performs statistical analysis of the pop in the Coke machine that it monitors. Most bank machines aren't this thorough.

If you'd like to check out Coke machines around the world, here's a list of several of the more interesting ones:

bargraph@coke.elab.cs.cmu.edu
coke@gu.uwa.edu.au
cocacola@columbia.edu
drink@drink.csh.rit.edu
graph@drink.csh.rit.edu
info@drink.csh.rit.edu
coke@cs.cmu.edu
coke@cs.wise.edu
coke@cmu.edu

COKE SERVERS

Not all these Coke servers are on line all the time. Finger them now and again to see what they're up to.

The file at the FTP site mentioned at the beginning of this section offers a brief history of the Internet Coke machines.

COMPACT DISCS

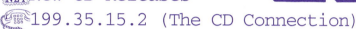

🛈 rec.music.cd
🕸 New CD Releases
☎ 199.35.15.2 (The CD Connection)

The CD new release mailing list is unquestionably one of the best mailing lists that I subscribe to. It appears about once a week, offering an extensive list of popular music compact disc titles that are about to be released. Each entry includes the date that the disc is due out, the artist, and the title. Re-releases, "best of" compilations, and foreign re-leases are designated. Discs with titles or other information that changes are tracked from list to list.

It's unclear where the contributors to this mailing list find out who's upcoming, but they're almost never wrong.

To subscribe to the new CD releases mailing list, e-mail a request to *new-releases-request@cs.uwp.edu*. You can find archives of back issues of the list at *cs.uwp.edu*.

The CD Connection is one of those little jewels of the Internet that one stumbles across after a while. It's an online database of over 80,000 compact discs, with a complete ordering service. You can browse the database by title, artist, song, and so on, flag the discs that you like, and place an order by credit card. The CD Connection's database includes discs from the larger North American labels and some of the most obscure imports that you can imagine.

In addition, the prices of discs from the CD Connection are pretty low.

You can access the CD Connection through Telnet to the address listed at the beginning of this section. In theory, Telnet to *cdconnection.com* also should work, although I've never seen it do so. I should note that I have actually ordered discs from these guys and received them, which is a good sign for a mail order company.

The *rec.music.cd* is a newsgroup of compact disc enthusiasts. It's a great place to check out rumors of new discs, inquire about rare or obscure releases, and keep up to date with the state of the aluminum.

Complaints

🛈 `alt.peeves`
🛈 `alt.flame`

There are times when you really just have to speak out about the dismal state of the oysters being served these days, how liberals have decimated the spotted owl population, the appalling state of the nation's graffiti, and any of countless other matters of import. Bitching is good for you.

Actually, bitching will usually get you stomped on in most newsgroups, especially if you like to do it incoherently or about topics that have nothing to do with the newsgroup in question. While complaining is easy, complaining with a purpose, a well thought out logical argument, and a worthwhile proposal for resolution of the issue at hand is a lot more work. It's very often just not worth the trouble.

The *alt.peeves* and *alt.flame* were newsgroups created especially to offer Internet users the opportunity for a good rant. Almost none of the rules of netiquette apply there. You can go on at length about any issue that you like. You can use language that would make a whore blush (that's a real whore, too, not one of those politically correct econo-sexually challenged individuals you hear about on the news). Your diatribes need not make any sense if you don't feel like it. You can even draw ASCII pictures of people that you don't like.

The only catch to all this is that most of the people who read your postings in *alt.peeves* and *alt.flame* probably are going to be in much the same frame of mind, and their replies might not make much sense. They also are likely to be somewhat coarse.

Of these two newsgroups, *alt.peeves* is arguably the less rabid. Some of the arguments postulated there are comprehensible, one occasionally encounters whole sentences that are printable, and now and again some pretty well thought out postings appear.

This is a newsgroup to air complaints in, rather than a place to take shots at things you don't like.

The *alt.flame* newsgroup is a sort of food fight undertaken with porcupines hidden in handfuls of hot cheese. Many of the postings consist of various participants calling each other names or speculating on their sexual practices. The average mental age of its regular users seems to be about six. It's a bit of mindless fun, as long as you don't tell anyone you've been there.

Perhaps the best comment about the *alt.flame* newsgroup is the list of more specialized sub-groups that it has engendered. They include *alt.flame.faggots*, *alt.hall-of-flame*, *alt.flame.roommate*, and perhaps paradoxically, *alt.flame.spelling*. The latter is indeed curious, as you'll rarely find any group of people less capable of correct spelling than the regular posters in *alt.flame*.

Concerts on the Road

CNS, Inc ¦ ENTER THE CNS GOPHER ¦ Entertainment ¦ Concerts on the Road

The Concerts on the Road listing is a decidedly incomplete list of major concert tours. Perhaps more fairly, it might define the word *major* differently than you would. Only fairly well-known bands seem to turn up in it. However, one of the perennial drawbacks to major concerts is that one rarely finds out about them until all the good tickets have long since been sold.

If you've ever experienced an evening in the cheap seats with a large telescope trying to decide if the moving dots on stage are the Grateful Dead or their roadies, you'll probably find this list to be a worthwhile resource. So armed, you can start nagging the ticket agencies before everyone else descends on them. Being in the same time zone as the musicians does so improve one's appreciation of a performance.

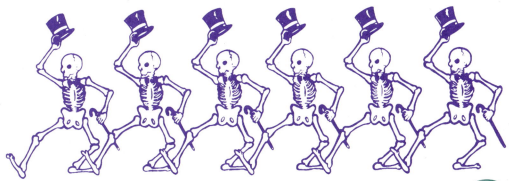

This was the list of available concert tours for the week that I wrote this section:

1. index.txt.
2. tour.clapton.txt.
3. tour.madonna.txt.
4. tour.paul-westerberg.txt.
5. tour.rod-stewart.txt.
6. tour.rush.txt.
7. tour.yes.txt.
8. tour.zztop.txt.

I should note that ZZ Top's local performance actually was sold out by then, this entry having been about for a while. Tickets for Yes still were available. We were going to be in Wales at the time, but had we wanted to fly back for the occasion, it looked like an outstanding concert. Perhaps not. The Toronto SkyDome is a sports arena with acoustics that probably will have made Jon Anderson eat his guitar by the time you read this.

✂ Excerpt from Concerts on the Road at the CNS Gopher

Note: This is a partial list. Downloaded toward the end of April 1994, it actually stretched to the end of July.

YES Tourdates

DATE	CITY	VENUE
June		
Thu 2	Binghampton, NY	Broome County Arena
Fri 3	Saratoga, NY	Performing Arts Center
Sat 4	Portland. ME	Old Orchard Barn
Sun 5	Mansfield, MA	Great Woods
Tue 7	Toronto, CAN	SkyDome
Wed 8	Montreal, CAN	The Forum
Thu 9	Quebec, CAN	Colesium de Quebec
Sat 11	Hartford, CT	Hartford Civic Center
Sun 12	Buffalo, NY	Darien Lake
Tue 14	Philadelphia, PA	Spectrum
Wed 15	Philadelphia, PA	Spectrum
Thu 16	New York, NY	Madison Square Garden
Sat 18	Wataugh, NY	Jones Beach Theater
Sun 19	Columbia, MD	Merriweather Post Pav
Tue 21	Pittsburgh, PA	Star Lake Amphitheater
Wed 22	Cleveland, OH	Blossom Music Center
Thu 23	Cincinnati, OH	Riverbend Music Center
Fri 24	Columbus, OH	Polaris
Sat 25	Clarkston, MI	Pine Knob Music Theater
Sun 26	Indianapolis, IN	Deer Creek
Tue 28	Moline, IL	The Mark
Wed 29	St. Louis, MO	Riverport Amphitheater
Thu 30	Milwaukee, WI	Marcus Amphitheater

Concerts on the Road

Condoms

 dixie.aiss.uiuc.edu:/pub/
cathouse/humor/sex/a.girls.guide.
to.condoms

One can but speculate on how a simple device with no moving parts can engender such widespread discussion and controversy. There's a lot of really serious documentation available for the selection, purchasing, storage, application, use, removal, and social implications of condoms. Happily, this section will concern itself with none of it.

The document mentioned at the beginning of this section, *A Girl's Guide To Condoms*, by Mimi Coucher, will help put the sexual derevolution of the nineties in perspective. It's brilliant.

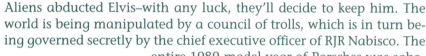 Excerpt from *A Girl's Guide to Condoms*

WARNING: Boys cannot read this. If you are a boy and are reading this, stop immediately. The following article is chock-full of highly intimate girl secrets that will be ten times more embarrassing than any TV commercial for feminine-hygiene products you've ever seen. So quit it. I mean it. You'll be sorry.

Conspiracies

 ftp.spies.com:/Library/Fringe/
Conspiry/

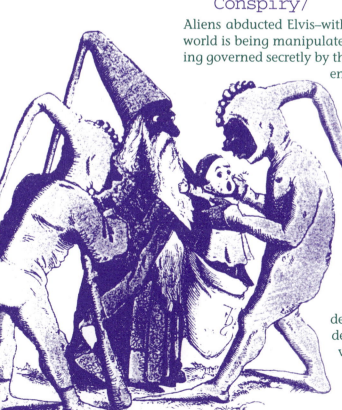

Aliens abducted Elvis—with any luck, they'll decide to keep him. The world is being manipulated by a council of trolls, which is in turn being governed secretly by the chief executive officer of RJR Nabisco. The entire 1989 model year of Porsches was sabotaged to make them emit barking noises at high speeds. All Pepsi-Cola commercials contain subliminal sexual messages that will cause otherwise rational people to take off their clothes in airports. The Gulf War never actually happened, but rather was an elaborate media event staged by the CIA. All telephone calls originating in the continental United States are being tapped and listened to by a group of puritanical librarians from Iowa. The secret ingredient in Mars bars is ginseng.

Conspiracy theories, paranoid delusions, and plots to overthrow all we hold dear are wonderfully common and make diverting entertainment for those cold winter nights when nude mud wrestling seems too cultural. There's a modest collection of particularly rabid conspiracy documents available at the FTP site listed at the beginning of this section. Anyone who takes this stuff seriously will probably find that his or her reality check has just bounced, but it's interesting to watch the minds of conspirists at work nonetheless.

As I write this, the selection of conspiracists for hire include the following.

OPAL.TXT—A long, rambling diatribe that links Aristotle Onassis, the Mafia, all of Japan, Rupert Murdoch, the IMF (that's the International Monetary Fund, not the Impossible Missions Force), Gulf Oil, the Chase Manhattan Bank, and countless other high profile parties in a massive conspiracy to do all sorts of ill-defined but clearly reprehensible things. A somewhat shorter but less well-edited version can be found in GEMSTONE.TXT.

BOOKFILE.TXT—It would be hard to describe this document more clearly than its author does: "The super radical file that uses real sources to document the CIA/BUXH/mob/Illuminati/Oil links to rape and steal from we the people!!!" Lock up your daughters.

AIDS-WAR.TXT—A somewhat circumstantial proof that the AIDS virus is an escaped manmade biological weapon, rather than a natural phenomenon. The argument has two principal foundations:

- Why did AIDS only appear recently, when there have been people around for 50,000 years?
- If scientists can invent and patent new bacteria, they certainly could have invented AIDS.

This treatise purports to have been written by an M.D. and jumps around more frequently than a cat in a mulching machine.

STARWARS.RUS—The Russians had a space-based defense system back when they still were the "evil empire"—at least, this document says they did. They put manned spacecraft into orbit with particle-beam weapons and blasted all the American spy satellites into neutrinos—even the ones that were later used in the Gulf War. The Russians then used these weapons to kill all the Americans on the moon and moved into their old digs. I won't spoil the surprise by describing their anti-gravity machines.

Lesser conspiracies include those surrounding the assassination of John F. Kennedy, secret plutonium deals, and J. Edgar Hoover. There's never a good alien around when you need it.

Crafts

 rec.crafts.misc

We live in a world of crafts. I mean that in a personal sense; if you reside in a more urban area, you probably haven't come to grips with quite as many door harps, wicker wine racks, hedgehog boot brushes, plywood lawn ornaments, and hand-thrown pottery dog dishes as we're confronted with during a typical afternoon in the nearest town. Perhaps in the absence of multiplex cinemas, video arcades, and theme parks, people out here have turned to making things.

Unlike more structured pursuits, crafts are very much an expression of their creators. There's something rather magical about transforming a pile of straw or scrap lumber into a recognizable, somewhat useful object. There's something quite a bit more magical about finding someone who'll buy the thing for more than the materials cost, too, but this is one of the less spiritual elements of crafts.

The *rec.crafts.misc* newsgroup offers a wealth of ideas for things to make, how to make them, how to peddle them, and what to do with the leftover green and purple ones that nobody wanted to buy. You can inquire about techniques, soak up the wisdom of craftspeople with whole barns full of unsalable items, and see what fellow artisans think about your latest project.

Now, if there was only someone who wanted all those hand-carved toothpicks…

Crowley

 slopoke.mlb.semi.harris.com:/pub/magick/magick/Crowley/

Aleister Crowley was a magician of a sort. He didn't do conjuring tricks with rabbits or cards, but rather sought knowledge of the ancient magick now largely lost to western civilization. He wrote a number of books about magick and related issues. He died in 1947 at the age of 72.

As an aside, magick of this sort is spelled with a *K* at the end to indicate its sexual nature. The *K* is the first letter of *kteis*, which is the Greek word for "vagina."

Crowley is a paradoxical figure; much of what can be said of him will contradict something else that can be said of him or something he

himself wrote. While raised by strictly fundamentalist Christian parents, Crowley had a vast interest in the occult. He was a member of several Victorian secret societies that were concerned with mystical and psychic research. In 1903, Crowley claimed to have been visited by a spirit named Aiwass, a facet of the god Horus, who over a space of three days dictated the "Book of Law" to him.

Crowley believed that to begin to understand women he must sleep with at least a thousand of them. This put some measure of strain on his marriage.

In his later life, Crowley established several small secret societies of his own, exploring sexual rituals and experimenting with drugs. He moved to Italy with his two mistresses at the time, but the rumors of the carryings-on at his villa there became a major scandal, both locally and in the British tabloid papers back home. He was eventually deported in 1923.

Many of Crowley's books have been transcribed into e-text files and lodged at the FTP site listed at the beginning of this section. Far from being the sort of weird, spooky stuff that frequently turns up on the net when the word "occult" gets bandied about, they remain captivating and occasionally disturbing in places.

See also the section of this book dealing with "Magick."

Cybersleaze

```
mtv.com:/pub/sleaze
MTV | sleaze
adam@mtv.com
hotlist@mtv.com
```

Cybersleaze used to be gossip about pop bands and musicians on MTV, as purveyed by video-jock Adam Curry. In addition to its manifestation on the tube, transcripts of cybersleaze were available over the Internet at the sites listed at the beginning of this section. Curry and MTV had a falling out, however, with the result that Curry departed for other climes. His Internet facilities remain at this time, although they're hotly contested by MTV, which wants him to stop using the letters "mtv" in his Internet addresses.

The FTP and gopher sites for cybersleaze offer transcripts of Curry's works on MTV, some new material, and quite a bit of writing about the ostensible reasons for his departure. You'll also find a few lawyers' letters there, which are typically a lot sleazier than anything rockers are likely to do.

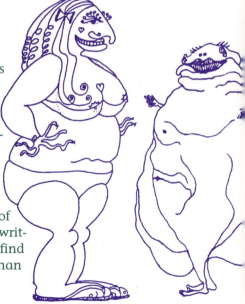

The Finger addresses listed here periodically generate quick digests of cybersleaze. At other times, they'll tell you about Curry's ongoing battle with MTV. In the absence of either of these, they'll suggest you connect with his gopher or FTP site.

Because of the tenuous legal character of these sites, they might have vanished or changed their names by the time you read this. Be prepared to quest for sleaze.

Answers

The *alt.answers* newsgroup seems rather Zenlike in its concept. It's a group of postings of all sorts of answers, including the frequently asked questions lists of many other groups. In it, you typically will find things like the guidelines for creating a new *alt* group, the FAQ list for Babylon-5, information on sending faxes over the Internet, and much more. It saves an enormous amount of searching. The *alt.answers* newsgroup is moderated and accumulates relatively few postings. As such, you can find quite a host of useful information there without having to weed through flames about users from America Online, advertisements for erotic sporting equipment, or long digressions on how best to prepare your cat before microwaving.

Other postings of note as I write this include a discussion about how to get less junk mail, information about the neo-pagan Church of All Worlds, and information about accessing a database of over 20,000 movies over the Net.

There are all sorts of unusual facilities on the Internet that you'll no doubt stumble across in time. The *alt.answers* newsgroup offers pointers to quite a few of them.

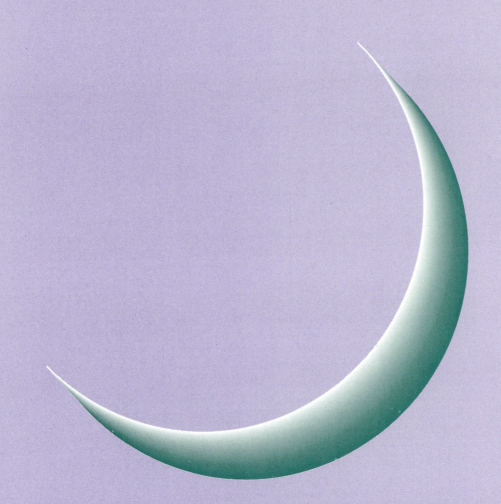

Dead Sea Scrolls

 ftp.loc.gov:/pub/exhibit.images/
deadsea.scrolls.exhibit

The Dead Sea Scrolls have engendered controversy on several distinct fronts since their initial discovery at Qumran in 1947. While in many cases badly damaged by the two millennia that have passed since their writing, they offer a glimpse into the lives and beliefs of the real people who inhabited the Middle East in biblical times.

The documents, which are now regarded as the Dead Sea Scrolls, are for the most part religious writings, probably written by a sect called the Essenes in the two centuries prior to the time of Christ. One likely explanation for their internment in stone jars in the caves above Wadi Qumran is that they were considered to be the word of God, albeit copies thereof, and one did not simply throw out the word of God when the paper it had been written on became worn.

The Christian Bible also is regarded as being the word of God and was copyedited from many far older manuscripts. The stories and traditions that formed the Christian Bible also appear in fragments of the Dead Sea Scrolls. However, in many cases, the biblical account of events in the Old Testament and those of the Dead Sea Scrolls are considerably at odds. While the Bible has clearly passed through many hands—and perhaps under many pens—in the nearly two thousand years since its creation, the Dead Sea Scrolls are as their authors left them. They have the ring of truth about them.

The first controversy that rose up in the wake of the discovery of the Dead Sea Scrolls involved a lot of questions about which word of God was the correct one. This quickly engendered a second and considerably less academic controversy. The Dead Sea Scroll fragments were ultimately to become the province of an international team of scholars who set to work putting them together and translating them. No one outside the teams was permitted access to the scroll material, and almost none of the translated material was released.

The second controversy largely diffused the first one, which was what it had been intended to do.

Over the decades since the initial discovery of the Dead Sea Scrolls, some photographs of scroll materials and some translations have emerged from the ongoing research into the scrolls. Various defectors from the scroll project over the years have suggested that this represents a tiny fragment of the writings from Qumran.

The FTP site listed at the beginning of this section offers several articles about the contents of the Dead Sea Scrolls and photographs of selected portions of the scrolls themselves and other artifacts found with them. While nothing in this material is likely to shatter the silence surrounding the scrolls to this day, it's a tantalizing introduction to the subject. If you download some of the GIF files from this archive, you can view words that were written over two thousand years ago.

Destroy the Earth

🛈 `alt.destroy.the.earth`

You'd probably think that a newsgroup with a name like this one sports would embody some sort of hidden message. It hints at being a radical environmentalist organization that has chosen an extreme name for itself to attract attention. This would have been a fairly clever thing to do, if in fact someone had done it. The *alt.destroy.the.earth* newsgroup, however, is just what it purports to be. It's a place to get together and trade suggestions for creative ways to destroy the planet or large sections thereof.

Some of the suggestions are extremely twisted and mightily improbable. Consider, for example, shooting the water from the earth's oceans into space to propel it into the sun.

The *alt.destroy.the.earth* newsgroup is a somewhat therapeutic experience should you find yourself stressed and really angry at absolutely everything. You can dream up a plan to have your revenge on civilization and actually share it with other people. No one will suggest that you seek counseling.

One of the sideshows that turns up occasionally in *alt.destroy.the.earth* is the advent of someone with a real environmental conscience who slips into the newsgroup by mistake. The regular users of *alt.destroy.the.earth* seem to treat these events about the way cats treat injured mice; tormenting the normals is clearly considered to be even more fun than planning manifest forms of destruction.

✂ Excerpt from `alt.destroy.the.earth`

I don't know if this has been proposed before, so please bear with me... has anyone done computations as to whether it is possible to use sea water as propellant (in effect make the Earth a giant rocket) and drop it into the sun or Jupiter?

In particular:

1. Would we be able to heat the water enough to shoot it into space?

2. Would we get enough thrust to kill the momentum we currently have going around the sun (if we are going to put the Earth into the sun).

We have a lot of water, we should be able to do some good with it.

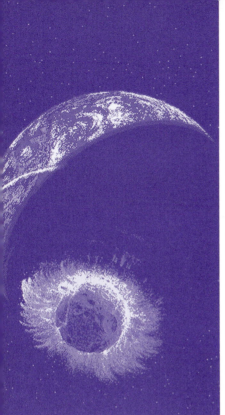

Hmm....how about a huge electrolysis reaction that converts millions upon trillions of gallons of water per second to its H_2 and O_2 states? That might be able to get some propulsion...

Of course, if you had all that explosive gas "happening" to be there, why not just explode the atmosphere? I'm sure that would work well enough...

Yes great. As we trail the gases behind us on our way to Jupiter someone could light a match and the earth would become a comet looking thing on its last voyage, streaming flame behind it like a Viking funeral pyre as it buries itself into Jupiter. If anyone is left after all this happens they could possibly be hit by Jupiter's or Earth's moons as they fly crazily around the solar system or otherwise the seismic disturbances on both planets would probably get them.

I can't think of a better way to go...

Yes! Let's fire the Earth into Jupiter... anything that survived the turbulence involved in passing through the Jovian atmosphere would probably get flattened by the gravity... how soon can we get this going?

Devilbunnies

 alt.devilbunnies

One of the really interesting things to do with the *alt.devilbunnies* newsgroup is trying to figure out precisely what it's about. The excerpt at the end of this section will avail you of some small measure of insight into it, but really pinning it down is a bit like attempting to use a squirt gun to shoot a charging rhinoceros that isn't really there. The principal characters involved are bunnies and Fudds. It's unclear which, if either, of these is intended to be regarded as a positive influence.

In an abstract philosophical sense, you can speak at great length of things that you know nothing specific about, as long as you understand some related facts, however groundless in reality they might be. Perhaps, in this light, it's possible for the participants in *alt.devilbunnies* to discourse about things cute, furry, and homicidal without anyone spoiling the fun by nailing down exactly what a devilbunny is.

Attempting to do so, by asking the obvious question in *alt.devilbunnies*, usually will provoke a variety of entertaining responses. It all sounds like a brainstorming session for a rejected Monty Python movie at times.

Excerpt from `alt.devilbunnies`

Will someone explain to me, either on here or via e-mail what in the living hell this group is all about? I bought myself an internet directory and the description of *alt.devilbunnies* was just "better left undescribed." My interest was piqued. What the hell is this group about? I must know.

Better left undescribed is correct. But since you must know, you will know, but you can't go back. Stop reading this now... or else face a lifetime of awareness of the evil that fluffs.

Going on? Too bad.

Devilbunnies are cute, cuddly, furry, little creatures that move at close to the speed of light and kill brutally and without regret. They would continue in this way until all of humanity was destroyed were it not for a band of people (sometimes known jokingly as "Fudds") who are aware of this horror and fight fire with fireax — or whatever else their skilled hands can get hold of.

Just think of the appealing things in your life that have turned out to be disasters. Or if you're that young, believe me there will be some. This is a reflection of the devilbunny style. All the disappointments, the entrapments, the bait-and-switch ploys — all the sorrow and pain and broken promises, are what devilbunnies personify.

LIES!!!!! ALL LIES!!!!!

Devilbunnies are your friends, Devilbunnies are good. Fudds are bad, very bad. Devilbunnies want to save mother earth, Fudds destroy mother earth. Devilbunnies are cute, Fudds are ugly.

Ah, yes, those jokingly referred to "Fudds"... who worship a god named Elmer — frequently mistaken for a glue bottle — who has a horribly serious speech impediment. You wascally widdo humans, who is yoo twying to foow, anyways?

Ah, how perfectly fascist of you... let's find a scapegoat for all our miseries and forget our own true responsibilities. I didn't know Canada *had* fascists, just a lot of really mean-spirited moose. Eh?

Devil's Dictionary

```
ftp.std.com:/obi/Ambrose.Bierce/
The.Devils.Dictionary.Z
```

Ambrose Gwinett Bierce was an American writer and journalist. He wrote a number of darkly humorous stories and a serialized collection of sardonic dictionary definitions that began appearing in 1881 and continued until about 1906. While originally entitled "The Devil's Dictionary," the morality of the time soon objected to this and many of the entries appeared as "The Cynic's Word Book," somewhat against the author's will.

Ambrose Bierce is another of those dead, dusty old authors who is in fact anything but. The Devil's Dictionary is periodically hilarious and useful for quoting from when you want to give someone a hard time, especially in print.

Eventually the entire Devil's Dictionary was printed in book form. It's this version that appears at the FTP site mentioned in this section. Of it—ultimately to be titled "The Cynic's Word Book"—Bierce noted:

This more reverent title had previously been forced upon him by the religious scruples of the last newspaper in which a part of the work had appeared, with the natural consequence that, when it came out in covers, the country already had been flooded by its imitators with a score of "cynic" books — The Cynic's This, The Cynic's That, *and* The Cynic's t'Other. *Most of these books were merely stupid, though some of them added the distinction of silliness. Among them, they brought the word "cynic" into disfavor so deep that any book bearing it was discredited in advance of publication."*

Also at the same FTP site is a document called *Can Such Things Be True*, a collection of some of Bierce's more scathing short stories.

Avoid the file DEVDICT.ZIP at the *ftp.std.com* site. This is a much abbreviated version of The Devil's Dictionary manipulated into a Windows help file.

Excerpt from `The Devil's Dictionary`

ABDOMEN, n. The temple of the god Stomach, in whose worship, with sacrificial rights, all true men engage. From women this ancient faith commands but a stammering assent. They sometimes minister at the altar in a half-hearted and ineffective way, but true reverence for the one deity that men really adore they know not. If women had a free hand in the world's marketing the race would become graminivorous.

ADMINISTRATION, n. An ingenious abstraction in politics, designed to receive the kicks and cuffs due to the premier or president. A man of straw, proof against bad-egging and dead-catting.

ALTAR, n. The place whereupon the priest formerly raveled out the small intestine of the sacrificial victim for purposes of divination and cooked its flesh for the gods. The word is now seldom used, except with reference to the sacrifice of their liberty and peace by a male and a female tool.

AMBIDEXTROUS, adj. Able to pick with equal skill a right-hand pocket or a left.

BACCHUS, n. A convenient deity invented by the ancients as an excuse for getting drunk.

BEARD, n. The hair that is commonly cut off by those who justly execrate the absurd Chinese custom of shaving the head.

BEAUTY, n. The power by which a woman charms a lover and terrifies a husband.

BEG, v. To ask for something with an earnestness proportioned to the belief that it will not be given.

CAT, n. A soft, indestructible automaton provided by nature to be kicked when things go wrong in the domestic circle.

CENTAUR, n. One of a race of persons who lived before the division of labor had been carried to such a pitch of differentiation, and who followed the primitive economic maxim, "Every man his own horse." The best of the lot was Chiron, who to the wisdom and virtues of the horse added the fleetness of man. The scripture story of the head of John the Baptist on a charger shows that pagan myths have somewhat sophisticated sacred history.

CHRISTIAN, n. One who believes that the New Testament is a divinely inspired book admirably suited to the spiritual needs of his neighbor. One who follows the teachings of Christ in so far as they are not inconsistent with a life of sin.

CRITIC, n. A person who boasts himself hard to please because nobody tries to please him.

DEBAUCHEE, n. One who has so earnestly pursued pleasure that he has had the misfortune to overtake it.

DELUGE, n. A notable first experiment in baptism which washed away the sins (and sinners) of the world.

FAITH, n. Belief without evidence in what is told by one who speaks without knowledge, of things without parallel.

Discographies

 ftp.spies.com:/Library/Music/Disc

There's a limited archive of discographies for popular musicians and bands at the FTP site listed at the beginning of this section. While the range seems to favor obscure metal bands, it offers lists of albums by a few somewhat more recognizable performers, such as Frank Zappa and the Grateful Dead. There's no mainstream pop in the list—hardly a loss.

While many of the bands in question are obscure, these discographies are exhaustive. The entry for the Grateful Dead, for example, lists both the mainstream Dead albums over the past few decades, early material by the Warlocks, other albums on which various members of the band have played, solo efforts, and a selection of bootlegs.

If you know of a record shop that will special order discs, these are the lists that you can use to really see what they're made of. Note that some of the albums in these discographies are available only on vinyl, and then only on very old, scratched vinyl found in moldering cardboard boxes at garage sales. While much of the history of rock has been remastered and released on compact discs, this process hasn't worked its way down to every experimental recording and bootleg of the distant past as yet.

Discordia

alt.discordia

There are a number of newsgroups that seem to exist primarily because they're extremely strange. Some, such as *alt.devilbunnies*, have a benign peculiarity about them, embracing the aura of the eccentric. There are a few really extreme groups that are a touch rabid along with being strange. The *alt.discordia* newsgroup seems to exemplify this quality.

Consider that:

It is a well known fact that Iceland eats bicycles.

Would you want Iceland to go hungry?

I wouldn't be surprised if a diet is in order.

Almost nothing in *alt.discordia* makes sense in the usual meaning of the word. The message threads are more like great tangles of blind-drunk polecats careening off trees in a petrified forest. A very brief sampling of the messages in *alt.discordia* will turn up dissertations on matters such as cheese, the four food groups of the apocalypse, barnacles, guilds, kielbasa, William Shatner's toupee, useless wishes, flat

earth, ScotchBrite masons, drive-by assaults with donut holes, and antivirgins. Actually reading some of the postings will turn up all sorts of other, tangential matters.

For example, consider the following exerpts from a thread in *alt.discordia*. While less than wholly lucid, the level of spontaneity is exemplary.

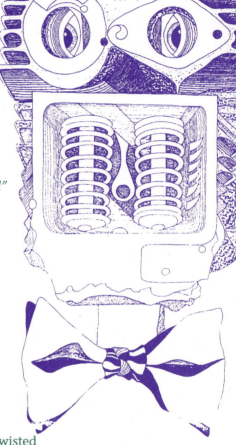

>   Gwork bobo no?
>
>   Ook *boba* no. Naba ook sa bobo *gro* na, aglas pib.
>
>   Abum sa!
>
>   Ook boba no *Gomi*
>
>   Ga, issu bob pib, naba ook sa Gomi, actu Klaatu barada nictanda es.
>
>   Aksa e Wik!
>
>   Don't forget to enjoy the sauce!
>
>   Wik boba sa Gomi?
>
>   Hek haki umpum lok putu mak bumbum zit ca "love child" ... Gomi bobosco.
>
>   Wik? ...gwork blep? Sa bekiboki boobocut?
>
>   Deeb kova, dahmae.
>
>   Mmmmmmm...Ga, ga boba.
>
>   Dem bepa, ga. Ke zeen boba sen Buha.
>
>   Agghk. Ke gwork _bleen_. Hep te blooba boobocut ahs alt.blenha.kubit.die.die.die!
>
>   O, rtranga ha, Wik. Orbi gra dahmum?
>
>   Ga, proba hes grinka plok, e nGomi sii glount.
>
>   hehehehehehe... se gruha!

It went on in this vein for some while.

You might well find that like many of the agreeably twisted newsgroups, *alt.discordia* is something of an inside joke. Be prepared to lurk around it for quite a while before you post anything, lest you be recognized immediately for someone nondiscordant. The regulars of *alt.discordia* don't seem to appreciate influences of normality in their alternate universe.

Dogs

rec.pets.dogs
rtfm.mit.edu:/pub/usenet/
news.answers/dogs-faq/

Few things are more sublime than the relationship between a dog and its master. Actually, "sublime" is probably a poor choice of words. Infuriating is frequently closer to the truth. While wonderful, loyal, and obedient creatures, dogs are less than optimally intelligent. At least, ours are. A mind is a terrible thing to waste, so they share one.

Dog ownership involves a lot more than reading the ingredients on the dog food bags carefully and going for a walk now and again. It's important to choose a dog that will suit your lifestyle and personality. Dogs are pretty demanding creatures in their own ways and require quite a bit of attention. Large dogs also require quite a bit of food. If you don't own a pickup truck now, be sure to put one on your shopping list.

There are all manner of books about dogs and dog care, but they tend to be written by veterinarians and dog breeders—people who have had years of experience with lots of dogs and periodically forget that many of the things that they take for granted are canine mysteries to the rest of us. For example, none of our dog books mentioned that labrador retrievers can chew through walls.

Here's an important tip for soon to be dog owners: labrador retrievers most certainly *can* chew through walls.

The files at the dogs FTP site at *rtfm.mit.edu* offer a number of lists of useful frequently asked questions and descriptions of many breeds; the latter will be informative for anyone considering a new pet. The *rec.pets.dogs* newsgroup is a great place to ask questions of other dog owners and pet care professionals.

One of the unfortunate aspects of dog ownership—especially if you're not on the Internet—is that there frequently is no one about to ask for advice if you don't know what to do with your beast. Vets, bless their pointy little heads, usually want $25 when you step through their doors. Commercial sources of information about matters such as nutrition usually have obvious axes to grind. Many important questions of dog owners go unanswered as a result. Subscribing to *rec.pets.dogs* cannot only allow you to share your experiences of owning a dog with others, but will allow you to periodically take better care of your pet.

Drinks

ⓘ `ocf.Berkeley.EDU:/typhoon/usr/local/ftp/pub/Library/Recreation/`

The use of alcohol predates most of the other inventive things that human beings are said to have done. Long before people had figured out indoor plumbing, stellar navigation, democratic principles, or paper making, they had a clear and well-rounded idea of how best to tie one on.

Mixed drinks are a somewhat more sophisticated art form than leaving some berries in a rotting log until they ferment, then drinking whatever oozes out. A mark of refinement and movement in fashionable circles, knowing how to mix exotic beverages can bring you respect—and unpaid bartender duties. People will tell you about their problems and nag you for peanuts. It's something worth knowing.

While there are a number of paper bartenders' guides available—the voluminous Mr. Boston books contain hundreds of drink recipes, for example—the mixed drinks available on the Internet are special. For one thing, they're free, leaving you with more money to spend on intoxicants. They also are somewhat weirder than most of what you'll find in commercial bar guides.

No one will forget your next party if you can mix a Screaming Orgasm, a Fred Fuddpucker, a Kiss In The Dark, a Sex On The Beach, or perhaps a Slow Comfortable Screw Up Against The Wall. The files at the FTP site mentioned at the beginning of this section will provide you with the details of all of these creations and countless more.

Political correctness bids me to note that none of these drinks are intended to help you get someone into bed, however much their names might suggest otherwise. Political correctness has a pretty unrealistic view of the world, mind you . . . .

Other notable recipes include a Ruptured Duck, a Hemorrhaging Brain, a James Bond Martini, and the legendary Vulcan Death Grip—one part Ouzo and one part Bacardi 151. Don't pour the latter around anyone you don't trust with your life.

Drugs

🛈 alt.drugs
🧘 ftp.spies.com:/Library/Fringe/ Pharm/

I consider it a sobering thought that most high school kids have much more ready access to drugs and drug lore than I do. If I suddenly decided to sell the house, abandon the cars, and give the dogs their freedom to allow me to pursue a life of vile, contemptible self indulgence and substance abuse, I wouldn't know where to begin.

One of the imponderable outgrowths of the explosive increase in the use of drugs in the nineties is the explosive increase in the number of politicians who want to be seen to be doing something about the problem. Usually, doing something involves printing a lot of pamphlets and T-shirts and showing up for as many photo opportunities as possible when the Coast Guard seizes another oil tanker full of cocaine. The level of hype surrounding the issue of drugs frequently obscures the realities involved.

One of the more enlightening resources of the Internet is the collection of documents pertaining to drugs and drug use at the FTP site listed at the beginning of this section. Very unsensational and factual, these files will tell you more in an hour about the realities of drugs than a week of propaganda on CNN. For most sentient life forms, they'll probably serve as a better deterrent to drug use, as well. However, unlike the government's literature on drugs, none of these files claim that you'll think you're a bat and throw yourself off the nearest high building the first time that you smoke something you shouldn't.

One of the best papers at the *ftp.spies.com* site listed at the beginning of this section is a translation of *Problem Child*, by Albert Hofmann. Hofmann is the Swiss chemist who discovered lysergic acid diethylamide, or LSD-25. While this document gets pretty technical in places, it's a lucid discussion of both the process by which LSD came to exist and the experiences of its creator as he experimented with the drug.

You might also want to look at Don Steiny's timeline of drugs and drug prohibition throughout human history. It begins with the earliest recorded use of opium in Sumeria, about 5000 B.C. and carries on with entries like:

1690 *The "Act for the Encouraging of the Distillation of Brandy and Spirits from Corn" is enacted in England.*
1691 *In Luneberg, Germany, the penalty for smoking (tobacco) is death.*

One wonders if they bothered with "no smoking" signs.

More specific documents at this site deal with marijuana, opium, heroine, and cigarette smoke, among many others. You'll also find a

number of tracts about drugs you probably have never heard of, such as Absinthe. In many cases, upon reading them, you'll probably never want to hear of them again.

The *alt.drugs* newsgroup offers a somewhat more interactive forum for the discussion of drugs. It's a pretty far reaching and eclectic arena, embodying everything from seriously spaced druggies to serious researchers and professionals. Plan to wade through the ravings from time to time, but there are all sorts of useful things to be learned therein.

✂ Excerpt from Problem Child

What seemed even more significant was that I could remember the experience of LSD inebriation in every detail. This could only mean that the conscious recording function was not interrupted, even in the climax of the LSD experience, despite the profound breakdown of the normal world view. For the entire duration of the experiment, I had even been aware of participating in an experiment, but despite this recognition of my condition, I could not, with every exertion of my will, shake off the LSD world. Everything was experienced as completely real, as alarming reality—alarming, because the picture of the other, familiar everyday reality was still fully preserved in the memory for comparison.

Another surprising aspect of LSD was its ability to produce such a far-reaching, powerful state of inebriation without leaving a hangover. Quite the contrary, on the day after the LSD experiment I felt myself to be, as already described, in excellent physical and mental condition. I was aware that LSD, a new active compound with such properties, would have to be of use in pharmacology, in neurology, and especially in psychiatry, and that it would attract the interest of concerned specialists. But at that time I had no inkling that the new substance would also come to be used beyond medical science, as an inebriant in the drug scene. Since my self-experiment had revealed LSD in its terrifying, demonic aspect, the last thing I could have expected was that this substance could ever find application as anything approaching a pleasure drug. I failed, moreover, to recognize the meaningful connection between LSD inebriation and spontaneous visionary experience until much later, after further experiments, which were carried out with far lower doses and under different conditions.

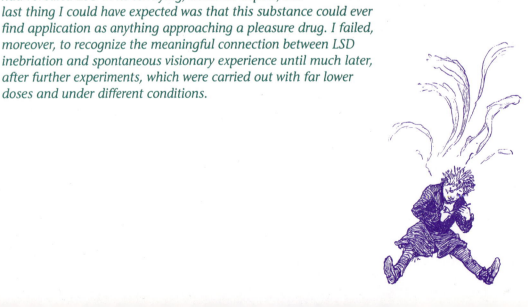

Early music

rec.music.early

There are some authorities who would have you believe that music was invented in the baroque period and that, prior to Bach and Pachelbel, the best musicians could aspire to was grunting with a pleasant rhythm. Most of these authorities, such as they are, seem to have had a hand in selecting the tracks for the "101 Classical Favorites" discs they flog at K-Mart.

Early music, or "preclassical music," is a vibrant and exciting form of music. It offers unusual tonalities and composition. While it might be a good six or seven hundred years old, it often sounds remarkably innovative because most people have never heard it before.

The other notable aspect of early music is that much of it has survived into the present day as tabliture and manuscripts, ultimately to be performed and recorded on compact discs. Because the halls and churches in which medieval and early renaissance music would have originally been performed typically were not constructed with an advanced understanding of acoustics in mind, listening to these pieces on your stereo probably will avail you of a much better performance than their original audiences could have hoped for.

The surviving manuscripts of early music composition suggest a sophisticated understanding of harmony and counterpoint, and the works often are fairly complex. What is lacking for all but the latest ones is much instrumentation, as the technology of instrument design hadn't quite caught up to the music being played. Most instruments, such as the earliest lutes and rebecs, were fairly quiet. The horns of the day were all natural; that is, they could play only a partial scale due to a lack of valves. They were useful for fanfares but rarely found their ways into performance.

Much early music, then, is entirely vocal. Instrumentation, when it appeared at all, was largely ornamental. This is rather the opposite of how music is performed today.

The rec.music.early newsgroup is something of a catchall for anyone interested in early music. In it, you'll find postings announcing early music performances, questions about the availability of early music on disc, discussions of musical theory, and odd bits of trivia. It's a great place to ask about recordings of specific works of interest.

✂ Excerpt from `rec.music.early`

What precautions, if any, does one need to take when air shipping a harpsichord? Is string tension a problem at higher altitudes during flight? Are all freight compartments on airplanes now pressurized? And second, what should one look out for when transplanting a harpsichord from a moist climate (SF Bay Area) to a higher, drier climate (Colorado Springs, CO)?

Detuning the harpsichord, in our experience, is not necessary. Air pressure does not seem to be a particularly important part of the structural integrity necessary for an instrument to hold tune. In fact, we are quite used to having instruments arrive more than acceptably in tune only to go out of tune when finally allowed to bathe in the new climate for four hours or so. The detuning leads to other problems, one of which is string breakage. As wire is generally on a one way street extension-wise, when you detune a string you allow wire with a long past history of flexing (around the tuning pin and past the nut & bridge pins) to go over some old ground. It is not uncommon to have strings break either when detuning or when tuning up again. Back before sliding keyboards, when transposing I found that strings would break more typically while letting them down than pulling them back up.

Be sure in constructing the crate that crush space is provided all around the instrument—sides, top and bottom. It is not uncommon for packers to put enough foam in the crate to bring the top of the instrument flush with the top of the crate and have the crate lid wedge the instrument into place. While we have had few problems with this practice, we recently had an instrument arrive which had been abused in transit and the bottom of the keywell had been popped off due to a blow sustained directly over the lockboard. Had there been an inch or two of rigid foam above the instrument the chance of this happening would have been much lessened. Further, the damage from the blow would probably have been much more apparent to the customer's eye and the crate would not have been discarded before the interior damage became apparent.

The claim process has hardly been worth the trouble.

Moist-to-dry climate. It could be worse, you could be going the other way. In general it is far easier to add moisture to dry air than to remove it from overly humid air. Try to recreate your present environment for the instrument when it arrives. In any case, you

should consider 40 percent Relative Humidity (R.H.) the floor percentage you wish to maintain. Your task will be to keep the R.H. up to this floor in the winter when it's cold outside and the absolute moisture content is quite low. When that outside air (which might display a healthy R.H.— outside) gets in and is raised to interior temperatures at which humans start to become happy, the R.H. can plummet to 10% (or less) if you don't add moisture to your air. Luckily, the moisture is good for you, your family, your pets, your plants and your furniture as well. If you add enough moisture (beyond 68% R.H. or so) it's good for all sorts of molds and buggy things that eat furniture, provide allergens, etc.

Moral: no overachieving is necessary — not like the instrument I once made whose owners did not understand this and provided it with a virtual Turkish bath in which to make its abode. All ferric materials were rusted (large stains around nails exposed on the bottom! of the instrument and at least four molds, each a different designer color. Very chic. In the winter you will probably have a hard time keeping the R.H. up to 30%. This is usually O.K. for very short periods. If you do get a crack (here beginneth the heresy) it probably doesn't matter to the sound. It might affect you, but it has better than even chances of not affecting the sound.

Best of luck. It will probably go swimmingly.

Electronic Frontier Foundation

 ftp.eff.org:/pub/EFF/

 Electronic Frontier Foundation

The Electronic Frontier Foundation is a curious institution. Founded in 1990 by Mitchell Kapor, the founder of Lotus Development Corporation, and John Barlow, one of the lyricists for the Grateful Dead, it exists to address the social and legal issues that have occurred as a result of computer-based communication and its headlong rush into the brick wall of society. While this has involved a good deal of education and such, it also has seen the Electronic Frontier Foundation helping with the legal expenses of hackers, cyberpunks, and other denizens of the fringes of computer culture.

Computer crime is a complex and pervasive issue, frequently obfuscated by the attempts of various branches of government to keep the whole sordid business secret.

While on the surface computer communications, such as things read on the Internet, would seem to be analogous to newspapers and radio broadcasts—and as such accorded the same freedoms and protections as other forms of expression—the unique nature of computers

has clouded this issue to some degree. The exact degree of clouding varies with the level of paranoia of the government agency involved. In several recent cases, government agents appear to have implemented a "seize first, ask questions later" policy, raiding suspected hackers and making off with everything that resembled a computer or a modem.

This has resulted in a number of innocent parties losing their means of livelihood.

To be sure, computer crime does exist—hackers breaking into sensitive networks and damaging the data there is far from unheard of. The Electronic Frontier Foundation isn't a blanket advocate for guilty criminals. It does seem to be actively involved in protecting those suspected of computer crimes from ill-informed, knee-jerk reactions of legal institutions not acquainted with the new frontier of computer communications.

For an introduction to the Electronic Frontier Foundation, have a look at EFF.TXT, the press release that announced its formation, and BARLOW.TXT, John Barlow's intriguing guided tour through his own personal corner of cyberspace. The Electronic Frontier Foundation FTP offers a wealth of additional documents, including information about various court cases it has been involved with.

✂ Excerpt from BARLOW.TXT

Howard: *Interesting couple of newusers just signed on. One calls himself acid and the other's optik.*

Barlow: *Hmmm. What are their real names?*

Howard: *Check their finger files.*

And so I typed *!finger acid*. Several seconds later the WELL's Sequent computer sent the following message to my Macintosh in Wyoming:

Login name: acid   In real life: Acid Phreak

By this, I knew that the WELL had a new resident and that his corporeal analog was supposedly called Acid Phreak. Typing *!finger optik* yielded results of similar insufficiency, including the claim that someone, somewhere in the real world, was walking around calling himself Phiber Optik. I doubted it.

However, associating these sparse data with the knowledge that the WELL was about to host a conference on computers and security rendered the conclusion that I had made my first sighting of genuine computer crackers....

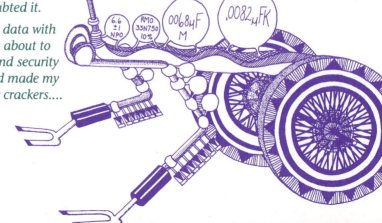

At first, I was inclined toward sympathy with Acid 'n' Optik as well as their colleagues, Adelaide, Knight Lightning, Taran King, and Emmanuel. I've always been more comfortable with outlaws than Republicans, despite having more certain credentials in the latter camp.... These kids were fractious, vulgar, immature, amoral, insulting, and too damned good at their work....

My own initial enthusiasm for the crackers wilted under a steady barrage of typed testosterone. I quickly remembered I didn't know much about who they were, what they did, or how they did it. I also remembered stories about crackers working in league with the Mob, ripping off credit card numbers and getting paid for them in (stolen) computer equipment. And I remembered Kevin Mitnik. Mitnik, now 25, is currently serving federal time for a variety of computer and telephone related crimes. Prior to incarceration, Mitnik was, by all accounts, a dangerous guy with a computer. He disrupted phone company operations and arbitrarily disconnected the phones of celebrities. Like the kid in Wargames, he broke into the North American Defense Command computer in Colorado Springs....

They finally got to me with:

Acid*: Whoever said they'd leave the door open to their house... where do you live? (the address) Leave it to me in mail if you like.*

I had never encountered anyone so apparently unworthy of my trust as these little nihilists. They had me questioning a basic tenet, namely that the greatest security lies in vulnerability. I decided it was time to put that principle to the test....

Barlow: *Acid. My house is at 372 North Franklin Street in Pinedale, Wyoming. If you're heading north on Franklin, you go about two blocks off the main drag before you run into hay meadow on the left. I've got the last house before the field. The computer is always on....*

Acid Phreak: *Mr. Barlow: Thank you for posting all I need to get your credit information and a whole lot more! Now, who is to blame? ME for getting it or YOU for being such an idiot?! I think this should just about sum things up....*

I spent a day wondering whether I was dealing with another Kevin Mitnik before the other shoe dropped:

Barlow: *...With crackers like acid and optik, the issue is less intelligence than alienation. Trade their modems for skateboards and only a slight conceptual shift would occur.*

Optik: *You have some pair of balls comparing my talent with that of a skateboarder. Hmmm... This was indeed boring, but nonetheless:*

At which point he downloaded my credit history.

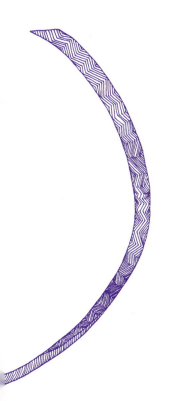

Electronic newsstand

 Electronic Newsstand

The electronic newsstand is a commercial entity to help you choose magazine subscriptions. It has a large and growing database of common and obscure magazines. Each one includes a gopher entry so that you can see what it's about. Typically you'll find the table of contents for current and recent issues and enough bits of articles to allow you to electronically browse a prospective publication and see if you like it. You also can browse the Electronic Newsstand by keyword searching.

Having found something that you like the look of, the Electronic Newsstand allows you to order single copies of magazines through a toll-free 800 number.

The list of publications available through the Electronic Newsstand is large and growing. Among the titles on hand as I write this are *Business Week*, *Canoe & Kayak*, *Decanter*, *Destination Discovery—The Discovery Channel Magazine*, *E—The Environmental Magazine*, *Inc. Magazine*, *The New Yorker*, *Saturday Night*, *The Times Literary Supplement*, and *Worth Magazine*. The list actually is quite extensive with new magazines being added periodically.

Enya

alt.music.enya

The *alt.music.enya* newsgroup is ostensibly a meeting place for fans of the Irish new age musician Enya—Eithne Ní Bhraonáin. Perhaps like Enya's music itself, however, it's singularly eclectic. A quick browse through it just before I wrote this section turned up references to Loreena McKennitt, Clannad, Elvis, and the Rolling Stones.

The usual discussion in *alt.music.enya* concerns translations of some of the Gaelic lyrics of the songs on Enya's albums, fragments of interviews, rumors of upcoming new discs, and tangential issues. Clannad, a band comprised of other members of Enya's family, turns up pretty frequently in the latter category.

As fan newsgroups go, this one is fairly well-mannered. The rabid flames and mutual abuse of newsgroups devoted to some of the more mainstream bands are largely absent. Largely. If you suggest that you didn't like Shepherd Moon, you'll get a sense of just how thin the veneer of civility is.

Equestrians

 `rec.equestrian`

It's been some while since horses were a serious form of transportation. One rarely finds a hitching post outside the local 7-11, and few roads are particularly accessible by anything born without wheels. However, with the demise of riding for practical reasons, it became something to do for recreation. To be sure, this seems to have suited the horses involved.

The world is a much more attractive place when it's seen from atop a horse. If you're reading this from deep in an urban wilderness, you probably will have to undertake a somewhat paradoxical journey to go riding—driving to where the horses are. A few hours in the saddle is arguably worth it.

If you have a look at the *rec.equestrian* newsgroup, you'll probably wonder how horses survived as long as they did prior to the widespread availability of Internet access. The acquisition, upbringing, feeding, outfitting, reproduction, and care of horses—and occasionally actually riding one when there's a moment left over—is a subject for infinite discussion. If you've been around horses all your life, you'll find *rec.equestrian* to be a comfortable place to exchange views and chat. New horse owners, or horse owners to be, can ask questions of veteran hands and avoid some of the problems that often confront the inexperienced.

The *rec.equestrian* newsgroup is one of the most well-mannered, laid-back newsgroups on the Net, with no meaningful amount of flaming or harsh language. It's very much a reflection of the serenity that grows from some time in a saddle.

 Excerpt from `rec.equestrian`

Note: The original question asked which plants are poisonous to horses.

Ornamental plants I can think of off the top of my head that are poisonous are azaleas (not too bad, a horse would have to eat a lot before you would see symptoms... like five percent of body weight)

I've been told that buttercups are also poisonous to horses. I didn't notice them on the list posted earlier. Has anyone else heard this?

Yup, but the waxy buttercups... and a regular yellow flower that is also called buttercup... also bracken fern, chive (causes liver damage), nightshade, nut trees, ornamental yew...

Common garden vegetables that I've been told were poisonous include tomato (plants) and rhubarb (leaves).

The following is quoted from "Livestock-Poisoning Plants of California", Leaflet 21268 of the University of California. Division of Agricultural Services (1982).

Larkspur – that's right, the flower. One book I have said that it is second only to locoweed in causing livestock fatalities. The stuff is an attractive garden annual that readily reseeds itself — not necessarily in the garden.

By the way, these are all bad for humans too. Did you know the honey from azalea flowers contains the toxin? Bad news in this area —we have wild azaleas all through the woods. Rhododendrons have the same stuff in them. The good news is that I've never heard of a horse that liked them.

"With few exceptions, livestock will not eat poisonous plants unless forced to by hunger. Thus, the single most important way to prevent poisoning is to use proper range management practices to provide ample forage and favor consumption of non-toxic plants."...

I'd like to point out that the "few exceptions" can be catastrophic. Horses will test various plants to see if they like them. Most will not eat deadly nightshade or its relatives (e.g. potato and tomato plants) However, some like the taste and become addicted to the plant...

Another exception to the "will not eat poisonous plants unless forced by hunger" generalization are plants such as alsike clover which causes death by liver damage. Alsike is poisonous to horses but cows eat it without harm.

Other toxic plant materials I've known well fed horses to eat include red maple leaves. The red maple is also known as the swamp maple or scarlet maple. It is *not* the decorative yard tree that has red leaves all summer. The red maple is native to the Eastern U.S. and is one of the most common and widely distributed trees in North America. The Latin name of the tree is Acer rubrum L.

Erotic literature

- 🛈 `alt.sex.stories`
- 🛈 `rec.arts.erotica`
- 🛈 `alt.sex`
- 🛈 `alt.pantyhose`
- 🐦 `Yellow Silk Magazine`
- 🐦 `Wiretap Online Library ¦ Articles ¦ Sex`

"The air was so close it was incestuous." I didn't write that. It was in one of the teasers in the Yellow Silk Magazine gopher service. It's an interesting image, nonetheless.

It's probably safe to say that more Internet resources are devoted to matters sexual than to any other single subject. The wonderful thing about the Net, after all, is that you can say anything you like, read anything you like, stare in dumbfounded amazement at anything you like... well, you probably get the idea. A section on staring in dumbfounded amazement, "Erotic pictures," follows this one.

Most of the stories in the erotic literature newsgroups listed at the beginning of this section are the work of amateur writers; what they lack in polish they frequently make up for by being very inventive. Many of the postings are fairly long discourses on various sexual encounters, kinky adventures, mild perversions, not at all mild perversions, and orgies. Frequently they run to multiple chapters. You'll also find threads discussing the stories, asking for more stories, or just rambling incoherently, probably the result of having read a few stories too many.

The definition of "adult" material seems to vary a bit these days. It seems worth noting that absolutely nothing is restricted in newsgroups like *alt.sex.stories*. There are sexual adventures described in some of the postings that you probably wouldn't undertake even after having consumed enough strong drink to drown a medium-size African elephant. Some of the people who write these things are truly twisted, which is what makes them such fun.

Every so often an emissary from one of the more restrained elements of the Net drops in and evangelizes for a while. This is entertaining as well.

One rather unusual aspect of *alt.sex.stories* is that it has a very pronounced conscience at times. The language in most of its postings is largely unprintable and the sexual appetites of its regular members are bizarre, but there's a singular sense of refinement about it nonetheless. Unlike most of the parties who drop by to flame and moralize, the users of *alt.sex.stories* just seem to want to be left alone to enjoy the pleasures of the written word. Consider the following excerpt:

> We are a British TV programme covering issues on net freedom/censorship. We are interested in talking to people who are involved in net porn.
>
> People of the internet, I address you now in the hopes of preserving the wonderfully free environment that has evolved here in cyberspace. We have achieved what 2000 years of "civilization" has failed to do — a truly free society where all members are truly equal, and no one can usurp or suppress the rights of others. Unfortunately, there is a threat to this world. It is the media, that evil entity which feeds on controversy and conflict. I have seen more requests by media representatives on the erotic groups than on all other groups combined. I have seen many 'objective' reports on the internet which always turn to "Young children can access porn on the internet" type drum beating. Sooner or later this is going to lead to either monitoring and/or erratication of these groups...
>
> I implore you, do not talk to the media! Do not talk to people who contact you spontaneously desiring information on these groups. Tell these people that these groups do not exist... We can survive, but only if we work together!
>
> Also, do not forget that while journalists are the absolute scum of the earth, British journalists are the absolute scum of journalists. British journalists are the most unprofessional, crackpot lot... our civilization has ever produced.

The *alt.sex.stories* newsgroup gets along by its own devices and is pretty wild at times. By contrast, *rec.arts.erotica* is moderated. It's considerably more civilized, although I feel that, on the whole, it's less interesting. There's a fair bit of erotic poetry, which is something of an acquired taste, I suspect. Amateur erotic prose is arguably more readable than amateur erotic verse.

The *alt.pantyhose* newsgroup is mostly about women's underwear and fetishes thereof. However, some really odd stories seem to appear in it from time to time.

The *alt.sex* newsgroup is for a general discussion of sex. Some erotic stories appear there as well, although you'll have to be prepared to work through a lot of other sorts of postings. This isn't as much of a chore as it might seem, mind ....

The Wiretap Online Library's articles about sex are an engaging sample of some of the sexually related texts that have appeared on the Net of late.

Here's the list as I write this:

1. All Time Favorite XXX Actresses.
2. An Essay concerning Nipples.
3. Artificial Eroticism.
4. Interracial Relationships.
5. Les/Bi/Gay & Transgender Glossary.
6. List of GLBO Celebrity/Historical Figures.
7. Natural Bears Classification System.
8. On Clothespins as Toys.
9. Playboy Centerfolds.
10. Playboy Centerfolds (with meas).
11. Polyamory.
12. Purity Test - 500 Q Version.
13. Review of Strip Joints.
14. Sexual & Gender Identity Glossary.
15. Smurfs Code.
16. Song of Solomon.
17. Surgeon General's Warning on AIDS.
18. The 100 Question Purity Test.
19. The 1500 Question Purity Test.
20. The 400 Question Purity Test (Best).
21. The alt.butt-harp FAQ (truly amazing).
22. Whore Prices.
23. Yoni Massage How-To.
24. alt.sex combined FAQ.
25. alt.sex.wizards combined FAQ.

I can't claim to have read all these, and I have no intention of stating which ones I have.

Finally, *Yellow Silk Magazine* is a commercial erotic literature publication. Its gopher service features a table of contents for the current issue and several past issues and some excerpts and teasers from its articles. This is probably not the sort of magazine you can get from Publisher's Clearinghouse.

EROTIC LITERATURE

Erotic pictures

- `alt.binaries.pictures.erotica`
- `alt.binaries.pictures.erotica.d`
- `alt.binaries.pictures.erotica.blondes`
- `alt.binaries.pictures.erotica.female`
- `alt.binaries.pictures.erotica.orientals`
- `alt.sex.pictures`
- `alt.sex.pictures.d`
- `alt.sex.pictures.female`

Honesty bids me to add that, in addition to the newsgroups listed here, there also are *alt.binaries.pictures.erotica.male* and *alt.sex.pictures.male*. One of the important attributes of this book is that I actually have had to dig through all the Internet resources listed in this book. I didn't check out these two newsgroups, nor am I likely to. This is a very sexist attitude and not all in keeping with the tolerance of the nineties, but I think I'll stick with it nonetheless.

The newsgroups listed at the beginning of this section are an unusual Usenet resource, in that many of their postings aren't human readable text, but rather pictures. These aren't crude pictures formed out of characters either, but data that will ultimately form high-quality scanned images. The process of retrieving them is a bit complex—it's discussed in detail in the introduction to this book—but it's not difficult to master. In technical terms, the files are uuencoded. The resulting images typically will be GIF or JPEG files. These formats are readable on most types of computers.

Of late, a number of erotic AVI files also have appeared in some of these newsgroups. These are animated video clips and are more or less specific to computers running Microsoft Windows.

You might well ask why erotic graphics are handled in this rather peculiar manner. It would seem as if they might be much more readily transferred from an FTP site. The problem is that doing so makes them a bit too readily accessible. Every FTP site that has thus far offered erotic graphics for download has been so swamped by people grabbing every file in sight that they've been forced to discontinue the service. There are no publicly accessible anonymous FTP sites that offer erotic pictures, as I write this, although rumors of secret ones persist.

Because scanned graphics are fairly large entities and there's a finite limit to the size of a single Usenet posting, you'll frequently find

pictures in the newsgroups split up into multiple postings. You'll require all the postings for a particular file to successfully decode it. The postings typically will be consecutive and named such that it's obvious which bits are required.

As with the "Erotic literature" resources of the Internet, there's effectively no restrictions as to what might turn up in any of these newsgroups. They range from bare-breasted women to people in positions that don't seem as if they should be possible without serious injury. Some of them would make a whore blush. (While I've not actually ever seen a blushing whore, I'm given to understand that it's not something that happens without considerable provocation.)

Also as with the "Erotic literature" resources, the occasional feminists and religious conservatives seem to stumble into these newsgroups from time to time and get generally worked up about the general state of the depravity. Me'thinks these people enjoy getting worked up. A good time can be had by all. (I wonder if one could pose as a "masculinist" and leave similar postings in *alt.sex.pictures.male*.)

Note that the newsgroups that end in *.d* are for discussion of erotic pictures, rather than for posting the pictures themselves.

All considerations of morality and decorum aside, erotica is fun. If you like this sort of thing, the effort involved in using a uudecoder and an image viewer to reconstruct and view the pictures probably is worth the effort, at least now and again. Life without a few occasional excesses would be very dull indeed.

Esperanto

 `ftp.spies.com:/Library/Article/Language/esperant.eng`

 `Wiretap Online Library | Articles | Language | Esperanto English Dictionary`

 `esperanto@rand.org`

 `esperanto-request@rand.org`

Esperanto is a language, just as English is. You might not be familiar with it, as, unlike English, it lacks a culture or nation that speaks it. You'll wander in vain across the planet looking for the land of Esperant or a people called Esperantii, Esperantites, or Esperantillians. Esperanto is a synthetic language, created from a fusion of the popular western languages. It was envisioned by its creator, Lazarus Zamenhof, as a common language that everyone could embrace.

Esperanto is almost a century old, and it would be hard to say that it has wholly eliminated the language barriers between people of different nations. It's a laudable undertaking nonetheless, however, and well worth having a look at if you like languages in general and want to try something unusual.

The *esperanto.eng* file at the FTP site and the gopher service listed at the beginning of this section is an Esperanto-to-English dictionary and a useful place to begin to study Esperanto. The Esperanto mailing list will put you in touch with other Esperanto speakers and help you find other Esperanto resources.

As an aside, Esperanto is somewhat infrequently encountered, but it does still turn up from time to time. Fans of the "Red Dwarf" television series, as discussed elsewhere in this book, will no doubt have noticed that all the signs aboard the ship appear to be bilingual. The second language is Esperanto.

Events of the Day

 copi@oddjob.uchicago.edu

The Finger site listed at the beginning of this section will send you a page worth of things that happened in history on this day. It's a curious mix of information, including some sports schedules, aphorisms and other bits of trivia. The excerpt in this section is the page for the day that I wrote this. Do note the author's conditions at the end of the excerpt. This is another instance of an Internet resource that works through mutual cooperation.

 ### Excerpt from Events of the Day

[oddjob.uchicago.edu]
Login name: copi   In real life: Craig J Copi
Directory: /home/oddjob/copi   Shell: /usr/local/bin/tcsh
On since May 6 09:38:36 on ttypc from onondaga:0.0
Mail last read Fri May 6 09:47:45 1994

Project:
Learning that we are only mortal—for a limited time.
        — Rush, "Dreamline", Roll the Bones

Plan:
Output brought to you courtesy of finger_monitor (beta0.9) CJC

    Was it love or was it the idea of being in love?
        — Pink Floyd, "One Slip"
    (current tally: 23 love, 38 idea of being in love)
    (Stand up and be counted; cast your vote today)

    And you can analyze this situation.
    To me it's all just mental masturbation.
        — Sammy Hagar, "There's only one way to rock"

Thank you for fingering me from accesspt.north.net (198.52.32.3).
Current time information:

Friday
May 6, 1994
9:52:18 AM (CDT)

Greenwich Mean Time: 2:52:18 PM
Day 126 and Week 18 of current year
10,835,538 seconds elapsed in current year
233 shopping days until Christmas
Phase of moon: waning crescent
Age of moon 4 days (to next new moon)
The year of the Dog

************************ Special Events
************** Birth: Sigmund Freud (138 years ago)
************* Birth: Willem de Sitter (122 years ago)
************* Birth: Rudolph Valentino (99 years ago)
*************** Birth: Orson Welles (79 years ago)
*************** Birth: Robert Dicke (78 years ago)
**************** Birth: Willie Mays (63 years ago)
**************** Birth: Bob Seeger (49 years ago)
*********** Death: Henry David Thoreau (132 years ago)
******** Death: Lyman Frank (Frank L) Baum (75 years ago)
Event: 1st athletic club in US founded (Olympic club) (134 years ago)
********** Event: Hindenburg explosion (57 years ago)
****

Please email me event (mm/dd/YYYY) information to add to my list

Here is a list of upcoming games (note: all times are EDT)

MLB schedule for today...

Red Sox	*at Yankees*	*(7:05 pm)*
Cubs (WGN)	*at Pirates*	*(7:35 pm)*
Indians	*at Orioles*	*(7:35 pm)*
Rockies	*at Padres*	*(10:05 pm)*
Astros	*at Reds*	*(7:35 pm)*
Royals	*at White Sox*	*(8:05 pm)*
Dodgers	*at Giants*	*(10:05 pm)*
Brewers	*at Blue Jays*	*(7:35 pm)*
Twins	*at Rangers*	*(8:35 pm)*
Expos (WTBS)	*at Braves*	*(7:40 pm)*
Mets	*at Cardinals*	*(8:05 pm)*
Athletics	*at Angels*	*(10:05 pm)*
Phillies	*at Marlins*	*(7:05 pm)*
Mariners	*at Tigers*	*(7:05 pm)*

With a large increase in the number of times I have been fingered I have noticed many repeat "fingerers." Since there is no need to finger me more than once a day here are some suggestions:

1) Do NOT finger me every time you log on (do NOT put it in your login file)
2) Have a cron/batch job finger me and pipe the results to a file. Define an alias to make it easy to page the file (page this file in your login file if desired).
3) Allow everyone on your system access to I have found that as much as 10% of all fin come from 1 site.
So far things have not gotten out of hand. I keep it this way.

alt.evil

The *alt.evil* newsgroup is a forum for a philosophical discussion of the nature of evil. Occasionally some real evil will find its way into the philosophy, however, and all this intellectual discourse will collapse into flames and harsh language.

Perhaps, as one might expect in dealing with so elemental a topic, much of the argument seems to fall into two camps: the Zenlike spiritualists who attempt to define evil in somewhat vague metaphysical terms and the hard-edged logicians who want to pin it down in concrete dimensions. All that Zen can get a bit tedious.

Elementary logic can be engaging, especially if you're able to find a few others who are capable of it. The *alt.evil* newsgroup will allow you to exercise your mind on problems more fundamental than who had the remote control for the television last. The first person to actually define evil in *alt.evil* should be in line for any number of patents and government grants.

Excerpt from `alt.evil`

Evil is an insidious truth that creeps past the intellect and stirs the primal fears. It cannot be stopped if it exists. And it cannot exist by itself.

We might be on to something here...

Evil preys on the ignorant and enslaves them. But knowledge of this is not enough... to be evil one must descend into the self-consuming circle while maintaining a belief that one will not be consumed, and thus become ignorant.

Only partial agreement on this point. I'd call the belief that one will not be consumed more arrogant than ignorant. I think part of what makes evil

"evil" is that it knows exactly what it is... there's no ignorance involved, and the enslavement is a willing one.

A few more thoughts on what evil is:

Easier for human language to define in terms of what it isn't than what it is. When it comes down to it, "evil" is the only word in English that describes evil. Beyond that, image and metaphor, parable, poetry, and art are the tools that come closest to enabling description...

Evil is undefinable. If I were to define evil...

I'm so glad that they are still teaching elementary logic in the universities...

They aren't, but some people have an intuitive grasp of it despite the omission.

Evil is a glitch in the human nature. The resolve to help others versus the resolve to help one self.

So, if I help someone else, but inadvertently through my assistance the other person ends up hurt by my actions... am I evil?

Look into a hit mans face as he kills. He doesn't care... he does not acknowledge the pain of death being inflicted. This is evil.

But neither are we acknowledging his reasons for being a hitman, so is our judgment of him also "evil"?

Evil isn't interested in inflicting pain. Evil has no concept of other's pain just one's own pain. Evil doesn't observe others as having needs. Evil doesn't observe other's desires, etc. Evil doesn't care if a persons life is destroyed. Evil doesn't acknowledge the pain other than his own.

Say someone sees an anthill and without pausing to consider the needs of the ants, smashes it with his foot, killing hundreds of them. Is this person evil? Was this an act of evil?

That's solipsism, which is selfish, but not necessarily evil. You seem to think that lack of compassion is evil. I'm not sympathetic to many peoples' trials, but I don't think that makes me evil.

Extremists and activists

- alt.activism
- alt.feminism
- alt.religion.christian
- alt.skinheads

There are a lot of extreme points of view on the Internet; perhaps this is inherent in its nature. Less extreme individuals would use CompuServe. Beyond the somewhat expressive nature of the Net in general, however, you can find a number of newsgroups that are decidedly volatile.

Extreme political and social views often are enlightening, even if you're unlikely to espouse them yourself. Rabid dogma leaves little room for ambiguities and gray areas.

One of the best places to go for a really extreme view of civilization is *alt.skinheads*. It's beyond the scope of this book to say anything judgmental about skinhead attitudes in general; that's the sort of thing that sociologists write magazine articles about and get to discuss in learned tones on "60 Minutes." However, whether or not you'd want anything to do with real-life skinheads, you might find the *alt.skinheads* newsgroup to be a diverting place to lurk for a while.

Skinhead politics are far enough right to allow most adherents thereof to see over the edge of the world. Skinheads typically are characterized as being racists if one is being polite or neo-Nazis if one is not. Skinheads themselves typically would not characterize themselves as such, which is why *alt.skinheads* is such an interesting place to kill time. While there are quite substantial flames there licking the walls and singeing the eyebrows of the unwary, you also will find some surprisingly coherent arguments espousing the skinhead perspective.

Having said this, the *alt.skinheads* newsgroup is arguably not for the faint of heart or for the easily enraged. The postings there frequently decry anyone who isn't white and Anglo-Saxon. Quotations from historical sources proving that members of various racial groups are somehow inferior seemed to be all the rage as I was writing this.

A less-intense introduction to the extreme groups on the Net can be found in *alt.activism*. The ostensible purpose of *alt.activism* is to discuss nonpassive methods for bringing about positive social and political change. Perhaps perpetually stymied by entrenched political and social institutions that want nothing more than to stay the same until the sun goes nova, activists in general are likely to be a somewhat violent lot. The regular posters in *alt.activism* are hardly an exception, and one senses a lot of pent up range and hostility in many of its postings.

A few creative ideas do seem to foment in this environment, however. On July 4, 1994, for example, thousands of e-mail messages were sent to Bill Clinton urging him to decriminalize marijuana, a project ostensibly initiated in *alt.activism*. Subsequent postings debated at length the matter of the White House's Internet mail address and whether messages sent to it were read by the President, read by anyone at all, or merely sent directly into oblivion. (See the sidebar on "Dear Prez" elsewhere in this book.)

The consensus was that no federal politician currently in office seems to have a clear idea what the Internet is, let alone how to actually use it to receive mail.

One of the most energetic of the extreme newsgroups is *alt.feminism*. It generally is pretty violent, with clouds of moral outage and the aroma of burning martyrs everywhere. It's a peculiar newsgroup, in that, while there are a substantial number of male posters visible there from time to time, most of the really nasty flames seem to be from women directed at other women. Perhaps this is between feminists espousing different degrees of extremism.

As with many other activist viewpoints, there's a large gray area between constructive feminism and rabid male-bashing. While the tenor of *alt.feminism* varies with time, it leans toward the latter.

As I write this, O.J. Simpson has just been charged with murdering his ex-wife. This has generated some pretty sensational postings, digressing into several threads about wife-battering and the abuse of women. The title of one of them was "Why men should be blamed." This seems to define the context for the discussion fairly well.

Perhaps because feminism in general has generated a great deal of social science over the past few decades—it is, after all, a subject in which at least half the human race might have an active interest—many of the postings in *alt.feminism* cite impressive lists of sources to substantiate their ideas. While one often has the sense that many of the regulars in *alt.feminism* would be unpleasant to encounter in a dark alley especially if you're male and only lightly armed, they do seem to be well read. Post at your own peril.

Finally, one of the most curious of the extreme groups is *alt.religion.christian*—perhaps as few of the regular posters there see themselves as such. Posts to this newsgroup seem to be of three distinct types: militant fundamentalist Christians, or "fundies," who will answer any question with a quotation from scripture;

nonchristians; or lapsed Christians who've just come for the collateral damage and flame bait. The latter is one of the more vandalous traditions of the Net. It involves choosing a newsgroup with an avowed cause and posting something certain to offend most of its users.

In most contexts, flame bait is spotted as such and ignored. The *alt.religion.christian* newsgroup is one of the few that still will get outraged by it, and one frequently will see long threads of vehement responses to postings like "Your god does not exist and you know it."

Unlike most of the extreme newsgroups, few of the regular users of *alt.religion.christian* argue very well, and it might well be said that taking shots at them is somewhat unsportsmanlike.

Fanny Hill

nic.funet.fi:/pub/doc/literary/
etext/fannyhill.txt.gz

The basis of several agreeably tawdry films and innumerable subsequent imitations, Fanny Hill: Memoirs of a Woman of Pleasure was written around 1749 by John Cleland. Cleland was a minor British diplomat and an employee of the East India Company, which ran most of the interesting bits of the known universe for several hundred years. Fanny Hill, one of his three surviving novels, was among the smash best-sellers of the eighteenth century.

Should you not have encountered it, Fanny Hill is one of the finest examples of the craft of writing erotic literature to be found. More to the point, it can be found on the Internet, so you need not skulk into some disreputable bookshop pretending your name is Smith. It's also a pretty well-written book. While a lot of old books read like old books, Fanny Hill holds up better than many novels a tenth of its age.

Perhaps its most notable credit is that, in 1963, over 200 years after its original publication, it was prosecuted in Britain under the Obscene Publications Act. While you can't always judge a book by its cover, you can certainly learn a lot from its coverage.

Anyone with an ounce of morality in them will be shocked by this book; be sure to print it out and leave it where they can find it.

Flying saucers

 ftp.spies.com:/Library/Fringe/Ufo/
🛈 alt.alien.visitors

After considerable reflection, I decided that entitling this section "Flying saucers" was a reasonable compromise. Putting it under *U*, for "Unidentified flying objects" just seemed to lend it entirely too much credence. Putting it under *C*, for "Crackpots," might have been potentially embarrassing in the admittedly unlikely event that real extraterrestrials appeared on Letterman in between writing this book and its release.

The FTP site listed at the beginning of this section offers a wealth of documents pertaining to aliens and their frequent peregrinations to earth. Some of them are eerily convincing if you like this sort of thing. Some are extremely flaky. Most are a good read, however, especially if you do it where no one else can see you. No one human, that is.

While there are all sorts of alien encounter stories about, the core of the UFO issue maintains that aliens have been showing up since at least the early part of this century. The United States government has recovered several damaged spacecraft, performed autopsies on the cadavers of extraterrestrial astronauts, held several live aliens in custody, and ultimately entered into a treaty with some of the aliens to buy their technology. Both sides have killed a lot of cows in Montana for no readily explicable reason. This whole issue has been kept absolutely secret for the past 50 years or so.

Aliens, it seems, appear in their spaceships and brainwash everyone who sees them into forgetting what happened. If you've never seen a flying saucer, you probably see them all the time.

Other documents of interest at this FTP site are a discussion of constructing your own flying saucer and a long paper dealing with the psychological characteristics of purported victims of alien abduction. The former document doesn't take itself too seriously; the latter is somewhat disturbing.

Finally, you'll find several accounts of people who claim to have had contacts with extraterrestrials at this FTP site. These stories are a bit spooky as well. Notably, there are no GIF files of the Martians involved accompanying the texts.

The *alt.alien.visitors* newsgroup will offer you a more interactive forum to discuss the arrival of people from outer space and the alleged government cover-up of their presence. Some of this stuff would sound far fetched to a staff member of the *National Enquirer*, but it's an interesting place to lurk for a while.

Food on the Internet

```
gatekeeper.dec.com:/
pub/recipes
ftp.neosoft.com:/pub/rec.
food.recipes/site
rec.food.recipes
rec.food.cooking
rec.food.drink
rec.food.historic
rec.food.restaurants
rec.food.sourdough
rec.food.veg
alt.food
```

Regrettably, you can't actually get food e-mailed to you, although it's likely that someone is working on the problem. Nonetheless, the Internet is a stunning gastronomic resource, with no end of discussions about food and enough exotic recipes to prevent you from seeing the inside of a Pizza Hut again until well into the next century.

One of the more voluminous recipe collections available on the Net can be found at the FTP site *gatekeeper.dec.com:/pub/recipes*. This archive includes not only recipes for dishes such as maple souffle, bouillabaisse, and chicken kung pao, but the software to access them as well.

A still more extensive collection of recipes—completely classified and with indices for every category—can be found at the *ftp.neosoft.com:/pub/rec.food.recipes/site*. This is an archive of the *rec.food.recipes* newsgroup. Unquestionably one of the best food resources on the Net, the only things not listed are entrees for extraterrestrials and the ingredients list for Purina Tiger Chow. Unlike the recipes at *gatekeeper.dec.com*, all these files are in plain text and can be read without special software.

There also are a number of lively newsgroups devoted to food. These include *rec.food.cooking*, *rec.food.drink*, *rec.food.historic*, the aforementioned *rec.food.recipes*, *rec.food.restaurants*, *rec.food.sourdough*, and *rec.food.veg*; the latter being for vegetarians. Also not to be missed is *alt.food*; you'll find a lot of interesting threads about food there, but with the occasional food fight included, as usually is the case for *alt* newsgroups.

Finally, there are several recipe archives available through gopher. A somewhat quirky one can be found at *Internet Wiretap ¦ Articles ¦ Food and Drink*. It includes articles about making beef jerky, but right along side them are features about issues like plant pain.

You also might want to have a look at the gopher at *Albert Einstein College of Medicine ¦ Internet Resources ¦ Miscellaneous ¦ Search the Food Recipes Database*. This is a searchable gopher item; it accesses a large database of recipes, but you'll need some idea of what you're looking for.

G. Gordon Liddy

alt.fan.g-gordon-liddy

Patrons of recent history will recall G. Gordon Liddy as being one of the original Watergate "plumbers," the alleged agents of the committee to re-elect then-president Nixon who broke into the Democratic campaign headquarters to have a look around. While others involved in Watergate have faded away, taken up religion, or written their memoirs, G. Gordon hasn't changed a great deal from those heady days. His autobiography, *Will*, is a somewhat disturbing work. The disturbing bit for some will be that people like G. Gordon are walking around pretty well armed.

Liddy claims to have told one of his superiors during the debacle following the disclosure of Watergate that he didn't want his family injured by stray gunfire and that, if he could be informed of a specific street corner and a time to be there, he'd allow himself to be shot without anyone else getting in the way. The offer appears to have been declined.

Subsequent to the publication of *Will*, G. Gordon wrote a number of spy novels, the most recent being *The Monkey Handlers*. They make light airplane reading if the in-flight movie is *Rambo III* and you've already seen it 8 or 10 times.

G. Gordon Liddy now hosts a radio show. Some of his views are slightly to the right of Genghis Khan.

Perhaps the most disturbing aspect of G. Gordon Liddy is that it's difficult not to agree with a lot of what he says, even if you'd never be caught dead telling anyone you know that you do. As such, the *alt.fan.g-gordon-liddy* newsgroup offers a comfortable place to commune with others who mourn the passing of an epoch of self-reliance, national identity, and liberal-bashing. Very little of what takes place therein could be said to be at all politically correct or in keeping with the spirit of the nineties, which is what makes it so appealing. Perhaps predictably, G. Gordon usually is referred to as the "g-man."

The intellectual level of the contents of *alt.fan.g-gordon-liddy* is usually pretty respectable.

Excerpt from `alt.fan.g-gordon-liddy`

During Liddy's 7 March radio program, he made the statement that some of the ATF agents involved in the Branch Davidian raid were killed or injured by bullets which pierced their bulletproof vests. Liddy further claimed that the Davidians did not have access to armor piercing ammunition.

Does anyone have anything that can back this claim up? I've heard precious little about the Branch Davidian raid/fiasco and it seems that there is a cover up. Does anyone know the basis for Liddy's claim?

If the Davidians were using rifle caliber weapons (Ak's, M16's, deer rifles, etc.) vests offer basically no protection. They are used to stop pistol caliber weaponry (pistols, SMG's) and shotgun pellets.

This is true for bulletproof vests but doesn't hold for "body armor." Looking at the videos I've seen it appears that some, if not all the agents were wearing body armor. A vest is difficult to discern while body armor is big and bulky and impossible to hide. While I can't remember exactly, but when I was in the service (70-74) body armor stops AK47 and M16 rounds with certain exceptions.

Grateful Dead

 gdead.berkeley.edu:/pub/gdead
 University of California Berkeley
 rec.music.gdead

The Grateful Dead is one of the more enduring bands, with one of the more unusual subcultures trailing in its wake. Deadheads are a pervasive phenomenon, both in the real world and on the Net. Some while back, *Time* magazine suggested that the community of fans that follow the Dead around on its tours supports itself by selling each other T-shirts, an interesting economic model.

One of the things that has made the deadheads what they are is the unique rapport that the band has with its audience. Unlike almost every other concert on the planet, the Dead encourage the use of cameras and tape recorders at their performances, usually setting aside a special section for the latter. Very nearly every concert the Dead have given exists on a bootleg tape somewhere, and swapping tapes is one of the pastimes of serious Deadheads.

The energy of the Grateful Dead in performance hasn't diminished over the several decades that they've been together, despite allusions to the contrary in some of the Grateful Dead's more recent songs—"Touch of Grey" and "Black Muddy River," for example, speak of advancing years.

Perhaps one of the most salient comments about the Grateful Dead is offered by the band itself, or rather by its marketing arm, Grateful Dead Merchandise. In addition to all sorts of posters and compact discs, the most recent full-color brochure offers both custom Grateful Dead Harley-Davidson clutch plate covers and Grateful Dead ties.

Imagine the chief suit in a corner office at some major law firm wearing the latter. It's a pleasing image.

The Grateful Dead archives at the FTP and gopher sites listed at the beginning of this section are a wealth of song lyrics, scanned photographs of the band, interviews, and other bits of Dead regalia. The *rec.music.gdead* newsgroup offers a lively discussion of upcoming concerts and rumors of new albums, the ongoing exchange of tapes, fragments of deadhead gossip, and other issues surrounding the band.

Guns

🛈 `rec.guns`
🛈 `talk.politics.guns`

The politicians who live for photo opportunities like to portray gun enthusiasts as rabid, deer-slaughtering anarchists who walk around with AK-47s. Gun control legislation has become very fashionable of late, and even if much of it doesn't make completely lucid sense when it's examined closely, it sounds convincing when it turns up on CNN. The thinking seems to be that if half the guns in the world are owned by

the aforementioned rabid, deer-slaughtering anarchists and the other half are owned by drug dealers, suppressing the guns of the former group immediately will reduce the number of guns by at least 50%.

Admittedly, you don't have to look very far to find a few holes in this argument. To begin with, it will really help reduce the crimes committed with guns only if all the drug dealers can be convinced to take up hunting, arguably an unlikely possibility.

The *rec.guns* newsgroup exists primarily for people who are interested in firearms for sport. If there are any rabid, deer-slaughtering anarchists there, they're keeping their heads down. One of the most well-mannered newsgroups on the Net, it offers intelligent advice about buying a gun, learning to shoot, dealing with the growing burden of gun legislation, reloading ammunition, storing and transporting firearms, and so on. You'll find the occasional diverting thread of gun trivia. This is the place to go to ask questions about guns or to trade ideas with other gun owners. There's pretty well none of the socio-political hysteria that surrounds the issue of gun ownership in *rec.guns*.

One recent *rec.guns* posting offered the following. It's not politically correct, but then, neither are guns.

I submit that guns are female, for the following reasons:
1) Each is different from all the rest.
2) Each has something beautiful, wonderful, and unique.
3) They are expensive and difficult to acquire and maintain.
4) They can be dangerous if handled improperly.
5) You can never have too many.

If you'd like to dabble in the socio-political hysteria that surrounds the issue of gun ownership, on the other hand, you'll find no better feeding frenzy than the ongoing movable feast in *talk.politics.guns*. While not as well mannered as the *rec.guns* newsgroup, *talk.politics.guns* is not the stew of flames and harsh language you probably would expect. Most of the postings are cogent, well-thought-out views about both sides of the gun control issue.

As I write this, President Clinton is pressing for a ban on assault weapons, and this has inspired a heated debate. It's curious how politicians can manage to be reviled equally by both sides of an issue. (Publisher's note: Passage of the assault weapons ban measure—part of the crime bill—was pending at the time that *Planet Internet* when to press.)

Firearms are an emotional issue and one that could often benefit by considerably more understanding of the realities involved. The two firearms newsgroups listed here are a good place to find out what guns *really* are all about.

Excerpt from `rec.guns`

I'd like to buy a .45 specially a Glock 21. Do any problems occur with this gun or is it just like the model 17 in 9 Para and are there also large 33-shot magazines as for the 17?

I have had one since last November. This gun works wonderfully well. In fact it is even better than then 9x19 models: it is much more accurate. Many people consider it as the best Glock and my experience confirms this opinion. I definitely recommend this gun.

Have you tried using 147 gr. bullets, either lead or jacketed in the Glock 17? It's like a different gun. A light load of Bullseye and a 147 gr. lead truncated cone is *very* accurate.

Questions:
1) Why do you like the G21 better than the G17 (just accuracy)?
2) What is the magazine capacity of the 21?

One criterion is the controllability of the two guns. Before I go on, let me state my opinions on the 9mm and 45ACP cartridges first. In general, a gun chambered 9mm Luger cartridge is easier to control than that chambered 45ACP cartridge. For example, I can shoot faster with a Beretta 92FS than a 1911A1, for a given accuracy index of course. Even though I can shoot faster with a Beretta, the recoil is sharper with a Beretta.

This is because a 9mm bullet generally travels faster than a 45ACP bullet. With a heavier gun like Beretta (as opposed to a lighter gun like Glock 17), this sharp recoil is not annoying. With a lighter gun, this sharper recoil tends to jerk the gun and thus increases the time needed for me to align the sights and the target.

The Glock 21 chambers 45ACP cartridges. Even though the Glock 21 is not as heavy as a steel frame 1911A1, its recoil characteristics are similar to that of a steel frame 1911A1. It kicks more than a Glock 17, but the muzzle rises at a slower rate and falls "nicely" into the sights and target alignment.

Heraldry

 rec.heraldry

Coats of arms began in the Middle Ages with the advent of armored knights and large-scale warfare among similarly equipped armies. By painting a readily identified symbol on one's attire, it became easier to identify the enemy. At least, it did if one had paid attention at the morning's briefing, as most knights had their own coats of arms, rather than one for the good guys and one for the bad guys.

As time went by, being a knight got to be exceedingly expensive, what with a lot of high-tech armor to pay for and keep up to date, heavy horses to rear and feed, and so on. The original mercenary knights, or "free lancers," gave way to knights who were commissioned and permanently in the service of the local nobility. The landed nobility was forever feuding and subsequently settling its disagreements with exchanges of territory and frequently of family members in political marriages. The coats of arms of the old European families reflect this. They became intricate devices, with each element chosen or modified by a generation of the family that they represented.

Many contemporary people of European descent can trace their lineage back to the medieval lords who gave rise to heraldic emblems and, as such, have justification to display coats of arms. While it no longer serves to help you decide who to run through with a lance, heraldry is an engaging expression of one's roots and culture.

The *rec.heraldry* newsgroup is a gathering place for heraldic enthusiasts, seekers after their personal lineages and coats of arms, and keepers of unicorns, gryphons, and lions *regardant*. Its regulars seem very knowledgeable about the intricacies of heraldry. There are periodic threads about the possible origins and meanings of specific heraldic devices—a fascinating glimpse into an almost forgotten past.

Herbs

ℹ rec.folklore.herbs

Long before there was conventional medicine, there were herbs. With the advent of medicine as a scientific discipline during the last century, the interest in herbal medicine diminished. If you visit a drug store in the nineties and ask for a bag of ginseng or a bottle of rosemary oil, you'll probably be referred to the front door. There are several reasons for this, not the least of which is that the patent on ginseng ran out shortly before 3500 B.C., and there's just no money to be made from it anymore. This is the problem with most herbs—at least from the point of view of the drug companies. They're so common that it's almost like they grow on trees.

An understanding of herbs is more than mere folk medicine. You can apply fresh herbs in cooking, to add pleasant scents to your home—ones that don't come from an aerosol can—and to improve your health without the use of chemicals. It's worthwhile to note that some of the synthetic drugs that drugstores won't refer you to the front door for asking about come from herbal sources or have been synthesized after analyzing herbs.

A good understanding of herbs requires at least a passing familiarity with the folklore behind them. There are certainly books on the subject, but the *rec.folklore.herbs* newsgroup offers the opportunity to actually ask other users of herbs about what they've learned or read. Like most folklore, opinions about herbs vary considerably—even among the participants in *rec.folklore.herbs*.

✂ Extract from rec.folklore.herbs

I have seen it written in this newsgroup that Siberian Ginseng is not really ginseng but has similar properties. I would like to know the advantages or disadvantages to taking Siberian Ginseng or Korean Ginseng or American Ginseng.

This is what I understand from different sources, some anecdotal: Korean Ginseng (Panax ginseng) is a major tonic and I think that in Chinese medicine it is mostly given to older people and to people who have been weakened by illness. Some people have written here that they find it has a stimulating effect that can be excessive if combined with caffeine.

You would not use it in conditions of excess like fever or high blood pressure but it might be suitable for someone cold-blooded and with a sluggish metabolism. I have also heard that it has some qualities analogous to male hormones, so its use can make men hornier; it's not supposed to be a good idea for women to take it on a regular basis, but taking it for a couple of weeks as a tonic now and then is OK.

Siberian Ginseng (Eleutherococcus senticosus) is a useful herb but hasn't the wide application of Panax. It seems to have the useful property of maintaining one's endurance while keeping one relaxed and one's mind alert.

I have used it often on days when I've had to work long hours and I can attest that it does keep me moving, without caffeine-type side effects and with no sleep disturbances.

Contrary to popular Western beliefs, though, I don't think anyone is meant to take these herbs every day like a vitamin pill.

Home brewing

- mthvax.cs.miami.edu:/pub/homebrew/
- nic.funet.fi:/pub/culture/beer/
- homebrew@hpfcmi.fc.hp.com
- homebrew-request@hpfcmi.fc.hp.com
- rec.crafts.brewing

Brewing beer, cider, and other fermented beverages is a time-honored way to get legless without having to pay the king's tax collectors for the privilege. However, more than merely being a way to save money on your drinks bill, home brewing offers a way to taste beer and other drinks that you'll never find in bottles.

Fermented drinks, such as beer, are made by letting yeast have a good time in a solution of sugar and other ingredients. The by-product of yeast is alcohol. Accomplished brewers can figure out how much sugar and yeast is required to achieve a particular sort of beer and a particular volume of alcohol before the yeast dies. This is actually fairly tricky, and natural beer tends to be a bit unstable as a result. It also varies from batch to batch.

Commercial beer—the sort they make in vats about the size of the containment building for a medium size nuclear power station—gets around this problem through pasteurization. Once the yeast has created the desired volume of alcohol, the beer is heated to kill the yeast and the resulting brew is bottled.

The drawback to pasteurized beer is that it's typically a bit watery and uninteresting. If you've gotten this far in life drinking nothing but commercial beer, you'll probably be unaware what real beer can taste like. Your first pint will knock you off your feet.

In addition to allowing you to create generally better tasting beer, home brewing offers a range of beers that you simply can't find commercially: pale ale, stout, porter, dopplebock, scotch ale, trappist ale, and brown ale, among others. You also can try your hand at other drinks, such as cider and mead.

While surrounded by a degree of mysticism and folklore, brewing isn't unreasonably difficult. It requires relatively little specialized equipment, and you can get started with kits of ingredients if you don't want to scare up all the requirements for your first attempt from scratch.

The home brewing resources of the Internet will prove equally useful to first time brewmeisters and long-time veterans of the specific gravity wars. The "Cats Meow" brewers book, which is available at the *mthvax.cs.miami.edu* FTP site, is a canonical collection of recipes for beer, cider, and other drinks. If you can't find your favorite beverage there, it's probably only available on the dark side of the moon.

The home-brew mailing list and the *rec.crafts.brewing* newsgroup are both valuable resources for anyone interested in brewing. You can use them to have your questions answered, locate unusual recipes, and swap horror stories of exploding bottles and yeast creatures from the eighth dimension. Now if there was only some way to upload actual beer to the Net.

Illuminati

alt.illuminati

The Illuminati is a somewhat mythical group of mystical freemasons postulated in Robert Anton Wilson's books. Originating during the Italian renaissance, they turn up in various secret societies, pulling the strings of governments across Europe, amongst the last of the medieval alchemists and with the founding fathers of the United States. Wilson likes to work a few facts into the story whenever possible. Consider, for example, the foregoing illustration. There's a considerable amount of masonic regalia on an American banknote—perhaps because many of the original instigators of the Declaration of Independence were in fact masons.

The proportion of fact to fancy in the Illuminati books is the source of inexhaustible discussion and speculation in the *alt.illuminati* newsgroup. If you have a taste for the esoteric, you'll find few more engaging places to kill a few hours. It's pretty well essential that you've read at least a few of the Illuminati books prior to doing so, however, or almost everything said there will sound like some sort of masonic code.

To some extent, *alt.illuminati* periodically becomes a discussion of masons and masonic ritual in general—perhaps more commonly during the intervals between the publications of Wilson's novels.

The intellectual level of *alt.illuminati* is somewhat higher than average for newsgroups. One encounters a lot of cogent arguments there and somewhat less verbal abuse and flaming than is usually the case. From time to time, *alt.illuminati* does seem prone to invasion by forces other than devotees of the Illuminati, who attempt to hijack it onto different topics.

Note that there also is a dedicated Illuminati bulletin board that can be accessed through Telnet at *illuminati.io.com*. Be warned, however, that it has the longest, most convoluted, and unpleasant logon procedure in the known universe.

Excerpt from alt.illuminati

Perhaps I'm way off, but a former freemason was through the area a while back speaking at lots of churches. I don't know what levels he was initiated into, but he said when you reached the higher levels you began to find out all this "secret" stuff, and part of it was that all this stuff they do (that they didn't know why) they do to worship the "goddess."

As I understand it, masonry does not involve any god or goddess other than the underlying unity of the godhead (the Grand Architect of the Universe), with no gender claimed or implied.

One of the problems freemasonry has is that too often it shrugs off the attacks on it. While not a "secret society," the Fraternity does pretend that it has secrets. Thus, the proper response to the random attacks of whatever group is attacking is to neither confirm nor deny but to ignore.

After all, if you say "that ain't it" often enough, sooner or later someone may by random hit on what it is.

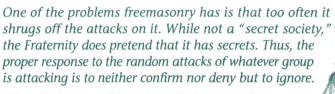

I am a thirty-second degree Scottish Rite (Southern Jurisdiction) Mason, and a Shriner. (The thirty-third degree is honorary, and I will not live long enough to get it.) Without doing violence to my vows of secrecy, I can say that nothing is said or done in any of the degrees which could be interpreted as "worship of a goddess."

You ever see those tall spike-like-towers that the masons are always building? According to him they were temples dedicated to this "goddess."

Can you give an example of such a tower? The only pointy thing on my lodge is the lightning rod.

Um, which ones? Most new lodge buildings are very plain. Older ones in the midwest tend to be the second or third story of a commercial building. (In Ashland, WI, I noticed that the lodge meets on the third floor of a building housing a pharmacy on the first floor; the second floor is a clinic.)

Scottish Rite Temples, built *ab initio* tend to imitate Roman architecture. (In Minneapolis, the Scottish Rite bought the old building of a Methodist Church, which had moved to new quarters. There are spike-like things, but left over.)

I find it difficult to believe the testimony of someone who is disclosing things imparted to him under vows of secrecy.

I have to disagree with you here. You are suggesting that freemasonry takes a syncretic viewpoint, in which all faiths are really the same. This is *not* the case. All we do is agree that all faiths can be used to improve their adherent's behavior towards each other. This in no way implies any 'underlying unity' in religion, beyond this social aspect. Thus, when a prayer is held in a lodge, Christians are praying to their god, Jews to theirs, and Muslims to Allah, without any suggestion that these are 'actually the same.' Masonry is not a religion, and has no deity of it's own.

This is a fairly subtle point, and widely misunderstood by anti-Masons, and even by some Masons.

The Internet Mall

taylor@netcom.com
ftp.netcom.com:/pub/Guides/

There are several rudimentary shopping services available over the Internet. In a real sense, the commercial aspects of the Net are just beginning to crop up as I write this, and many long-time users of the Internet seem to be rather upset about this. The obvious catch in Internet "shopping" is that, while it's handy to be able to Telnet over to a book shop or an online ordering system for compact discs when you actually want something, few of us would wish to be bombarded with electronic junk mail or the digital equivalent of advertisements and billboards throughout our use of the Net.

Large commercial interests don't seem to be able to resist this sort of thing; at least, they don't if they think they can get away with it. Not only would McDonald's buy advertising space on the side of a yak if it were available, but rumor has it that they're investigating the possibility of breeding genetically engineered yaks that grow up with the golden arches naturally embossed on their hides.

At the moment, all the commercial activities on the Net are limited to things that you have to go looking for, rather than advertisements that come looking for you. This has the advantage of keeping the Internet relatively free of billboards, but perhaps the disadvantage of making it less than obvious where some of the genuinely useful shopping resources are to be found. However, as tradeoffs go this seems like a pretty manageable one.

The Internet Mall is a list of services available on the Net, or at least accessible through e-mail. It's updated monthly by Dave Taylor and represents one of the more diverse commercial catalogs on the Internet. The quickest way to locate it is to finger the following location: *taylor@netcom.com.* This will generate a listing informing you of how to access The Internet Mall over World Wide Web, by FTP, and through e-mail. At present, it can be found at the following FTP site: *ftp.netcom.com:/pub/Guides/.* Be warned; the *ftp.netcom.com:/pub* directory is absolutely huge, with hundreds of subdirectories.

The Internet Mall file is organized in floors, as a large urban department store would be. Here's what you'll find in it as of this writing:

First floor: Books—This is a diverse list of book sellers that can be contacted over the Internet. It includes several mainstream bookshops, such as Book Stacks Unlimited, which is discussed elsewhere in this book, as well as specialty dealers offering technical books, rare books, and books about specific topics. It even includes Statistics Canada, the Canadian government agency that other Canadian government agencies use to explain why their election promises can't be kept after all.

Second Floor: Personal Items—This floor includes things like European perfumes—suitable for saving your skin in the aftermath of a forgotten anniversary—games, jewelry, and sex toys. Used correctly, the latter might be more effective than European perfume.

Third Floor: Software—You'll find all sorts of software on this floor, ranging from discount general software dealers to specific applications. An annex lists several suppliers of interesting CD-ROMs.

Fourth Floor: Services—This floor includes suppliers of numerous business services, such as contracts, credit checks, telemarketing, a travel agent, and international trade advisers. An annex to this floor deals with training and education.

Top Floor: Food—This floor offers a wealth of ways to gain weight, eat improperly, and subsequently overwork your exercise equipment. It includes suppliers of gourmet popcorn, chocolate, exotic coffees and teas, herbs, and home-brew beer making supplies.

The Internet Mall is perpetually under construction, with new features added monthly. Items that have been added to the current issue are so designated.

Japan

 `ftp.spies.com:/Library/Article/Language/grammar.jap`

 `ucslex.sdsu.edu:/pub/doc/etext/japan-that-can-say-no.txt`

 `f.ms.uky.edu:/pub3/mailing.lists/japan/japanno.Z`

 `f.ms.uky.edu:/pub3/mailing.lists/japan/japanyes.Z`

 `f.ms.uky.edu:/pub3/mailing.lists/japan/japanyes.reply.Z`

There are numerous resources on the Internet pertaining to Japan and Japanese culture. Some of them are extremely exotic. Actually, some of them are in Kanji and will be largely inaccessible to English-speaking users.

The Japanese language itself is exceedingly difficult to learn to speak well. If you'd like to pick up a few phrases, the *grammar.jap* file listed at the beginning of this section will avail you of enough Japanese to order dinner at a sushi bar or ask for directions if you wake up unexpectedly in downtown Osaka tomorrow. The Japanese word for non-Japanese people is *gai jin*, which can be translated as "foreigner" if you're being charitable or perhaps as "barbarian" if you're not. Realistically, the *grammar.jap* file will not teach you enough Japanese to change anything in this regard.

Japanese trade practices over the past few decades have become a subject of considerable interest of late. Several bits of popular media have centered upon them, such as the film *Rising Sun*. The drawback to discussing this issue in the popular media is that it will have you roundly criticized for "Japan bashing" about 15 minutes after your words are printed. The pseudo-sensitivity of the nineties is almost as easily manipulated as international trade restrictions.

The Internet is about as far from being politically correct as any medium can come, and you can pretty well say what you like therein about issues such as this one. The FTP site listed at the beginning of this section offers an intriguing look at some of the attitudes behind the workings of

east-west trade policy. The Japanese are of the opinion that "business is war." You'll find some of this stuff very warlike indeed.

To begin with, there's an unauthorized translation of "A Japan that can cay No." The original document, written in Japanese by Shintaro Ishihara, a member of the Japanese parliament, and Akio Morita, the chief executive officer of Sony, describes in fairly blunt terms how its authors feel that Japan will supersede the United States as a world power. Ishihara caused a degree of international consternation some while back by proclaiming "Americans are lazy, ignorant, and stupid." Note that, while a translation of this document has appeared in book form, it's said to be incomplete, having been edited by Akio Morita to avoid impacting Sony's North American sales.

Once you've grappled with "A Japan that can say No," you also should read Louis Leclerc's article "Does America say yes to Japan?"

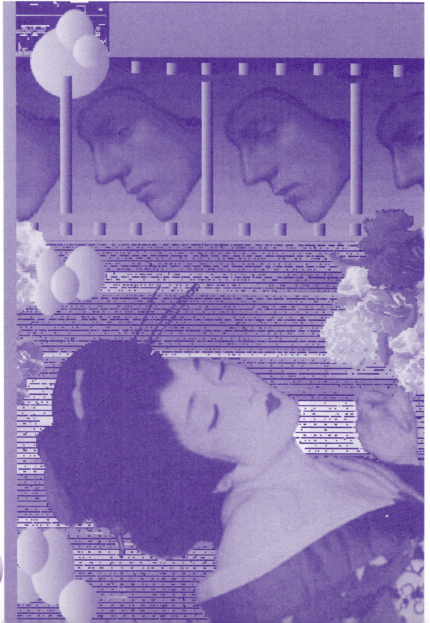

This is the sort of stuff that really gets the Japan-bashing activists white hot and nasty. It's a somewhat unflattering analysis of Japanese trade policy, industrial practices, and culture as they affect Japan's actions in the West. While exceedingly dull in theory, the author's presentation is intriguing and the document, well over 100K in length as of this writing, is eminently readable. It's a lot more readable than "A Japan that can say No," for example.

Finally, you might want to have a look at the reply to "Does America say yes to Japan?" by Dr. Andrew Jennings, a senior staff member at the research laboratories of the Australian and Overseas Telecommunications Corporation. Jennings brands the Leclerc article "inflammatory" and sets about to refute select bits of it—perhaps not all that convincingly.

The realities of trade between the West and Japan are, in a sense, one of the dark and grotty aspects of free trade. These documents might change your mind about this issue, as well as affect what you buy in the future and who you buy it from.

Jazz

rec.music.bluenote

Jazz and blues are timeless, nationless musical forms. Actually, perhaps more to the point, jazz has never had the apparent commercial potentials of popular music and, as such, has been left alone by the producers and record companies to a much greater extent. Jazz sounds like it has been played, rather than engineered.

The *rec.music.bluenote* not only concerns itself with jazz, but it also kind of reads like jazz, too. It's unmoderated and flows freely between topics. It offers discussions of jazz recordings, announcements of concert dates, discussions of jazz clubs, some periodically incisive bits of musical theory, and references to more detailed books about jazz and jazz performance. It supports a truly outstanding FAQ about jazz.

Perhaps because they don't have anything like the marketing machine behind them that popular music does, jazz and blues seem to be seething with obscure artists and performances, stunning recordings that you probably will never encounter in record shops and so on.

Merely lurking in *rec.music.bluenote* will avail you of a casual discography of great bits of jazz to look out for. It's a bit like overhearing the muttered conversation of a crowd of horn players between sets, talking about their music.

Juggling

 `rec.juggling`

You probably wouldn't think that juggling requires much discussion, let alone a whole newsgroup devoted to the subject. Actually, the *rec.juggling* newsgroup is a pretty lively arena for people who like to keep a lot of things in the air at once. Whether you juggle professionally, juggle to work off the stress of the day, or just like to watch Cirque de Soleil, you'll find something of interest here.

There's quite a bit to juggling when you get into it. The *rec.juggling* newsgroup periodically includes threads on such subjects as breaking the three-ball limit and breaking the five- and seven-ball limits thereafter, alternate juggling patterns, and what to juggle when balls just aren't interesting enough.

Chainsaws are only for the extremely extroverted, and then only if you're not all that fond of your extremities.

The *rec.juggling* newsgroup will offer you ways to improve your juggling and stretch yourself into new patterns or new objects to swing. You'll find announcements of professional juggling performances and juggling on the tube there as well. Finally, *rec.juggling* includes frequent discussions of serious juggling paraphernalia, which I confess I never knew existed. One such thread appears in the excerpt in this section.

 Excerpt from `rec.juggling`

I recently received a catalog from Infinite Illusions. It was quite surprising to see such a puny catalog. However, I did find torches in their "brochure" and noticed that they were rather inexpensive. The description for them was pretty convincing in terms of their quality. They cost about ten dollars less per torch than Dube's torches. But I'm hesitant to buy them for fear that they might be significantly inferior to Dube's torches (which I've juggled and liked). Can someone please help me out? Has anyone ever seen Infinite Illusions' torches? If so, would you recommend them?

For what it's worth I learned to torch with IF torches. They are very durable, and I have no complaints about them. They are balanced much like my clubs (Dube's) but slightly heavier (of course). If you were worried about them falling apart on you, you do not have to as mine have been through the ringer and come out none the worse for wear.

I met Gregg (of Infinite Illusions) at the Montreal convention (92). He showed his torches to me and a friend, and I was quite impressed with the torches as well as his testing methods. I remember him talking about spinning them at high speeds off a balcony onto

concrete—the Dube's torches he tested tended to break on the first hit, but his would take ten or so hits before breaking (kids—don't try this at home!). I may have the details a little off, but you get the idea. My friend bought torches from him then, and I bought some a few months later. We've both been quite happy with them. In fact, I know a few other people who own sets, and I can't recall ever hearing any complaints. Not only are they durable, they look really cool! They have a somewhat slenderer handle and slightly smaller knob than Dube's or Todd Smith torches, and may weigh a little less, although they still weigh a little more than a club. I use them for juggling and club swinging, and they're great for both.

Jumping from great heights

rec.skydiving

There's something decidedly unnatural about throwing yourself out of a perfectly good airplane for no sensible reason. Nonetheless, people do so regularly. Skydiving is a popular and growing sport. Other, tangentially related activities, such as bungee jumping, also seem to be attracting all sorts of adherents.

The *rec.skydiving* newsgroup is a place to discuss most aspects of hurling yourself into oblivion. It's worth noting that, while bungee jumping is somewhat beyond its purview, it still is a subject that comes up periodically there. One thread that seemed to be of considerable interest as I was writing this dealt with potential eye injuries caused by the rapid deceleration of bungee jumping. Keep in mind that, unlike as with skydiving, bungee jumpers can expect to have their eyes facing downwards when they decelerate. This can result in such nasties as detached retinas.

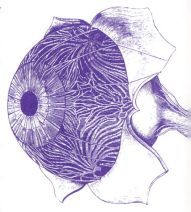

There are numerous postings in the *rec.skydiving* newsgroup about the all-important hardware required to get down safely. Parachutes are a complex technology, and you'll find all sorts of experienced skydivers to discuss the matter with.

Perhaps the largest aspect of *rec.skydiving*, however, has little to do with falling. Much of this newsgroup seems to be dominated by the social—and frequently sexual—aspects of the "drop zone," or DZ. You'll find numerous threads about sexual harassment while skydiving, and the hotly debated issue of gay skydivers.

I confess to preferring to stay in airplanes once they take off, and I've never actually been skydiving. Nonetheless, I've seen skydivers; they look like they're wearing enough body armor to survive a week in downtown Beruit. Somehow this would seem to preclude any possibility of sex entering into the sport. If you're equally curious about this issue, make sure you lurk around *rec.skydiving* from time to time and see how it turns out.

Laser discs

alt.video.laserdisc

If you're old enough to still have a crate of vinyl records buried in your basement, you've probably experienced the sensation of replacing some of them with rereleased compact discs and hearing your favorite albums again for the first time. Laser disc video is something like this, only considerably more effective.

Broadcast television over cable typically offers unbelievably bad image quality. The only other popular medium for video, VHS tape, usually is just a bit worse. Many television viewers rarely get to see high-quality video. For most of us, the only two media likely to provide it are satellite television, which is discussed elsewhere in this book, and laser discs.

Laser discs are leading-edge video—pictures with compact disc quality.

Laser discs are considerably more expensive than VHS tapes, and they require a laser disc player. The latter start at about $500. They also double as audio compact disc players. While there are outlets that rent laser discs, they're nowhere near as common as VHS video rentals.

It's worth noting that, unlike VHS tapes, laser discs do not deteriorate with use. Most larger cities have shops that sell used laser discs; the prices for these are pretty reasonable.

There are two notable characteristics of movies on laser disc. To begin with, they offer image and sound quality that will knock your socks off and clear into the next room. Many films are available in letterbox format on laser disc. Secondly, you can usually get movies on laser disc that include footage not included in the original theatrical or tape releases. This often is more than merely scraps from the cutting room floor.

Two such films that come to mind are *The Abyss* and *Aliens*. The plot of *The Abyss* makes a great deal more sense on laser disc with its extra footage included, and *Aliens* includes all sorts of interesting new scenes. Both discs also include extensive "behind the screen" documentaries about their creation; the creation of *The Abyss* is a story almost as intricate as the film itself.

The *alt.video.laserdisc* newsgroup will be an invaluable asset to anyone with a laser disc player. A singularly well-informed group, it offers discussions of laser disc player hardware, new releases of titles on disc, laser disc trivia, and frequent mention of the minutiae of different releases of popular films on disc. This latter point is more than idle chatter, considering the cost of some laser disc editions.

If you spend five or six hours a day before your 10" portable television in a catatonic stupor, you'll probably want to ignore laser discs entirely. If you regard television as something to be experienced only at its best, however, you'll find laser discs in general and the *alt.video.laserdisc* newsgroup to be as much a part of your living room as the tube itself.

Excerpt from `alt.video.laserdisc`

Here's a complete list of the Star Wars THX set flaws: read on, but be warned! 'tis not for the light hearted!

Star Wars: The THX Definitive Collection Box Set: Flaws

Overall box set complaints:
1. Large individual sleeves falling apart due to inadequate glue.
2. Early editions of the box set exhibited a much too snug fit of LD's, the Creative Impulse book and supplemental liner notes.

Star Wars:
1. Misprinting in liner notes: Liner reads chapter 19, but actual interview is on chapter 18; side 2.
2. Loud clicking as scene is cut: side 3; frame #33250.
3. Misprinting in liner notes: Liner reads chapter 2, but actual interview is on chapter 1; side 5.
4. Missing liner note for interview on chapter 19; side 5.

The Empire Strikes Back:
1. Missing seven seconds of Leia welding: side 3; beginning of side 3 (Fox is recalling discs for this flaw, amazingly enough.)
2. Two chirping noises in left channel: side 3; frame #23892-#23920.
3. Three other chirps in right channel: side 3; frame #24080-#24120.
4. Misprinting in liner notes: Liner reads chapter 16, but actual interview is on chapter 17; side 4.
5. Misprinting in liner notes: Liner reads chapter 17, but actual interview is on chapter 18; side 4.
6. Upside down still photo in supplemental section: side 6; frame #47235.

Return of the Jedi:
1. Subtitle misspelling of Wookiee: side 1; frame #21895
2. Subtitle misspelling of Bantha: side 1; frame #30350
3. Digital ghost image of Shuttle: side 3; frame #3249-#3251
4. Digital noise on Chewbacca: side 4; frame #22743-#22746
5. Digital noise on Luke: side 5; frame #5025
6. Digital noise on Emperor: side 5; frame #15488-#15489

Not to flog a dead horse even more, but I think you missed a flaw: in Star Wars, when they are standing around in the control room of the Death Star and R2 is looking through the schematics for the location of the tractor beam power system, C3PO's line of dialogue is missing when he says something like, "Loss of power at one of the terminals will shut down the entire system."... It really isn't vital to the story, only serving to fill in a moment with no speaking.

I was under the impression that that dialogue was not in the original version of Star Wars. It was added to the video versions and maybe even some of the later theatrical releases that it enjoyed. The way I look at it is that it doesn't belong, even though the other LD versions have it. This way it is like the original theatrical release.

This is correct. The line appears in the original script but for some reason the line never made it to the theatrical release. In video releases after 1986 the line was included. I always hated it because you could distinctly tell the difference in Anthony Daniel's voice in that line from the surrounding lines...

Letterman

 `alt.fan.letterman`

 `quartz.rutgers.edu:/pub/tv+movies/letterman`

 `listproc@mot.com`

If you spend your days in blissful anticipation of the pleasures of the night—and if your idea of the "pleasures of the night" is parking yourself in front of the tube and figuring out which network David Letterman's leaning toward this week—the *alt.fan.letterman* newsgroup should be the ideal place to wile away the daylight hours. A gathering of Letterman fans, it features lively and periodically coherent discussions of what Dave said and what it meant.

For a more archival sense of Letterman, be certain to stop by the Letterman FTP site at *quartz.rutgers.edu*. It offers transcriptions of some of the truly memorable events of the Letterman show.

For those less enamored of Letterman as an institution, the FTP contents include transcriptions of all of Dave's top-ten lists. Even if you can't sit through an entire show without wanting to get up to attend to some important sock polishing responsibilities, the top-ten lists are singularly amusing. Included are numerous classics, such as "top ten words that sound great when spoken by James Earl Jones," "top ten signs you have a dumb cat," and "top ten things Gore does when Clinton is out of the country."

For those who absolutely must keep up on the top-ten lists, there's a mailing list devoted to them. To subscribe to it, send some e-mail to *listproc@mot.com* with the body of the message beginning "SUBSCRIBE LETTERMAN-TOP-TEN" followed by your first and last names.

Lewis Carroll

 nic.funet.fi:/pub/doc/literary/etext/carroll/

Charles Lutwidge Dodgson was born in 1832. His more renowned pseudonym was derived from his name: Lewis is the anglicized version of Lutwidge, and Carroll is a variation of Charles. While inarguably best known for *Alice in Wonderland* and *Alice Through the Looking Glass,* which were published in 1865 and 1872 respectively, he was a prolific author and a man of many facets. He wrote several books on higher mathematics, was an early practitioner of the then-nascent art of photography, and a wry and inventive poet.

Many of Dodgson's photographs survive, including pictures of Alice Liddell, upon whom the books were based. The unforgettable illustrations of Alice's adventures were created by the English painter and cartoonist Sir John Tenniel. In more recent times, a number of letters and papers belonging to Charles Dodgson have appeared. Among other things, they suggest that Tenniel also had an editorial function in the stories of Alice in that he refused to illustrate chapters that he didn't feel were appropriate. At least one complete missing chapter, entitled "The Wasp in the Wig," has recently come to light.

The FTP site at *nic.funet.fi* includes a number of transcriptions of Lewis Carroll's works. You'll find the complete text of both Alice books, as well as several other files. Don't miss *The Hunting of the Snark,* an excerpt of which follows.

The source of most of the Internet transcriptions of Lewis Carroll's works is Project Gutenberg, which is discussed in detail elsewhere in this book.

✂ Excerpt from *The Hunting of the Snark* at `nic.funet.fi`

"Just the place for a Snark!" the Bellman cried,
    As he landed his crew with care;

Supporting each man on the top of the tide
    By a finger entwined in his hair.

"Just the place for a Snark! I have said it twice:
    That alone should encourage the crew.

Just the place for a Snark! I have said it thrice:
    What I tell you three times is true."

The crew was complete: it included a Boots—
    A maker of Bonnets and Hoods—

A Barrister, brought to arrange their disputes—
    And a Broker, to value their goods.

A Billiard-maker, whose skill was immense,
    Might perhaps have won more than his share—

But a Banker, engaged at enormous expense,
    Had the whole of their cash in his care.

There was also a Beaver, that paced on the deck,
    Or would sit making lace in the bow:

And had often (the Bellman said) saved them from wreck,
    Though none of the sailors knew how.

There was one who was famed for the number of things
    He forgot when he entered the ship:

His umbrella, his watch, all his jewels and rings,
    And the clothes he had bought for the trip.

He had forty-two boxes, all carefully packed,
    With his name painted clearly on each:

But, since he omitted to mention the fact,
    They were all left behind on the beach.

Library of Congress

 `locis.loc.gov`

There actually are a number of ways to search the records of the Library of Congress over the Internet. It's available in a somewhat modified form as a gopher server as well. The search engine at the Telnet address listed at the beginning of this section is very fast, exceedingly easy to master, and capable of finding just about anything in the Library of Congress except for stray congressmen and the mice that live under the shelves. It's an invaluable reference for anyone who's looking for a book.

As of this writing, it also allows you to search a huge database of various types of copyrighted entities as well, including audio recordings, films, and multimedia presentations.

The book search engine allows you to search by a number of criteria, including authors and titles. I decided to look up myself to see what I'd been up to recently. It turns out that Rimmer isn't as uncommon a name as I'd been led to believe.

```
B01+Rimmer, David//(AUTH=1)
B02 Rimmer, Douglas//(AUTH=10)
B03 Rimmer, E. M//(AUTH=1)
B04 Rimmer, Edward Johnson//(AUTH=1)
B05 Rimmer, Eve//(AUTH=1; SUBJ=1)
B06 Rimmer, Frederick//(AUTH=1)
B07 Rimmer, Gordon, 1925-1990//(AUTH=1)
B08 Rimmer, Harry, 1890-1952—//(SUBJ=1)
B09 Rimmer, Ian, 1955-//(AUTH=1)
B10 Rimmer, J. A//(AUTH=1)
B11 Rimmer, J. G//(AUTH=4)
B12 Rimmer, Joan//(AUTH=4)
B01+Rimmer, John//(AUTH=1)
B02 Rimmer, John Osborne//(AUTH=1)
B03 Rimmer, Joyce//(AUTH=1)
B04 Rimmer, Lesley//(AUTH=1)
B05 Rimmer, Malcolm//(AUTH=2)
B06 Rimmer, Peter James//(AUTH=11)
B07 Rimmer, Peter, 1937-//(AUTH=1)
B08 Rimmer, R. J//(AUTH=1)
```

B09 Rimmer, Robert H//(AUTH=1)

B10 Rimmer, Robert H., 1917-//(AUTH=18; SUBJ=1)

B11 Rimmer, Robert H., 1917- Harrad experiment//(SUBJ=1)

B12 Rimmer, Russell//(AUTH=1)

B01+Rimmer, Russell J., 1948-//(AUTH=1)

B02 Rimmer, Stephen J. (Stephen John), 1961-//(AUTH=1)

B03 Rimmer, Steve//(AUTH=20)

B04 Rimmer, William, 1816-1879—//(AUTH=2; SUBJ=2)

I don't know who most of these people are, except for the last two. William Rimmer is a great, great uncle, I think; he was a sculptor toward the end of the last century. I wasn't aware he'd written anything.

Having found the author that you're looking for, you can have the search engine list all the books pertaining to him or her. It then will display a capsule description of any entry that you like. For example, this is what turned up when I asked for books by Boris Vallejo, the fantasy artist:

(DESCENDING ORDER)

1. 85-11106: Vallejo, Boris. Fantasy art techniques / New York : Arco Pub., c1985. 127 p. : ill. (some col.) ; 29 cm.
  LC CALL NUMBER: ND237.V14 A4 1985

2. 84-90812: Vallejo, Boris. Enchantment / 1st ed. New York : Ballantine Books, 1984. 107 p. : ill. (some col.) ; 31 cm.
  LC CALL NUMBER: PS3572.A413 E5 1984

3. 82-90217: Vallejo, Boris. Mirage / 1st ed. New York : Ballantine Books, 1982. [90] p. : chiefly ill. (some col.) ; 31 cm.
  LC CALL NUMBER: ND237.V14 A4 1982

4. 79-101629: Vallejo, Boris. The boy who saved the stars / New York : O'Quinn Studios, c1978. 32 p. : col. ill. ; 22 x 26 cm.
  LC CALL NUMBER: PZ7.V254 Bo

5. 77-82693: Vallejo, Boris. The fantastic art of Boris / 1st ed. New York : Ballantine Books, 1978. 12 p., [40] leaves of plates : ill. (some col.) ; 31 cm.
  LC CALL NUMBER: NC975.5.V34 A4 1978

The Library of Congress server is a great research tool should you be confronted with doing some serious work, but it's also a wonderful way to locate obscure books just because you want to read them. Coupled with a good bookshop, it will provide you with access to millions of volumes. See the section of this book dealing with "Books" for the Telnet address of a bookshop on the Internet.

CNS, Inc. gopher service

A lot of gopher servers are somewhat specialized. Actually, a lot of them are pretty dry. If you didn't know that Arizona has a university, you probably won't care to know that its university also has a gopher server.

The CNS gopher is an exception to the oftentimes unadventurous nature of gophers in general. A vast collection of resources, all thoughtfully organized and menu-driven, as gophers usually are wont to be, CNS is worth browsing even if you have no idea what you're after.

A list of everything on the CNS gopher would run for pages. It accesses dozens of Internet resources to provide selections that are both useful and entertaining. Many items in its extensive menus are cross-referenced in multiple categories to make finding things more intuitive.

Among the more interesting resources available through CNS are:

- ASCII clip art—pictures drawn with text characters.
- Access to numerous electronic publications, or paper publications with gopher servers. These include *Mother Jones*, *Wired*, the Electronic Newsstand, and the Online Book Initiative (the latter two are discussed elsewhere in this book.)
- A vast selection of files designed to be purely entertaining, organized by topic. Among the current topics are guitar chords for popular songs, humor, movie reviews, and recipes.

As with much of the Internet, the scope and diversity of the CNS gopher can't be properly described in words; it cries out to be experienced. Plan on having a lot of time to kill when you set about to experience it, however. It just seems to go on for miles.

Note that some of the resources accessible through the CNS gopher—most notably the news servers—typically will not be available to users accessing the Internet from somewhere outside a college campus.

Limericks

 `ftp.netcom.com:/pub/jvasquez/dirty.limericks`

 `ftp.quartz.rutgers.edu:/pub/humor/limericks`

It seems fair to note that Limerick is a county in Ireland, aside from being a type of vulgar poetry. It's unclear how the place name came to be associated with five-line poems.

Composing limericks is an art form. Composing extremely vulgar limericks is a very refined art form. The degree of refinement increases with the level of vulgarity. Out of deference to the publisher, only fairly unrefined limericks will be printed here. For example:

A remarkable race are the Persians,
They have such peculiar diversions.

Actually, I don't think we'll finish that one. In it's place, consider:

There was a young lady of Clewer
Who was riding a horse, and it threw her.

On second thought, that doesn't look like the sort of thing they'd want in this book either. Perhaps this one:

There was a young lady named Smith
Whose virtue was largely a myth.

In reflection, I suspect it's somewhat hopeless. The problem is:

The limerick form is complex.
Its contents run chiefly to sex.
It burgeons with virgins
And masculine urge'ins,
And swarms with erotic f/x.

The best way to really get a feel for limericks on the Internet is to go find the two references mentioned at the beginning of this section, make sure no one else is looking, and read them. The first of them is by far the most extensive and, to be sure, the more vulgar of the two. While perhaps not very well edited—most of the better verses appear two or three times throughout its length—a thorough reading of it will certainly be time well spent if you like this sort of thing. You'll be well spent, too, if you try any of the situations described therein. For the more modest devotee of light verse, the *limericks* file at *quartz.rutgers* is somewhat shorter but doesn't involve quite as many acts of perversion. It also is somewhat better maintained, and few of the entries show up on multiple occasions.

Excerpt from limericks

There was a young lady named Clair
Who possessed a magnificent pair.
At least so I thought
Till I saw one get caught
On a thorn, and begin losing air.

A bather whose clothing was strewed
By breezes that left her quite nude,
Saw a man come along
And, unless I'm quite wrong,
You expected this line to be lewd.

A pretty young maiden from France
Decided she'd just take a chance.
She let herself go
For an hour or so
And now all her sisters are aunts.

A team playing baseball in Dallas
Called the umpire blind out of malice.
While this worthy had fits
The team made eight hits
And a girl in the bleachers named Alice.

A wanton young lady from Wimley
Reproached for not acting quite primly
Said, "Heavens above!
I know sex isn't love,
But it's such an entrancing facsimile."

There was a young girl of Darjeeling
Who could dance with such exquisite feeling
There was never a sound
For miles all around
Save of fly-buttons hitting the ceiling.

Lute music

 `lute@cs.dartmouth.edu`
 `lute-request@cs.dartmouth.edu`
 `cs.dartmouth.edu:/pub/lute/`
 `cs.dartmouth.edu | Lute Files`

The lute is a medieval and renaissance instrument. It finds its origins in the Arabic Oud. While a stringed instrument like a guitar, it's characterized by pairs of sympathetic strings, a short neck with a raked head block, and a round back. Unlike a classical guitar, a lute is properly played with the flesh of one's fingers, rather than with fingernails.

One of the reasons that guitars supplanted lutes in more recent times is that the former are very much more difficult to construct. It's interesting to note, however, that contemporary Ovation guitars have adopted the round back of a lute, albeit made of injection molded plastic, rather than strips of bird's eye maple.

Because lutes predate the technology required to make extruded fret wire—by about a thousand years—the frets on a lute are created by tying lengths of gut string around the instrument's neck. Unlike brass frets, which can be expected to stay put once they're hammered into a guitar's neck, tied gut frets have a tendency to slip. Part of the exciting quality of lute performance is learning to thumb the frets back into place without anyone noticing.

While originally a solo instrument, the lute really flowered during the Renaissance and became a consort performance instrument. Lutes of varying sizes and keys appeared. At the height of its popularity, lutes with eight or nine courses—that is, pairs of strings—were common. Keeping 18 gut strings in tune is a bit like trying to convince colonies of earthworms to form themselves into recognizable typography.

While lutes are less common than they once were—the likelihood of Fender building a Stratocaster lute, for example, is right up there with that of responsible government and soda crackers that don't contain unpronounceable ingredients—lute music never really went out of fashion. Contemporary lutes are made of materials that serve to render them more stable, and the replacement of gut strings with nylon ones has made keeping a lute in tune long enough to get through a reasonable performance nothing like the nightmare that it once was.

The relatively small size and delicate construction of a lute makes it a much more responsive instrument than a classical guitar. While you can play a lot of the extant lute music on a guitar if you really want to, it takes a lute to give it the fluidity and grace it deserves.

There are some excellent compact discs of lute music available should your interest in lutes extend no further than listening to them.

Actually playing a lute is a rather more involved undertaking. Lutes are by no means easy to locate, a situation which is confounded somewhat by the profusion of lutelike creations that periodically turn up in antique shops. There are several contemporary lute makers who produce stunning instruments, but it's unlikely that you'll find one in the yellow pages under *L*.

There's a common sentiment amongst serious performers of lute music that truly authentic performance of Renaissance lute music can be accomplished only with completely authentic instruments. This can be troublesome for contemporary lute players. For example, the lowest strings on a bass lute a few hundred years ago would have been treated with mercury to increase their density. Mercury is rather nasty stuff. This was less of a concern during the Renaissance, both because no one knew this and because it was likely that all but the most avid lute players would die of something else before they succumbed to mercury poisoning. The same cannot be said for contemporary performers.

Learning to play a lute, like locating one, also is an undertaking. Many lute players are to a greater or lesser degree self taught, for obvious reasons. Lute music usually is written using a specialized lute tablature, rather than conventional sheet music. There is a considerable wealth of extant lute music.

The lute music mailing list at *cs.dartmouth.edu* is a superb resource for anyone considering taking up lute playing, as well as for serious musicians. Its members include numerous lute players, and it offers buckets of useful advice about things like obtaining a lute, locating particular scores, performance technique, and historical issues pertaining to authentic lute playing.

 ## Excerpt from the `lute@cs.dartmouth.edu` mailing list

Is a seven-course lute better for a beginner to start with, or should I begin with an eight-course lute? I've been told eight is better, but have a line on a seven-course lute.

Of course, (no pun intended) it all depends on the music you are most interested in. I have an eight-course lute, but since I am playing mostly sixteenth-century music these days I almost never touch the seventh and eighth. A lot of seventeenth-century English music can be played with a seven course instrument...

I would recommend starting with a six- or seven-course lute. There is an enormous amount of music written for the six-course instrument. It has been my experience that a fair number of the works composed for eight- or nine-course lute can be played on the seven-course lute, although you run into problems with later works composed for these instruments.

I would recommend a seven- or eight-course lute for a beginner, because it allows you to range over the various repertoires of the sixteenth and early seventeenth centuries. The repertoire for eight-course can be played on a seven-course with a marginal increase in difficulty, because the low F's have to be fingered on the seventh course rather than played as an open string. Later, if you decide that your heart lies in the early music that only requires six courses, you can get a six-course lute with appropriate barring pattern.

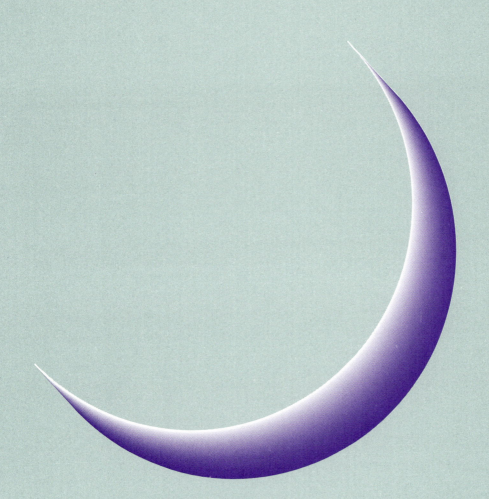

MAGICK

🛈 alt.magick
🛈 alt.magick.sex

Having been raised in a generation that watched *The Wizard of Oz* a bit too frequently as children, many North Americans remain ignorant of the genuine occult traditions. At various times—and to some extent depending upon who you listen to—these have embodied alchemy, sorcery, satanism, and a whole pantheon of extremely peculiar cults. Magick frequently is confused with pagan fertility worship, which is discussed elsewhere in this book. It's arguably fair to say that the two are fundamentally different. Magick is associated with the study and ultimate control of the physical world through energies as yet undescribed by science.

The word *magick*, spelled with a *k*, is considered to be distinct from the word *magic*. The former denotes the manipulation of occult energies, and the latter amusing card tricks and prestidigitation involving bunnies.

Many of the occult traditions remain—as in the true meaning of the word *occult*—largely hidden from modern readers because little of what they embodied was written down. While some of the ostensible knowledge of the occult seems decidedly suspect, a great deal more of it can't be easily discredited. The traditions of alchemy, for example, are clearly a lot more than old men with long beards chanting in the dark, even if it's unclear what they are.

One of the frequent threads of magick is that of sexual magick. It turns up independently, for example, throughout Medieval and Renaissance Europe and in the Tibetan *Tantra*, among other places. The traditions of sexual magick imply that great energies might be commanded at the moment of climax, if one is sufficiently disciplined. Actually, perhaps "disciplined" is a poor choice of words under the circumstances. Many of the threads in the *alt.magick.sex* newsgroup run to long tales of bondage and submission. They're pretty lurid in most cases; depending upon whom you ask, they're also somewhat off topic.

One of the most famous proponents of magick as something more than folk tales and B movies was Aleister Crowley, who was born in 1875 and died in 1947. You'll find him mentioned frequently if you go exploring in *alt.magick* or *alt.magick.sex*. His writings are discussed elsewhere in this book. He was a magician, occultist, and perhaps one of the few people ever to bring a truly scientific approach to the understanding of the occult.

Crowley also practiced quite a lot of what he perceived as being magick. He was expelled from The Order of the Golden Dawn, a prominent esoteric society of his day, and later from his adopted home in Italy for his "extreme practices." Several of his books have turned up in reproduction of late. *Magick in Theory and Practice*, now published by Castle Books, is a worthwhile introduction if you'd like to make immediate sense of *alt.magick*.

The *alt.magick* newsgroup tends toward a serious exploration of magick, with quite a bit of scholarly reason brought to the subject. The *alt.magic.sex* newsgroup, while ostensibly an aspect of *alt.magic*, is somewhat less credible and frequently something you'd only want to read when you were sure no one else was looking.

It seems worth noting that some of the traditions associated with magick are a bit nasty; necromancy and satanic beliefs often turn up in *alt.magick*. Whether or not you choose to believe the postings about these issues, they can be a bit disturbing just in considering that someone thought them up. Unlike the aforementioned B movies, much of the material in *alt.magick* reflects someone's perception of reality.

Excerpt from `alt.magick`

Note: O.T.O. is Order of the Temple of the Orient, another occult secret society.

I asked this long ago and got no answer, so I'll ask again... maybe someone new has an answer. Anyone know what was the dispensation of Crowley's body after his death? Was he cremated? If so, where were the ashes scattered or interred? If not, where was the body interred?

By his request, Crowley's remains were cremated at Brighton, England on December 5, 1947, and the ashes shipped to his successor in the O.T.O., Karl Germer. Germer subsequently buried them at the foot of a pine tree on his property in Hampton, New Jersey, 111 miles from New York City. When Germer moved to California c. 1956, he tried to retrieve the box of ashes, but the box had disintegrated — according to one version of the story he told. In another version the ashes were scattered at the base of the tree. A.C. had requested in his last will that his ashes and his seal ring be preserved.

Crowley was cremated and his ashes were scattered on Long Island. They were shipped to that OTO fellow, Gardener? who lived in the NYC area. Can't remember where I read this, so take it with a grain of salt.

He was probably cremated due to lack of money.

Can't remember. Check Symmond's biography *The Great Beast*.

Sorry to say it's true, but when I knew Kenneth Grant he did show me a few fragments of Shri Crowley's ashes left unburnt from Hastings Crematorium.

How can ashes be left unburnt?

When you've had five pints of lager at the pub and then attempt to post intelligent replies to postings.

I published the initial account of the scattering of Crowley's ashes by the Germers in New Jersey. That was printed in the old O.T.O. Newsletter in the 1970s e.v., under my editorship.

Grady McMurtry gave the account, based on a discussion he had with Germer at the Germer home in New Jersey. Germer had just pointed out a tree to Grady and said "That's the Crowley tree."

The rest of the story comes from K. Germer's explanation to Grady. There are two versions:

1. Germer told Grady that Germer's wife had simply grabbed the cigar box used to hold the ashes and tossed them at the base of the tree.

2. Germer later told other members of Agape Lodge O.T.O. that the box was deliberately buried but decayed before it could be dug up when the Germers moved to Calavaras County in California.

Grady figured that story number one was the truth and story number two was invented to make the stupid action by S.Germer look better.

Cremation is the traditional final disposition preferred by many O.T.O. members. I've specified it in my own LWT, and Crowley specified it in his LWT. It's neater and quicker.

Speculation only, but Crowley did write a story or two about the consciousness surviving until the death of the last cell in the body, a matter of months. He got the idea from a story by Poe, but may have believed it himself. Cremation is also common in Masonic traditions.

McDonald's

 alt.food.mcdonalds

It's been said that anyone who likes sausage and respects the law shouldn't watch either of them being made. This clearly holds true for fast food as well. A visit to the *alt.mcdonalds* newsgroup will likely prove to be hundreds of times more effective than Dexatrim for keeping your appetite in check.

There are several broad classes of people in *alt.mcdonalds*. They include former burger-slingers with horror stories to tell, a few McDonald's managers vainly attempting to put their fingers in the crumbling dike of bad press that this newsgroup represents, and finally the occasional curious, rabid, or dissolute passer-by with a taste for gastronomic terrorism. Very few of them have anything genuinely positive to say about McDonald's.

One recent message thread dealt with the expression "pure beef" as it applies in McDonald's around the globe.

According to one authority, pure beef in Great Britain consists of everything inside a cow ground up, with a few nominal exceptions. The only condition is that no component appear in greater abundance than it would within a basic type-A cow. This is the sort of thing one can imagine a government allowing.

The remarkable thing about *alt.mcdonalds* is that it's a fairly old newsgroup; its regulars never seem to run out of things to say about Big Macs. This is not a venue for the faint of heart or the weak of stomach. The language used is reminiscent of graffiti rejected for being too crude. However, if you think you can take it with the best of them or if you genuinely dislike Macs and want to have a shot at the golden arches amongst peers who'll be certain to applaud your choice of targets, *alt.mcdonalds* is an engaging little time-waster.

Excerpt from `alt.mcdonalds`

Hello, friendly McCustomers(tm). I've just been around Europe testing different McDonald's restaurants. The number on the first column are my rating which goes from 1-10 where 10 is the best. Here's the results:

1	Mcdonald's Copenhagen	Too lame BigMac(tm) it looked as if the man behind the desk had walked over it.
3	Mcdonald's Eindhoven	They had this very good sauce with the fries.
1	Mcdonald's Paris	And I was looking for French food. Expensive it was too.
1	Mcdonald's Wien	They served curry with the fries.
2	Mcdonald's Budapest	I was extremely hungry.
?	Mcdonald's Munchen	I didn't find the damn thing.
1	Mcdonald's Oslo	They didn't have the guts to serve McWhale.

The good news is that we don't have McDonald's here in Tromsoe and I hope that we never will have McDonald's here because their bread is so dry, their burger meat is okay, but what good is that when their burgers looks like they've been driven over by a Mazda? The combination pickles, salad and something undefined is too sour. The fries are seldom fried enough and these chicken nuggets are tasteless. I think that McDonald's is a big firm that exploits its customers to the most. By selling cheap hamburgers, whose meat have been taken from animals who are grassing from areas where there used to be rain forest, they are exploiting their employees by putting 'em to hard work, without paying them anything than nickels (compared to what they get back from customers).

Monty Python's Flying Circus

- `bigbang-ether.berkeley.edu:/ftp/pub/Library/ Monty_Python`
- `monsoon-ether.berkeley.edu:/ftp/pub/Library/ Monty_Python`
- `maelstrom-ether.berkeley.edu:/ftp/pub/Library/ Monty_Python`
- `tsunami-ether.berkeley.edu:/ftp/pub/Library/ Monty_Python`

Comedy has gone the way of rock 'n' roll to some extent. As rock impresario Bill Graham once said of the latter, the learning amateurs have all been replaced by slick professionals. Like popular music, contemporary comedy frequently seems to have the taste of something mass produced.

Before the days of comedy on Arts and Entertainment, there was comedy on the BBC. While certain similarities between the two forms exist—the word *comedy*, for example—"Monty Python's Flying Circus" predates the corporate humor of the nineties by a couple of decades.

"Monty Python's Flying Circus" is more or less disbanded now, but its legacy in television episodes, films, and bits of the English language that will never be the same is seminal. Almost a quarter of a century after their creation, the old sketches still hold up pretty well. Dead parrots, book shops, cheese shops, questionable policemen, and shrieking middle-aged "pepperpot" housewives are an ineffaceable part of our culture.

If you occasionally long for an argument, notice that your hovercraft is full of eels, find

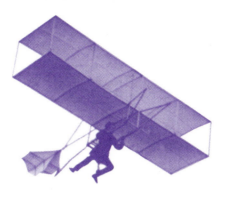

that you can't pronounce the letter C, or fancy a quick bite of crunchy frog, you'll find no small end of comfort in the darkened halls of the Monty Python archives at any of the FTP sites listed at the beginning of this section.

The Python archives include a vast selection of transcribed sketches, bits of songs, and other minor copyright violations from the original programs, the later films, and a few of the solo efforts by various members of the troupe. Included are both bookshop sketches: the original television version and the Hollywood Bowl version.

Notable by its absence is the parrot sketch. It was so often requested when Monty Python went on the road that its performers eventually ran out of ways to modify it, got thoroughly sick of it, and swore not to trot out the demised Norwegian Blue ever again.

MOVIES

rec.arts.movies

There's so much to say about the movies, and it's constantly changing. There's movie gossip, nagging trivia questions to be posed and answered, predictions of new movies in production, and the quest for obscure films on videotape or laser discs. Really avid fans of movies who linger in *rec.arts.movies* might not actually have time to make it to the flicks, with all the other cinema-related activities available.

The *rec.arts.movies* newsgroup offers a place to exchange information and questions about the twentieth century's most prevalent art form. It includes reviews of new movies—typically ones written by other users, rather than professional critics. It seems fair to observe that its users seem to include a satisfactory number of devotees of the art of B movies; films can be good by being bad.

Immediately upon browsing through *rec.arts.movies*, you'll probably observe that many of its regulars clearly spend a lot of time in darkened rooms with buttery fingers. There's a lot of minutiae and insight about movies in this newsgroup. It's a great way to choose the films that you want to see or ones you'd like to buy or rent on tape.

One area of discussion common in rec.arts.movies is lists, such as the one in the following excerpt.

Excerpt from rec.arts.movies

Does anyone know which film has been remade the greatest number of times? For this, you can include various adaptations of the same original story — e.g., the various versions of MacBeth, or of Dr. Jekyll and Mr. Hyde, etc. Thanks!

Dracula's been done at least 6 times... 1919, 1931, 1957, 1973, 1979 and 1992.

If anything goes, then the answer has got to be *Dracula*, in its many, varied, and (just occasionally) good forms.

Story remade that stuck even vaguely close to the original? *Brewster's Millions* has got to be a contender, but I don't know what the winner is.

I don't know the answer, but how about *Mutiny on the Bounty*, off hand I would say there are five versions.

To my knowledge, there have been 27 versions of *Les Miserables* by Victor Hugo, although I'm sure that more common stories can beat this.

While attending the play *Les Miserables*, they gave a brief history of the story in the program. I seem to remember a highly unusual number (50!!) that this story had been made into a movie.......

I heard there were more than 40 movies about Joan of Arc.

Yeah, but that ain't the same. They're movies about the same character, not remakes of the same story.

There have been at least 94 versions of *Cinderella*, including parodies, cartoons, etc.

Another candidate is *Cyrano de Bergerac*. I've seen the basic story from it reused in a lot of contexts, including TV sitcom episodes, and movies that don't acknowledge the original in any way.

I'd go for *Dracula*... about a 100 times methinks.

Going by memory, *The Three Musketeers* is the most often made film, having been filmed something like 35 times. I believe *Robin Hood* follows a close second. No idea about *Dracula* but you can't really count all vampire movies, just adaptations of Stoker's novel.

Scandal Rocks Toontown

One day in the middle of March 1994, a rumor appeared in the rec.art.movies newsgroup that there was more to Who Framed Roger Rabbit than meets the eye. At least, there was unless you played the laser disc version of the film one frame at a time.

As the rumor told it, Jessica Rabbit wasn't wearing any underwear under all that ink and paint. In the scene toward the end of the movie where she and Eddie Valiant are thrown from Benny the cab, the animator had drawn three frames wherein it's possible to see up Jessica's dress.

Elsewhere in the scene, the home telephone number of Michael Eisner, chief executive officer of Disney, can be found spray-painted on a wall, looking like graffiti. Eisner's number is said to have since been changed.

The story began as an Associated Press newsfeed on ClariNet. The scene involving Jessica's lack of knickers was described as "You can see clear up Broadway." — those AP writers have a blistering command of English. The images in question are on side three of the standard play laser disc version of the film, frames 2110, 2111, and 2118.

While licentious visions of Jessica Rabbit seem somehow in keeping with the generally raunchy undercurrents of Who Framed Roger Rabbit, one wonders if this is the sort of thing Walt would have agreed with. Actually, this may be somewhat immaterial — it seems unlikely that Walt would have agreed with much of what goes on at the studio that bears his name. Consider the matter of booby traps, for example.

In fact, wild frames in animated cartoons have been a tradition since their inception. As one respondent to the initial messages in rec.art.movies suggested, the nude frames of Jessica should probably be regarded as an homage to the 'toons that came before.

Perhaps more interesting than the existence of Jessica's

naughty bits is the passage of this fragment of gossip through the net. Within a day or two, the initial message asking if it were true had engendered dozens of responses. Several people with laser disc players had investigated the relevant scenes to ascertain the veracity of the matter. Someone had tried calling Michael Eisner. A great deal of moralizing took place.

As the thread progressed, other ostensibly titillating sections of Who Framed Roger Rabbit came to light. One message offered the following: I can't confirm the nude Jessica Rabbit, but I've heard from a friend (who is an animator and so knows these things) that in the scene where Betty Boop is waitressing, her short skirt billows up around her waist to reveal that she isn't wearing any underwear...

On March 17, the front page of USA Today carried the following story:

RABBIT REDUX: If you haven't yet hit your favorite video haunt in search of Who Framed Roger Rabbit, you could be out of luck. Retailers are reporting a run on the 1990 animated flick... While unnoticeable at the usual 24 frames per second, the scenes are visible when viewed frame by frame, as is possible with laser disc players and some four head VCRs... "We've received calls from all over the country asking for the disc," said Ken Crane, of Ken Crane's, an audio/video chain in Los Angeles. A television program in Britain actually showed one of the controversial frames of Jessica Rabbit. Old ladies must have been fainting for hours afterwards.

The scandal and sordid goings on of Toontown weren't restricted to rec.art.movies. Mention of Jessica's lurid secret spread to other newsgroups. I'm told it appeared in alt.sex.movies and alt.sex.pictures.female, although I confess I didn't go find out in person. Honesty bids me to confess I did watch the laser disc again.

35 versions of *The Three Musketeers*? I think I have only encountered about 5–6 starting with Douglas Fairbanks, and going through Gene Kelly, Michael York, and Chris O'Donnell, with a few cheepys thrown in. How could there have been 35?

I think the posters who mentioned *Les Mis* are closer to the mark as for a single story being re-made into multiple films. But of course if you loosen the idea of a re-make *Dracula* has to be pretty close to a winner.

Well as I recall there were at least 7 different versions of *Jeckyl and Hyde* made by the time the Barrymore version came out in 1920.

I don't know about Musketeer movies, but I do know that in the pre-sound era, stories like these were remade many many times. If memory serves, there were a good six or seven silent versions of *The Hunchback of Notre Dame*. I know of a couple other stories that were remade many times in the silent era, but my mind has gone blank.

You forgot the Bugs Bunny cartoon.

Hound of The Baskervilles has been filmed over 130 times.

Murphy's Laws

dixie.aiss.uiuc.edu:/pub/
cathouse/humor/murphys.laws/

Murphy's law states "anything that can go wrong will," addressing the general perversity of the universe with a simple explanation for its frequently bad behavior. In the wake of Murphy's generalized law, countless more specific laws and axioms have been developed to further explain the nature of bread to land with the buttered side down more than half the time, why experiments fail, how consultants defy numerous physical limitations of space and time, and so on.

The Murphy's Laws FTP site at *dixie.aiss.uiuc.edu* includes several exhaustive lists of Murphy's laws and all manner of dependent laws, theorems, axioms, postulates, observations, conundrums, mottoes, and other bits of folk wisdom. None of this actually will make you better able to cope with reality, of course, but at least you'll know why nothing ever works as it should.

 ### Excerpt from Murphy's laws at dixie.aiss.uiuc.edu

Trust everybody... then cut the cards.

Two wrongs are only the beginning.

If at first you don't succeed, destroy all evidence that you tried.

To succeed in politics, it is often necessary to rise above your principles.

To steal ideas from one person is plagiarism; to steal from many is research.

He who hesitates is probably right.

A clean tie attracts the soup of the day.

If it says "one size fits all," it doesn't fit anyone.

You never really learn to swear until you learn to drive.

Life can be only understood backwards, but it must be lived forwards.

Interchangeable parts won't.

No matter which way you go, it's uphill and against the wind.

If enough data is collected, anything may be proven by statistical methods.

Progress is made on alternative Fridays.

No man's life, liberty, or property is safe while the legislature is in session.

The hidden flaw never remains hidden.

People who love sausage and respect the law should never watch either of them being made.

A conclusion is the place where you got tired of thinking.

A free agent is anything but.

Never do card tricks for the group you play poker with.

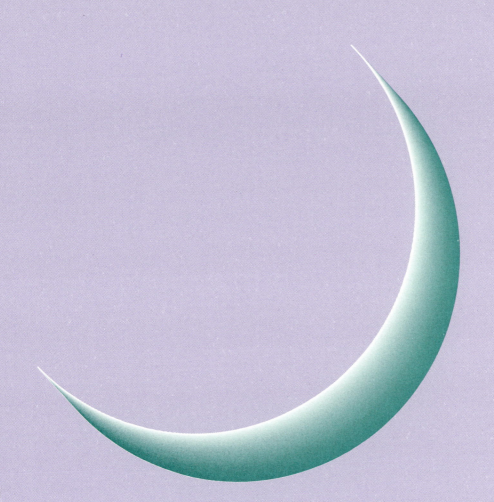

Oculis Exciditis Porcus Dimidius Facti

 wiretap.spies.com:/Library/
Article/Food/oculis.rcp

The phrase *Oculis Exciditis Porcus Dimidius Facti* is Latin; it means "when the pig's eyes fall out, it's half cooked." A more literal translation would be "eyes exit the pig [when] half done," although the former version is arguably closer to the reality of this wonderful document. The Oculis includes the complete plans and recipes for a medieval pig feast, adapted by Leigh Ann Hussey. It feeds about 130 guests.

There are numerous extant documents discussing the preparations for medieval feasts; however, to a large extent, they're more curiosities than practical instructions. The language alone makes them a bit tricky to implement, and many of the ingredients widely available a millennium ago are no longer easily obtainable at your local supermarket. A few have merely changed names, but it often is impossible to know what they're called now.

Consider the following directions—all this is correctly spelled middle English:

> *Pigge ffarced. Take rawe egges, and draw hem yorgh a streynour, And then grate faire brede; And take saffron, salt, pouder ginger, And suet of Shepe, And do medle all togidre into a faire vessell, and put hit in the pigge wombe Whan he is on the brocche, And then sowe the hole togidre; or take a prik, and prik him togidur, And lete him roste.*

The Oculis is actually workable because it includes translations for the middle English recipes and common replacements for all the ingredients. It also discusses preparation techniques not listed in the original treatises from which this document was constructed, things which the cooks of the time probably considered so common as not to require recording. Aside from *Pigge ffarced*—stuffed pig, should you have been born after 1450—it includes numerous other dishes popular back then. While we've not actually tried roasting a whole pig as discussed there, some of the less adventurous entrees worked out very well. Everything tasted decidedly unique.

Male diners should be cautioned to resist the temptation to chuck the bones over their shoulders and refer to any women present as "wenches."

The references in the Oculis all date back to before the middle of the fifteenth century.

✂ Excerpt from `Oculis Exciditis Porcus Dimidius Facti`

Note: This is the contemporary English version of the directions for *Pigge ffarced*, which was given earlier in Middle English.

Stuffed pig. Take raw eggs and run them through a strainer, and then grate nice bread, and take saffron, salt, powdered ginger, and sheep suet, and mix all together in a bowl, and put it in the pig's cavity when he is on the spit, and then sew the hole together, or take a spike and spike him together, and let him roast.

Origami

 `origami-l@nstn.ns.ca`
 `origami-l-request@nstn.ns.ca`
 `rugcis.rug.nl:/origami/`

Origami is a Japanese art of folding paper into figures, such as birds, trees, and so on. Somewhat removed from making paper airplanes, creations of origami can be impossibly intricate and look just plain impossible.

Creating complex origami sculptures only seems as if it should be easy. It takes considerable patience. Diagrams of what to fold and where are a considerable asset as well.

The FTP site mentioned at the beginning of this section offers a wealth of articles about origami, scanned photographs of origami creations, and PostScript files that can be sent to your PostScript laser printer to generate folding diagrams for numerous origami projects. You also will find archives of the origami mailing list there.

Excerpt from the Origami Mailing List

Does anyone know of some good videos on origami? I recently rented one from the local Blockbuster and it was... how can I put it... well... pretty sad. Any good ones out there?

That's a new one. Can you describe the video a bit? Was it step-by-step instructions with pauses in between for you to complete the folds? Who was doing the folding?

I really shouldn't name the video out of simple courtesy, but there was two main problems with it. 1. It didn't give the folder enough time to watch the fold and then do the fold themselves. I didn't have trouble with the timing but then I have experience with origami. The models were the type for beginners, so they would have trouble. Since the models were the very basic ones, it was boring for me. The second problem was the background music. Music sets a mood for the viewer and all I wanted to do was groan. (my 14 year old son's reaction was not so pleasant).

Since I don't have any experience at making videos I hesitate to criticize to harshly, but this one did not create any excitement for origami. Origami for me is magical. I would like to see a video that inspires and creates excitement for all the possibility origami holds.

I don't know if it is on video, but I originally learned origami from a TV program from the late 60's or early 70's called simply "Origami." The host was Samuel Randlett, and it aired on PBS. I have been trying to find out if it is available on video, if it was aired nationally, or just locally (Mr. Randlett makes his home in the Milwaukee, WI area), and if it is not available on video, is the original film stored someplace. If any of you heard of this program, remember it, or have found it on video someplace, please let me know.

I would love to see a video by Randlett also! I think his books I've seen in the library are wonderful! I wish that I could order them from the book store. Does anyone know of any books by Akira Yoshizawa besides the (I think) Origami Museum 1.? I can't seem to locate any anywhere. I'd be willing to try a book written in Japanese.

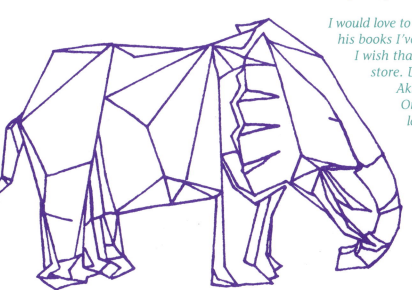

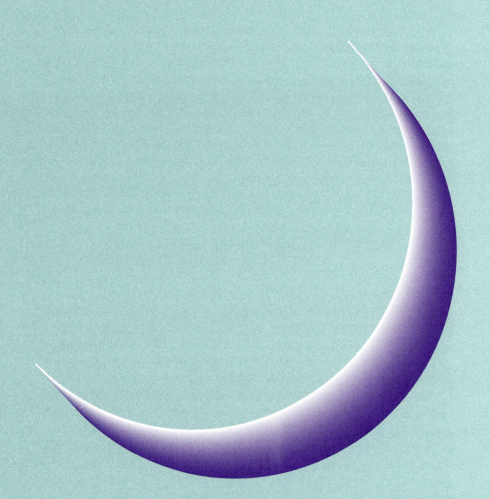

Pagans

 `alt.pagan`

The word *pagan* means a lot of different things to a lot of different people; you'll find quite a few of them in the *alt.pagan* newsgroup. Most of them are pretty serious about what they believe, and the discussions in *alt.pagan* will appeal to anyone with an interest in religions other than the ones that typically engender the construction of large places of worship.

The basis of a lot of pagan beliefs is worship of the old fertility gods. This is to some extent what medieval Christians called witchcraft. Quite a number of other cults and traditions grew out of this, and you'll find people interested in deities from places as diverse as ancient Egypt and prehistoric Scandinavia in *alt.pagan*.

Except perhaps to religious conservatives and other extreme parties, most of what appears in *alt.pagan* is fairly benign. There's a great deal of discussion about various aspects of the goddess—typically with relatively little resolution, as pagan beliefs vary widely.

One of the basis of fertility worship is the belief in a goddess of the land, for fecundity and children, and in a god of the hunt. In Celtic traditions, the goddess is called Anui or Rhiannon, and the god is Herne. Herne usually is portrayed as having the skin of a slain animal, such as a ram or a stag, wrapped about himself.

If you imagine doing the same, you'll appreciate that you'd wind up with horns on your head. Quite a lot of Celtic tradition involves a horned man or a horned god.

The rites of medieval fertility worship frequently were somewhat orgiastic, something the Christian church frowned on. The image of the Christian devil—that badly sunburned fellow with horns on his head—appears to have been drawn from the pagan image of Herne.

The notion that Christians could find an evil spirit in the god of the hunt will prove somewhat inexplicable to most pagans—something of a contradiction in terms, along the lines of another Christian image, that of a pregnant virgin.

As a rule, the pagans in *alt.pagan* are a relatively restrained lot, and the discussions in this newsgroup are agreeably esoteric. You'll encounter frequent mention of books that you've never heard of—many of them being worthwhile references if some of the foregoing has gotten you curious about pagan beliefs. You'll also no doubt come across periodic arguments about what might best be described as pagan theology. Unlike their Christian equivalents, pagan theologists don't seem to feel that profanity need be excluded from heated discussions of the divine.

Excerpt from `alt.pagan`

I am an ex-Christian interested in expanding my awareness of other beliefs and practices. I wanted to know how much "witchcraft" plays a role in this newsgroup and in the lives of the people who support it. I am not the sort of person who would place judgment upon anyone else's belief system, yet I am definitely interested in chatting with people who feel about things in somewhat the same manner as myself. Although this appears to be a very limited way of trying to unwrap the complexities of the universe, I have a very strong belief system that I have adapted to fit the world as I see it and I would like to pursue this first before seeking logic in other established practices. So I ask about witchcraft because I don't believe in it and if it is a primary belief of everyone on this newsgroup then I will look elsewhere. I am, however a naturalist. What this means will be played out if I feel this is the forum I need. Any responses are welcome.

Perhaps it might be helpful for you to tell us what you mean by "witchcraft." You may find people on this group who will say they are witches, but whether they would fall under what you think of when you hear the word "witch" is a different matter. So, let us know and then we might be able to answer your questions better.

Perhaps you would be surprised at what "witchcraft" actually means to those who practice it.

I too would fall under a Christian origin but have since realized that there is so much more to life and the world. I am too interested in learning about witchcraft, but I do not have a view of someone in a black pointy hat, long black gown, green skin, and lots of warts (too many children's books). I do realize that witches are normal people with different beliefs. But I want to learn more. Can anyone help me?

Witches don't really exist. They exist in literature. It would be nice to believe that some people have control over spirits and magic and what not but people don't. Witchcraft, like alchemy and neoplatanism was phased out around the seventeenth century. There is a resurgence of this stuff due to certain postmodern feminist readings of medieval European histories. Witches though, as most people understand them do not exist. This is also much different than saying God does or does not exist, because this question due to most definitions of God is still very unanswerable. The question of witches though is different. Witches are supposed to be people who have access to certain spiritual forces giving them control over laws which govern the psychological and physical domains of the universe and human behavior. Much of modern science has uncovered laws to explain what was once attributed to the malicious will of the witch. Basically the more we learn about the world the less we need to explain it in terms of simple moral paradigms like angels, witches, heroes and other characters best left to mythology.

Oh go away.

Good job, much more concise than I would have been. I say FAQ that puppy.

Pave the earth

alt.pave.the.earth

One of many newsgroups that seems dedicated to the prospect of environmental catastrophe, *alt.pave.the.earth* offers a place to discuss the available technologies for and possible outcomes of paving the earth. A lesser tangential topic that turns up from time to time is that of chrome-plating the moon.

There are numerous facets to the discussion of paving the earth. Consider the effects it would have on our climate; black surfaces absorb a lot of heat, for example. Consider also the prospect of being able to drive anywhere you like. This would have immense social impact, to be sure, not to mention affecting gasoline prices somewhat.

Don't subscribe to *alt.pave.the.earth* if you have an ounce of environmental conscience; you'll probably become outraged, say something everyone else will regret, and get roundly flamed. However, if all the green sensitivity of the nineties has begun to grow a bit tiresome and you'd like to spend half an hour being revenged upon the chanting hoards of Gucci-encrusted environmentalists, there are few better places.

 ### Excerpt from alt.pave.the.earth

Just wondering what would happen to the climate after we pave the whole thing over with asphalt. Even the oceans. That would be the greatest engineering achievement ever, no?

Assuming the earth becomes a giant, smooth, black ball, I'm guessing that the climate will become much warmer. All that black, you know. I'm concerned because I'm wondering if the air conditioner in my car is going to be powerful enough. If it's going to be like 150 degrees F. outside, I want to make sure it's plenty cool in my vehicle as I cover the vast beauty of asphalt at very high speeds. Could this perhaps be an oversight?

Ever heard of black body radiation? A black object will expel heat faster... therefore the Earth will cool off much faster... of course all the super hot cars will help balance it out...

There will be no cars. No people. No nature. Face it.

Of course there will be cars, probably nuclear powered. And there will be people, driving them. Nature. Who needs it when a nuclear powered car can break the sound barrier in a coast to coast drive across Asia?

Perhaps we need to build a great big solar reflector... perhaps a chrome one...

Have no fear of global warming, that's just a simplification. The sissy climatologists refuse to see the full picture: an opaque, semi-reflective party atmosphere, similar to the L.A. basin. Any needed adjustments will be handled by large charcoal braziers (mobile of course) emitting vast clouds of volatile organic compounds, CO_2, and vaporized cholesterol from the vast globs of bio-reengineered beef sizzling on each grill. Finally man will be able to obey the maxim that steak should be breathed and not eaten, as should most petroleum derivatives.

The left half (formerly North/ South America) will be paved in grey concrete, while the right side (Formerly Eurasia/Australia) will be paved in black asphalt. Now, if you grow tired of one side, just simply "Head for the Border" and live on the opposite side for a while. Another idea, for those competitive people who feel that asphalt-based cars are faster than concrete-based cars (And vice versa of course), they can have a trans-global race side by side right along the borders, to see who can circle the globe in the shortest period of time!

PAVE THE EARTH

It disgusts me how low humanity has sunk. Unaware of their true purpose they defile the sacred Usenet group. Chrome mooners, concrete fanatics. The next thing you know it'll be cobblestones. Or worse yet — grass! Woe is me. The hour is dark. I must hold fast to the true faith. It will rise from the ashes someday. For now I pave in secret.

Personal ads

🛈 alt.personals
🛈 alt.personals.misc

It would be difficult to say anything flippant or sarcastic about the Usenet personal advertisements if they took themselves seriously; lonely people seeking love in a cruel, inhospitable world is not a matter for jest. Fortunately, most of the people who frequent this newsgroup seem to be into bondage and phone sex, which does tend to blow some of the respectability from the proceedings.

The *alt.personals* is a place to begin a relationship if you feel that picking up partners in a bar is too low-tech for someone with a $5000 computer on his or her desk. You can post a message to this newsgroup describing your perfect man, woman, or perhaps both. Amidst the hoots of derision and cranks, you might even encounter someone serious. You're guaranteed to have at least one thing in common: if conversation fails, you can talk about the Net.

The arguable drawback to *alt.personals* as a substitute for the real, cruel, inhospitable world is that it's easily as cruel and inhospitable itself at times.

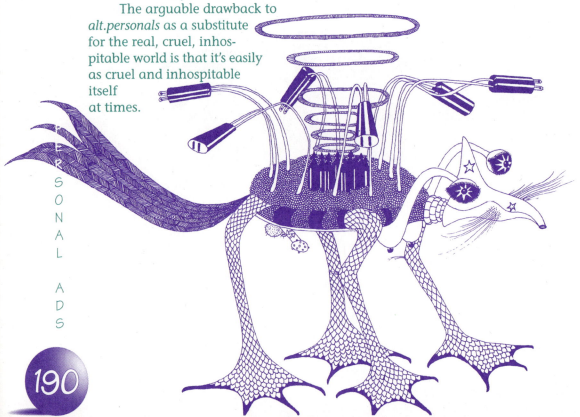

Fragile egos need not apply.

Unlike the personal ads in your local paper, there's nothing you can't say in *alt.personals*. Even if you have no interest at all in meeting someone over the Internet, consider lurking in this newsgroup as a test of your nerve. See if someone manages to post something that damages your mind.

There are a lot of abbreviations used in *alt.personals*, by the way. I haven't worked them all out myself. Among the obvious ones are:

SWM—Single white male
SWF—Single white female
SBM—Single black male
SBF—Single black female
SLM—Single latino male
SOM—Single oriental male
SOF—Single oriental female
MWM—Married white male
MLF—Married latina female
DBM—Divorced black male
DBF—Divorced black female
DOM—Divorced oriental male
GWM—Gay white male
GLF—Gay latina female
BiWF—Bisexual white female
BiWM—Bisexual white male
BiOF—Bisexual oriental female
WM/TV—White male transvestite

Other less specific abbreviations are B&D, which probably does not require an explanation, or soon won't if you frequent *alt.personals*, and ISO, which means "in search of."

Not all the ads in the *alt.personals* newsgroup involve unusual things to do in bed, although honesty bids me to say that it took me awhile to find one that didn't.

I am looking for a female companion to run the Paris-Dakar or Australian Safari Raids with. Sex is not necessarily involved but hard work, training, and marketing (we have to raise the money) is involved. Besides the race(s) we will be producing several films, writing magazine articles and doing a book, all in order to help pay for the adventure. Rallying experience would be helpful.

It will be an adventure, it will be hard work but fun. Also consider that the Paris-Dakar requires you to spend about 18 days in the cockpit of a race truck traveling across the Sahara at speeds in excess of 100 mph. There are no showers or porta-potties in the desert.

Princess Caroline tried it but didn't finish. Generally 400 vehicles start and about 50 cross the finish line; the rest either drop out or fail mechanically.

This next one sounds like somebody with a death wish or, at least, somebody who likes the insides of prisons:

Good-looking guy, living on Long Island (Nassau County) would like to hear from hot [young] girls . . . who would like to get together for some fun...

BTW, any cheerleaders out there?

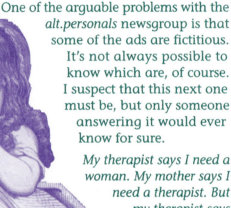

One of the arguable problems with the *alt.personals* newsgroup is that some of the ads are fictitious. It's not always possible to know which are, of course. I suspect that this next one must be, but only someone answering it would ever know for sure.

My therapist says I need a woman. My mother says I need a therapist. But my therapist says of my mother, "get over it," and I say I love her, but not *that* way. So then this guy sends me a filament and Ranger Rick builds a bonfire underneath the front porch. All the while the lady next door is sunbathing with an inner tube strapped to her eyelids and keeps proclaiming that the sun is making her feel like a bottle of Tylenol with a child protection cap. Later the doorbell rings and the mailman starts whipping me with his kneesocks all the while singing a medley of Broadway Show Tunes. Can I borrow a dollar?

I am a 22 year old tall, dark, handsome, interesting, eccentric male from the Northeast. If you are an attractive, tall (preferably), eccentric, intelligent female from somewhere in the Northeast, please let me know. I am looking for that special someone to write to and perhaps meet if things go along well.

A quick lurk in *alt.personals* probably will suggest that most of the participants are either guys or very, very strange women. On this premise, this next posting must surely be someone's fantasy.

Hi! I'm 18 years old, 5'8" tall, long blonde hair, bluish-green eyes, tan, weigh 125 lbs. I'm in good shape, do aerobics several times a week, and look good enough that I notice the heads turning......

My measurements are 36c-23-35. I've done some swimsuit modeling here in Southern California, and like to wear tiny bikinis and get all the attention... but when it comes to talking with guys, I break down, and crawl up in a shell. I need someone who can help me learn to be a little more fearless, who can free me up. This is really a problem, because I know I'm hot enough to have any guy I want, but something holds me back. Yet I'm horny all the time, and all I think about is being sexual with someone, and meeting their every desire.

If you can help, please write back...

If you felt that the foregoing was not only too good to be true but also too wholesome to be bearable, you probably will like this next posting. It was unclear whether this one came from a man or a woman. Civility prohibits me from suggesting that it might have been unclear to whoever posted it as well.

I am looking for a dom to fulfill some very kinky fantasies for one night. I would definitely want to be the submissive and be treated without any respect. Is there anyone that is looking to do just this? I am from the Western NY region so please don't respond if you aren't, or if you can't travel here.

Finally, this next guy sounds a bit like a stock quotation; one wonders if he carries on conversations in acronyms. So you'll be able to decrypt the entire message, keep in mind that MWF is a married white female, WM is a white male, and YO is "years old."

Looking for MWF's in central PA

Why MWF's you ask? Because at this moment I am currently not capable of searching for a relationship, but I am searching for some intimate physical contact.

I'm a WM, brown hair, brown eyes, 6' 1", 175 lbs., 25 YO, without trying to sound vain, I have been told that I am attractive.

You're a MWF (single is OK, but I prefer married females because it assures "no strings attached"), 22–45 YO, you do not need to look like a model, but you must be somewhat attractive with weight proportionate.

Email me for details. I'll be waiting.

I wonder if anyone has posted a message seeking after a SFFAW; that's single Fijian female alligator wrestler.

The *alt.personals.misc* newsgroup purports to be somewhat less specific than *alt.personals*, although I confess that I couldn't tell the difference.

Photography

 rec.photo

Photography is a complicated undertaking if you want to do it with something that doesn't have a plastic lens. High-end photographic equipment offers a bewildering array of body types, lenses, lens mounts, exposure modes, and options. As traditional photographic technology becomes more comfortable with computers—in such developments as digital cameras and Photo-CDs—the situation is only likely to become more confusing still.

Every year, about half a dozen hot new camera designs wash up on these shores. Some of them are brilliant. Some of them probably should be allowed to wash back out to sea. The best way to find out which is which is to buy one and see if you like it. This could get a bit expensive should you guess incorrectly.

The *rec.photo* newsgroup offers a forum in which you can ask questions of numerous serious amateur and professional photographers. It will avail you of advice on things like the best choice of lens for your camera, how to light difficult subjects, how best to work with a Photo-CD, and so on. You also will find lots of advertisements for cameras and related hardware there.

As with so many specialized hobbies, photography typically suffers from a lack of advice, especially if you're just getting into it. Unlike the people behind the counter at your local camera shop, the regular users of *rec.photo* will answer your questions without an ax to grind.

 Excerpt from rec.photo

I will travel to Europe soon. I want to buy a wide angle lens and wonder which one is the best. Can anybody comment on the lenses listed below?

SIGMA 15mm f 2.8 fish-eye   HK$3300 (about US$400)
SIGMA 18mm f 3.5   HK$2700 (about US$340)
TOKINA 17mm f 3.5   HK$2700 (about US$340)

I have both PENTAX P-30 and CANON EOS630 so I can bring the P-30 together if the fish-eye is the best choice.

You might want to consider the Tamron 17 3.5. Since it has an interchangeable mount, you can use it on both cameras. Also might be easier to sell. I use one on my Nikon and am very happy with it. It's not really a fisheye, just super wide. Not sure of current price but probably between $350–400 mailorder.

I don't think there is a Tamron Adaptall-2 mount for EOS cameras.

There is an Adaptall mount for EOS! I use it myself with the 500/8 mirror lens and the 17/3.5 wide angle. Manual focus and stop down metering of course, and you have to depend on the image on the screen for focus (no "green dot" in focus indication).

The 17mm is a good lens. There's a bit of lateral color at the edges of the frame and it's not real easy to tell when the image is in focus on a standard EOS screen (everything looks in focus with a 17mm lens! It is a rectilinear lens (not a "fish-eye"). On a 630 you can use the split-image viewfinder screen which helps focusing.

The 500/8 mirror also works on an EOS just fine. It's as good as any mirror lens (which is not very good), so I don't use it unless I have no other choice. Even then I might not use it!

If you want wide on an EOS, Sigma have a 14mm f3.5 (not a fish-eye) for about $450. It's supposed to be quite good, but I've never used one myself.

Pirate radio

ℹ alt.radio.pirate

The Usenet description for the *alt.radio.pirate* newsgroup is "Hide the gear, here come the magic station-wagons." This seems singularly appropriate.

Pirate radio is the practice of setting up unlicensed radio-broadcasting stations and doing radio the

way that you want to. Pirate radio is very much an underground culture. Because pirate transmissions tend to come and go at irregular intervals, you'd either have to know when a clandestine station will be broadcasting or you'd have to play with the dials a lot and hope to come across one. The latter is relatively unlikely.

Pirate stations can range from very simple transmitters to very elaborate systems. They're usually mobile to avoid detection.

In most western countries, the public airwaves are anything but. Governments typically sell the privilege of broadcasting at a pretty high price and as such expend considerable effort in locating pirate transmitters—hence the magic station wagons.

The *alt.radio.pirate* newsgroup is a curious patois of technical discussion on how to construct a radio transmitter, rumors of the emergence and silencings of pirate stations, and diatribes about the politics and philosophy of pirate radio. Here's what one posting in *alt.radio.pirate* said about the Zen of clandestine broadcasting:

> *Pirate radio is the most satisfying, and least rewarding of undertakings I have ever pursued. You never know if people are listening, there is no direct feedback for your efforts, there are no "babes at your feet," no instant stardom, no adoring fans, nothing. There is however the satisfaction of doing a job that the [real] stations are too pussy to undertake.*
>
> *So why do I do it? Simply, because the radio stations around here are too scared of the FCC to play the music that I like to listen to. In fact, others like to listen to it too. It's nice to be able to tune into a radio station that doesn't avoid songs that contain expletives, and especially one that doesn't bleep out the words that the FCC (and only the FCC) finds offensive.*
>
> *I am not doing this because of political reasons, I have nothing important to say. What I do care about is the truth, an open mind, saying what comes from your heart, spontaneously, and without cue*

cards, without play lists. I talk to the microphone like I am talking to my soul. I open myself up to the world and let the world inside me. I talk about my fears, my pain, my emptiness, and if I can touch just one other person who can connect and say "Yea, I feel that way too, I'm not alone," then I have done my job.

You will never hear this kind of air play on a commercial station. It makes people sad, it may even make people angry, but it makes them think. Thinking is not good for commercial radio, mindless robotic and spontaneous purchasing of the advertisers product is. I have nothing to advertise, nothing to profit by, I have no reason to be fake, "up-beat" or happy. I can be myself, speak my mind, be honest for once in my life.

There's a fair inferno of flames dancing through alt.radio.pirate, most of it directed at the authorities that control radio broadcasting and at the commercial radio stations themselves.

If you're looking for an unusual hobby, you *might* find some inspiration here—although juggling chainsaws is probably less likely to get you into trouble. While the degree of energy and spirit found in alt.radio.pirate is admirable, the cause seems a bit lost at times. There seems little point in the sheep passing laws supporting vegetarianism when the wolves are of a different opinion.

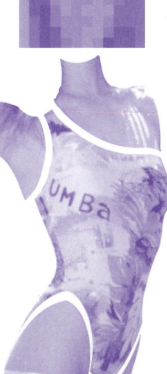

Political correctness

dixie.aiss.uiuc.edu:/pub/
cathouse/humor/politically.correct

Political correctness is among the most offensive affectations of the nineties, making BMWs, power lunches, and shoes by Gucci almost acceptable by comparison. While proponents of political correctness will tell you that it's the result of an era of heightened sensitivity and awareness of the sensibilities of others, most of the rest of the western world seems to regard it as something that would probably be more useful in making the grass grow.

The premise of political correctness is that most of us would feel a great deal better if everything said, written, or spray-painted on a wall were done so using neutral, somewhat meaningless language. In a politically correct world, then, one would say "spouse" rather than "wife," "challenged" rather than "disabled," and so on.

The Internet, of course, isn't anything like politically correct. Given a medium in which they can say what they want to say, most people will express themselves in the same politically incorrect terms that we all grew up using. Far from merely ignoring political correctness, the Net occasionally takes a few shots at it. There's a collection of some of the finest examples of political correctness bashing at the FTP site listed at the beginning of this section.

This is the sort of thing that will plunge our civilization into chaos that will make the dark ages or the advent of program stock trading—your choice—look like mere pub brawls. At least, it will if you believe all those BMW owners wearing out their Guccis running from one power lunch to the next. It's a good laugh for the rest of us.

 Excerpt from the political correctness documents at dixie.aiss.uiuc.edu

New Official Politically Correct Terms

conservative	reactionary
hearing person	temporarily aurally abled
sighted person	temporarily visually abled
blind	visually challenged
mute	vocally challenged
deaf	aurally challenged
dead	metabolically different
alive	temporarily metabolically abled
ugly	aesthetically challenged
fat	gravitationally challenged
heavy-set	people of mass
rude	politically correct (tm)
psychopath	socially misaligned
crooked	ethically challenged
bald	follicularly challenged
short	differently statured
weird green freak	person of color
female	person of gender
drooling drunk idiot	person on floor
minority group	under-represented population
woman	womyn
women	wymin
girl	pre-womyn
man	oppressor
boy	oppressor-to-be

The Prisoner

 alt.tv.prisoner

"The Prisoner" is one of the most esoteric television cults. A British television series from the sixties, it continues to be aired to this day. As of this writing, its North American rights are owned by the SciFi channel.

"The Prisoner" was created by actor Patrick McGoohan, who also starred in the leading role of "Number Six." The first episode was shown in Britain on October 1, 1967. The plot of "The Prisoner" is deceptively simple: Number Six is a secret agent who wished to retire. His former employers didn't want him at large with a head full of secrets, so he was abducted and transported to "The Village," a town of miniature houses and decidedly peculiar characters. Some of them are prisoners as well, but it's typically difficult at best to know which ones. Through various means, the authorities of The Village attempt to manipulate Number Six.

The Village actually is a real location, by the way; it's the town of Portmeirion in England. It's almost as unworldly in real life as it was in the television programs.

"The Prisoner" consists of seventeen one-hour episodes. They've recently been released on videotape and as laser discs as well as being rerun.

The *alt.tv.prisoner* newsgroup is a little village of its own, a place for fans and analysts of "The Prisoner" to exchange interpretations of the more inscrutable aspects of the episodes, to seek after minutiae of the creation of the show, and to locate "The Prisoner" on tape, disc, on the air and so on.

A considerable amount is known about the production of "The Prisoner," and to some extent about the thinking behind it, because its creator has given numerous interviews about it and at least one book has been written about it. However, far from revealing all, these fragments of insight into the program seem to have added fuel to the controversy that surrounds it.

Excerpt from alt.tv.prisoner

Note: A posting in *alt.tv.prisoner* asked about the meaning of the pennyfarthing bicycle symbol that appears periodically throughout the episodes. One reply offered the following explanation for it.

The answer comes from Patrick McGoohan, who originated it complete with the canopy over it: "I came up with the pennyfarthing bicycle because I thought it was an ironic symbol of progress. The feeling is that we are going too fast — we don't have time to assimilate as much as we should. Every year, one has to learn quicker and quicker, because there is so much information pouring out in every direction. So that was a symbol of progress to me. I wish we could go a bit slower, but we can't. Also it had a sort of elegance about it — think of a beautiful line drawing of the large wheel and small wheel, and sitting on top of the large wheel is a gentleman in a frock coat, with his nice trousers and patent leather shoes, top hat and gloves, and always beside the pennyfarthing was a beautifully dressed lady. I liked this sort of symbol of gentility, of another age."

Regarding the canopy: "That's protection, you see. That's safety belts. They're compulsory in some places, you know. I think we're being overprotective."

Quotations

 quartz.rutgers.edu:/pub/
computer/fortune/

There's nothing more up-market than being able to quote Sophocles; with a few well-chosen words from a Greek tragedy, you can transform yourself from just another toad in the hole to someone who belongs on "Masterpiece Theater." It doesn't even matter that most people have no idea who Sophocles was. They all know they should.

He was a playwright, by the way. He wrote *Oedipus Rex*, among many others.

Aside from being a fast track to ersatz respectability, if you spend a lot of time amongst people who eat more books than they read, quotations are amusing. Almost everyone says something witty and incisive once in a while; lists of quotations allow you to enjoy these sparks of brilliance without having to wade through a lot of intermediary prose that might be fairly dry.

To be sure, this is a very superficial attitude, but we live in a very superficial age. Let's enjoy it.

Fortune cookie programs have been around almost as long as computers have; they're applications that put something clever on your screen every morning. Having an insatiable requirement for clever things to say, they typically involve large lists of quotations.

There are a number of exhaustive lists of quotations at the FTP site listed at the beginning of this section. They're stored as readable text files. If you don't have a suitable fortune cookie program, you can just read them with a word processor.

✂ Excerpt from `quartz.rutgers.edu:/pub/computer/fortune/`

"On the day of victory no one is tired."
　— *Arab proverb*

"A specification that will not fit on one page of 8½ by 11 inch paper cannot be understood."
　— *Mark Ardis*

"The gods are too fond of a joke."
　— *Aristotle*

"The art of living is more like wrestling than dancing."
— Marcus Aurelius

"The danger from computers is not that they will eventually get as smart as men, but that we will meanwhile agree to meet them halfway."
— Bernard Avishai

"On two occasions I have been asked [by members of Parliament!], 'Pray, Mr. Babbage, if you put into the machine wrong figures, will the right answers come out?' I am not able rightly to apprehend the kind of confusion of ideas that could provoke such a question."
— Charles Babbage

"There's nothing remarkable about it. All one has to do is hit the right keys at the right time and the instrument plays itself."
— J. S. Bach

"I want to find a voracious, small-minded predator and name it after the IRS."
— Robert Bakker, paleontologist

"Every crowd has a silver lining."
— Phineas Taylor Barnum

"Thus the metric system did not really catch on in the States, unless you count the increasing popularity of the nine-millimeter bullet."
— Dave Barry

"Die? I should say not, dear fellow. No Barrymore would allow such a conventional thing to happen to him."
— John Barrymore's dying words

"Love thy neighbor as yourself, but choose your neighborhood."
— Louise Beal

"It is difficult for me to comprehend the fact that some people actually do not consider all uses of explosives to be recreational."
— Ragnar Benson

"There are four types of homicide: felonious, excusable, justifiable, and praiseworthy."
— Ambrose Bierce

"True, money can't buy happiness, but it isn't happiness I want. It's money."
— Bizarro

"Never before have I encountered such corrupt and foul-minded perversity! Have you ever considered a career in the Church?"
— Black Adder II

"The Bible doesn't forbid suicide. It's Catholic directive, intended to slow down their loss of martyrs."
 — Ellen Blackstone

"The fool sees not the same tree that the wise man sees."
 — William Blake

"Most human problems can be solved by an appropriate charge of high explosive."
 — Blaster, "Uncommon Valor"

Raves

🛈 `alt.rave`

🧘 `techno.stanford.edu:/pub/raves`

It's difficult to describe raves in 25 words or less. A rave is a long party with techno-music, visual effects, and usually some smart drugs. Most raves are public, typically with a cover charge to get in. However, more than all this, raves are a culture, and those who frequent raves have a perception all their own.

The rest of western civilization might ascribe this "perception" to all those visuals and smart drugs, but this is a matter of some debate.

If you've not been to a rave, many of its elements might be unfamiliar. Techno-music is, as its name implies, music that is highly electronic. It has a predominate beat, usually in the range of 115 to 160 beats per minute. The instruments used are often machines—drum machines, bass line machines, and synthesizers.

One of the central figures at a rave is a disc jockey. Especially on the west coast, there are "celebrity" disc jockeys with their own followings. Hiring one for a rave pretty well guarantees a substantial crowd. A good disc jockey will be able to mix his or her selections to keep the pulse of the music continuous and hypnotic.

The visual effects at a rave can vary from strobe lights to 10-watt lasers, fluorescent tubes, and large-screen televisions to elaborate computer-generated graphics. Visuals are a seminal element of a rave.

Drugs also are a seminal part of raves. Ecstasy and acid are popular, as are some of the less intense drugs, such as marijuana and alcohol. Also popular are "smart" drinks, alcohol combined with other substances, such as amino acids.

The combined elements of a rave, and their hypnotic assault on several senses at once, can seriously distort your sense of reality. While usually an all-night affair, some raves last several days. Your mind can become pretty distorted in that time.

There's an archive of rave-related documents available at the FTP site *techno.stanford.edu:/pub/raves* and a newsgroup to discuss raves, *alt.rave*. You can learn about raves in general, find out about upcoming raves that you might want to attend, and gain some insight into staging a rave of your own by checking out these resources.

Red Dwarf

alt.tv.red-dwarf

toaster.ee.ubc.ca:/pub/red-dwarf

"Red Dwarf" is a British science fiction comedy series with one of the most virulent cult followings this side of "Star Trek." The premise of the program is relatively easy to understand. Dave Lister, a pudgy maintenance technician on the galactic mining vessel Red Dwarf, is put in suspended animation for refusing to dispose of his pet cat. While he's in the deep freeze, the ship develops a radiation leak which kills the rest of the crew. The ship's computer keeps Dave in stasis until the radiation dies down—about three million years.

When Dave emerges from suspended animation, the ship is deserted except for himself, a hologram of one of his former crewmates named Arnold Rimmer—absolutely no relation—and an exceedingly vain creature that has evolved from Dave's cat. Also present is Holly, the ship's computer. In the early episodes, it's a male face on a monitor; however, it later appears to have undergone a sex change, becoming a blond airhead.

Finally, as the series evolved the crew acquired an exceedingly timorous android named Kryton.

In the photograph, the cat is to the far left, Dave Lister is in the foreground, Arnold Rimmer has an H on his forehead, and Kryton is the fellow with the somewhat angular features. Holly, the computer, appears indistinctly on several monitors in the background.

Originally created in the late eighties, "Red Dwarf" still is in production in Britain. It appears sporadically on public television in the United States. If you have a satellite dish, you can find it on KRMA, F1-3, at 12:00 midnight EST Sunday nights as of this writing. It also is widely available on videotape. It's inadvisable to watch "Red Dwarf" with a full stomach.

The *alt.tv.red-dwarf* newsgroup offers lively discussions about the Red Dwarf series itself, tangential bits of British culture—or perhaps more correctly, subculture—and the ongoing search for "Red Dwarf" tapes, "Red Dwarf" books, and other bits of "Red Dwarf" paraphernalia. Trivia from the episodes frequently reaches galactic proportions; the closing song lyrics, for example, periodically incite discussions that run for weeks.

There's a particularly good "Red Dwarf" FTP site at *toaster.ee.ubc.ca*. It features scanned pictures from the program, sound bites, transcribed scripts, gossip, and numerous documents of interest to fans.

Anyone with an ounce of upbringing will regard Red Dwarf as utterly tasteless, politically incorrect to the point of obscenity, vulgar, periodically incomprehensible, and a thorough waste of time. Smeg 'em all.

Excerpt from `alt.tv.red-dwarf`

I want to change my signature... and I want a great quote from RD...

My favorite quote (well one of them anyway) is not from Rimmer. In Meltdown, Lister says to Rimmer, "Is that Mahatma Ghandi in hand-to-hand combat with a nun?"

"The Committee for the Liberation and Integration of Terrifying Organisms and their Reintroduction Into Society. Of course, the one drawback to this is that the acronym spells CLITORIS."

One of my favorite is "Oxygen's for losers!" by Confidence in "Confidence and Paranoia."

My favorite quote is by the Cat in "Demons and Angels" in RDV. The engines are on overload and the Cat appears in the doorway of the scanning room and says: "Hey, they're playing our tune, the awooga waltz. Anybody care to join me in the quick step?"

When you're younger you can eat what you like, drink what you like and still climb into your 26 inch waist trousers and zip them closed. Then you reach that age, 25, 26, when your muscles wave a little white flag and without any warning you're suddenly a fat bastard.

Rimmer: After intensive investigation comma of the markings on the alien pod comma it has become clear comma to me comma that we are dealing comma with a species of awesome intellect colon

Holly: Maybe they could help you with your punctuation.

Rocky Horror Picture Show

alt.cult-movies.rocky-horror

Breathes there a soul in the western world who has not watched, nay, participated in the *Rocky Horror Picture Show*? In reality, there probably does, but they can't be breathing very hard.

One of the most successful low-budget flicks in history, *Rocky Horror Picture Show* is unique in that not only do audiences still queue up to see it, but they come dressed for the occasion and participate in the performance. To properly be a part of a showing, you should know all the lines from the film and plan to shout them at the top of your lungs as they're spoken by the actors.

If you've never been to a screening of the *Rocky Horror Picture Show*, be prepared for the occupant of the next seat to be dressed as a transvestite from Transylvania.

More experienced audiences usually have bits of dance and performance art to go along with the spoken lines, as is discussed in the excerpt for this section. The *alt.cult-movies.rocky-horror* newsgroup is a place to trade bits of "Rocky Horror" trivia and to share your experiences at the local rep theater with virgins around the world.

Excerpt from alt.cult-movies.rocky-horror

Note: These are some responses to the question of what sort of audience participation various regulars at *alt.cult-movies.rocky-horror* perform.

When Brad and Janet are in the car, and we see the windshield wipers, we move our arms in sequence with the wipers.... What do you do?

Someone gets up and leads the audience in doing windshield wipers on different forms of drugs... i.e.: "Windshield wipers on speed" (wave arms real fast) "Windshield wipers on acid" (Randomly wave arms) "Windshield wipers on qualudes" (Wave arms slowly) "Windshield wipers on uppers" (Move arms up and down) "Windshield wipers on crack" (Fall over dead)

After this whole exchange, someone usually chimes in "Windshield wipers on PMS: I don't do... windows!"

We do the "two arms mimicking the wipers" stuff, going "shhh, shhh, shhh, shhh." I guess it's kind of boring when you think about it. But, in the middle of all this, I usually put one arm down and continue, initially shouting, "Look! I'm a BMW!"

My favorite variant of this, as performed by the inimitable Fuchsia McFarln of LipSync: "Okay folks, here it is, the part of the movie that *all of you* can do! (Move arms back and forth in rhythm) Left, right, left right... For those of you on uppers (double time) leftrightleftright... For those of you on downers, (half speed) leeeeft...riiiiight... For those of you on acid, (mistimed) Red, yellow, blue, yellow... For the spatially-impaired, (cross and un-cross arms) Left, right, left, right!

Rumors

 `talk.rumors`

The problem with facts is that they have to be true. By comparison, rumors need not be even close to being true. By definition, the more interesting ones are outright lies that only seem as if they could be true. A clearly false rumor all by itself is easy to spot. Allow it to associate with numerous other rumors of questionable veracity, however, and its obvious falsehood will become far less obvious. With a bit of luck it will turn up on CNN, and some senators will deny it publicly.

The *talk.rumors* newsgroup is a forum for the initiation and spreading of rumors, true or otherwise. In the twisted alternate universe of this newsgroup, the distinction between "true" or "otherwise" is somewhat less significant than the distinction between "liar" or "liberal." Neither is measurable.

Rumors in *talk.rumors* range from the highly improbable to the plausibly deniable. It's up to you to decide which is which, of course. Consider this one:

Ozzy is in hell and he's having sex with Rush Limbaugh! (That sounds redundant — having sex with Rush Limbaugh would be hell.)

> But all this talk of Ozzy makes me wonder about what Harriet's doing?

This is seriously warped, but one can take comfort in knowing that it has a very low order of probability as it's unlikely that Rush Limbaugh is particularly dead. The same cannot be said for this next one:

> *Michael Jackson's Genital Tattoo*
>
> I don't want to say too much about where I heard this, but a friend of a friend explained what the LA District Attorney's office found when they executed the warrant that allowed them to photograph Jacko's genitalia. It seems Mr. J. has a tattoo of Tigger's tail that begins on his lower abdomen, and then extends onto his penis. My friend was not sure if the rest of Tigger's body was present. Nevertheless, it seems that the young boy who has since settled his lawsuit was the one that told them about this tattoo. The mental picture of this, and my twisted imaginings of the predator's dialogue using such a tattoo, are revolting to say the least. Any other rumors on this subject?

The disturbing thing about this rumor is that, while it might make your eyes water just thinking about it, it's hardly surprising.

Not all of the rumors in *talk.rumors* are sexual, by the way, although rumors about other subjects seem far less juicy and interesting. Rumors about who Bill Clinton might have played golf with just don't seem to elicit the same interest as rumors about who he might have slept with.

Here's a bit of nonsexual hearsay that did ripple through *talk.rumors* for some while; you might well decide that it's a pity that it isn't true, although if it were, you'd probably be confronted with the untenable prospect of going down to the local pub for a pint of ZIMA. Polish those Guccis first....

> I heard a rumor that people who are intoxicated after drinking ZIMA don't register as drunk on a breath-a-lizer. I thought it was bullshit, but I wanted to know if anyone's heard anything similar?
>
> I heard the same rumor about ZIMA but it has turned out to be false. A cop was on a local morning show and they did an experiment to show that it does register the same as other alcoholic products. Bummer for the drunk drivers out there, great for us responsible drinkers.
>
> A possible explanation for why anyone would drink the stuff!
>
> It's true, but there's a tradeoff. You're more likely to suddenly combust while talking to the troopers. And there's nothing that's more of a give-away that something's wrong than if you burst into flames.

As with so much of the Internet, there's nothing that you can't say in talk.rumors. Profanity is certainly acceptable, although your fabrications will sound a lot more plausible if they're written in printable, moderate English.

Rush Limbaugh seems to turn up in *talk.rumors* more often than most personalities these days, although it's rare indeed that anything complimentary is said about him.

> AUTHORITIES CALL FOR CALM AMID OUTBREAK OF FLESH-EATING BACTERIA
>
> *common bacterium that dissolves fat*
>
> *Good news for fat people like Roseanne Barr and Rush Limbaugh!*
>
> *You've got to be kidding! His head would be the first thing to go! Followed rapidly by the rest of his body and Vic Healey.*

The best rumors are the ones that touch us all and speak to the completeness of the human condition. This one, for example, is truly disturbing:

> *I hear from this guy down the road that if you are born then after a while (varies between 0.0000001 to approximately 110 years) you will die. Is this true?*

You won't find any useful news in *talk.rumors*; it's sort of like reading the *National Enquirer* while you wait to pay for your groceries. However, unlike that august journal, no one has ever threatened to sue *talk.rumors* for libel. As such, none of the people posting articles there need be fettered with any sort of nonsense about integrity, sources, or journalistic ethics. This is one of the most entertaining little time-wasters on the Net.

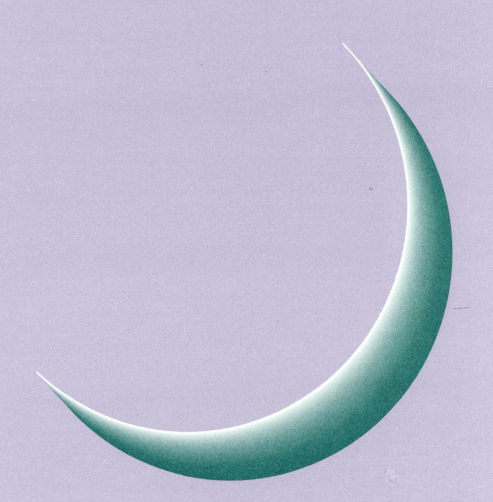

Satanism

 `alt.satanism`
 `wiretap.spies.com:/Library/Zines/Watcher`

Out of deference to whatever satanists might be reading this, it seems fair to point out that there's a clear distinction between satanism and devil worship. The former is a somewhat extreme and oftentimes questionable view of the order of the universe. The latter typically is people who really don't like the Catholic church very much getting together for some mutual loathing and mayhem.

In its most elemental sense, satanism is a manifestation of black magick and other occult beliefs. Rather than venerating the devil per se, it views the universe as the ongoing struggle between primary good and evil forces. This struggle turns up in a number of non-Christian religions as well.

Most satanic cults are heavily involved in occult practices and what the popular press likes to characterize as "black magic." In many cases, this also is what the popular press likes to characterize as "meditation," "yoga," and other far more benign-sounding practices when it turns up in other contexts.

One of the unfortunate aspects of satanism is that it spans a pretty broad range of beliefs. There are some fairly extreme satanists about who are genuinely into blood sacrifices, antichristian ritual and such. Their slightly psychopathic exteriors typically hide very much more psychopathic interiors; all but the extremely curious or the unbelievably foolhardy will do well to stay away from these guys.

Less extreme, more moderate satanists can be genuinely interesting; you don't have to agree with anything they espouse to find satanic publications an enlightening read. One of the best of the satanic 'zines available on the Internet is *The Watcher*, the "New Zealand Voice of the Left Hand Path." A voluminous mixture of press clippings about satanic groups, thoughtful philosophical texts, and bits of black magick for dilettantes, it belies its somewhat remote origins. It's available at the FTP site listed at the beginning of this section.

I confess to finding most of this stuff a bit improbable, but it's engaging nonetheless. The best bits are Uncle Setnakt's handy tips for using black magick around the office, some of which are reproduced here.

The *alt.satanism* newsgroup typically manages a somewhat less intellectual tone than *The Watcher*, although it's considerably more interactive. While *The Watcher* offers a perspective of moderate satanism—if that's not a contradiction in terms—much of what takes place in *alt.satanism* seems drawn from all the nasty things that the newspapers have to say about satanic practices. Be warned.

✂ Excerpt from *The Watcher*

Uncle Setnakt would like to share a few tips about timing in lesser and greater black magic.

1. When you need to establish yourself as a control figure, arrive early. It may seem boorish, but if you help the host do the set up, you can greet each newcomer with phrases like, "we have decided to" or "we were just talking about"—this sets you up as being a member of the inner circle and also lets you set the agenda for the evening.

2. When you need to discover the true leaders of a group, arrive late. Simply ask a few people what you've missed. If anything has been said rather than their simple human venting of hot air, they'll point it out not only with their words but with their tone and body language...

3. When you have an agenda to pass on to your business, pick a time when your co-workers are sleepy. When I want to get something started at work—rather than brainstorm on a topic—I schedule my meetings after lunch, in a slightly too warm conference room (if it has flickering fluorescent lighting this is a plus)... People are full and sleepy. They want the meeting to be over, and if I talk smoothly, distinctly, and in three quarters time they absorb my suggestions as though I've hypnotized them. Which in fact I have.

4. If you want to gain more self knowledge, occasionally radically alter your biological rhythms. Sleep, food, and sex are the keys here. Take a nap in the afternoon (if you already don't) and be sure and record the strange dreams that come in your dream diary. Fast until you feel deliciously faint, and see how your consciousness both is and is not a product of your body. Have sex much more in a single session than you do normally and study the powerful lucidity that exhaustion brings. Abstain from sex until you become a walking flame of desire...

5. If you want to train your will, test your concentration against the clock. Like the athlete trains his body, the magician must train his psyche. Many beginners find that they cannot concentrate for more than seconds at a time. They perceive this as a failure rather than the natural outcome of societal training (docile sheeple aren't supposed to concentrate). A simple and powerful exercise is to put aside nine minutes a day to meditate on projecting your godhood from the realm of Being into the realm of Becoming. During this active meditation hold a long leather thong with a few beads on it. Every time you find that your concentration has wandered, move a bead from one end to the other. Don't nag yourself, just return to the process. At the end of the exercise note in your magical diary how many beads you've had to move. In a short time you'll find that you're moving fewer and fewer beads.

Uncle Setnakt hopes you have a pleasant day.

Satellite television

 rec.video.satellite

The rumor that satellite television is dead was started by cable television companies some years ago and represents more wishful thinking on their part than fact. Offering hundreds of channels, near-laser-disc picture quality, and programming prices typically competitive with what cable companies charge, a satellite dish can revolutionize what you watch. It also can revolutionize when you watch it; what satellite television offers in picture quality and selection, it often takes back in convenience.

Almost as important as a television, a VCR is an essential adjunct to a satellite receiver.

Satellite television programming falls into two basic categories. There's a great deal of commercial programming available by satellite; you can receive HBO, MTV, ESPN, Arts and Entertainment, and numerous commercial broadcast stations through the use of a VideoCypher, a descrambler. This allows you to purchase the programs that you're interested in watching. Ignoring the cost of the VideoCypher, the cost to subscribe to something like HBO over a satellite downlink typically is considerably less than the cost to subscribe to it over cable. (This assumes that you actually have cable television available where you live, of course.)

The other group of programs are wild feeds and backhauls—transmissions that aren't specifically intended for end users per se. Many of these are uplinked without scrambling. Most weekly television programs produced by independent production companies are delivered to the stations that will air them over satellite. Most of the news services and many sports events use private uplinks to move raw footage around—usually without scrambling.

For example, as I write this it's possible to see the uplink of "Star Trek: The Next Generation" on Saturday afternoons, typically several days to a week before it's broadcast commercially. The picture quality is notably better than even a satellite retransmission, as it's one generation newer than one would normally see it. It's on at an inconvenient time; that's what a VCR is for.

Unlike the paid-for, commercial programming packages, wild feeds are only somewhat predictable. While they don't tend to change from week to week, it's not uncommon to discover that one of your favorite programs has changed satellites, time slots, or transponders without warning.

The *rec.video.satellite* newsgroup is a great place to find out about satellite television technology—which dish and receiver to buy, for example—but its real worth is as a place to keep up with the available programming and the migrations of programs across the sky. It's rich with tales of program surfers—people who wander about the arc looking for unscheduled feeds. It also reflects a variety of tastes in television viewing, as illustrated by the following excerpt.

As you might imply from the following, one of the less frequently mentioned elements of satellite television programming is erotica. It ranges from the mildly titillating to movies capable of melting your monitor.

 ### Excerpt from `rec.video.satellite`

I nearly drowned while satellite surfing late last night. My board and I nearly got sucked under when I hit a French Canadian shark named TVA on G6-9. Since the waves were totally in the clear I should have been more careful. I thought for over an hour that I was never going to escape as this shark's sharp porno teeth stared me right in the face. It was quite a struggle to escape but now I'm back in calmer waters.

Surfers beware. Stay away from G6-9 late at night unless you bring your no-leak life preserver.

Or at the very least, your inflatable Bible belt (beats the Tammy Faye Bakker blow-up doll — now *there's* an ugly thought!).

I gotta hand it to Michael, though — at least when he moralizes, he keeps his sense of humor intact. I wonder if he's written any of those Grammys sponsors yet.

Science fiction

- rec.arts.sf.announce
- rec.arts.sf.fandom
- rec.arts.sf.marketplace
- rec.arts.sf.misc
- rec.arts.sf.movies
- rec.arts.sf.reviews
- rec.arts.sf.science
- rec.arts.sf.starwars
- rec.arts.sf.tv
- rec.arts.sf.written

While not quite up to the number of individual newsgroups offered in *alt.sex*, science fiction on the Internet is singularly well represented. You'll find discussions of science fiction novels, movies and television programs, bits of science fiction esoterica and trivia, and postings of original science fiction short stories in these newsgroups.

The *rec.arts.sf.announce* newsgroup features announcements of soon-to-be-released books and movies and other things of interest to fans of science fiction. The *rec.arts.sf.fandom* newsgroup is a place to trade gossip with other fans of your favorite flicks or episodes; books turn up occasionally as well. The *rec.arts.sf.marketplace* newsgroup is an unusual institution of Usenet; it offers a place to buy and sell science fiction paraphernalia, such as movie posters, videos, film props, and so on. One thread, as I write this, concerns the sale of *Star Wars* light sabers. These are, says their owner, authentic but nonfunctioning. Considering that the light sabers in *Star Wars* actually were painted in with a rotoscope, this seems a bit suspect.

The *rec.arts.sf.misc* newsgroup is an undirected forum for anything having to do with science fiction. It's an interesting place to lurk but about as well organized as Toontown on a Saturday. You can find some really interesting discussion of science fiction cinema in *rec.arts.sf.movies*. This includes discussions—and oftentimes just mere rumors—of soon-to-be-released films and details about the classics. The *rec.arts.sf.reviews* newsgroup is for posting reviews of science fiction; much of its contents have to do with books, rather than films.

The *rec.arts.sf.science* newsgroup is for the discussion of the "real" science that appears in science fiction. This is an engaging topic, as most science fiction at least attempts to have a foundation in real science. If you're sufficiently adept, you can spot perversions of natural laws along with the best of them. One long thread as I write this has to do with the fluid breathing system that appears in The Abyss. Apparently the scene in which the rat appears to be breathing liquid actually took place, although Ed Harris used a prop when it came to be his turn. Quite a bit of real-world research has been done on the subject.

The rec.arts.sf.starwars newsgroup exists to discuss the universe of Star Wars.

The rec.arts.sf.tv newsgroup is among the liveliest of the rec.arts.sf groups. Television science fiction appears to have been enjoying a renaissance over the past few years. Perhaps because of the immediate nature of television, there seems to be a lot more to discuss about science fiction on the tube than science fiction in films, for example. The following is the sort of posting one finds in rec.arts.sf.tv. These are excerpts from a release written by Joe Straczynski, the executive producer of "Babylon 5."

> I have some news that must be imparted. I think that the best way to convey that news is to start at the end of the story, make my way to the middle, and end at the beginning. So: the end of the story. Everything is okay. Nothing major really changes. All is well. Now the middle of the story. I've been asked, several times, what happens if something happens to me, or one of the cast members, during the five year arc, since this is a fully-worked-out novel. Generally, I blow off the question with humor. But the truth is, obviously, I've taken every possible step to make sure that no one is disappointed. In my case, I've made sure the story is available somewhere. The trouble, of course, is that unlike writing a novel, where the characters exist only on a sheet of paper, actors and writers are some discussion on the best of days). They can get sick, they can get into contract disputes, they can be hit by meteors, they can decide to buy a house in Cambridge and raise hedgehogs under an assumed name.

> There are, in short, always unpredictable elements in any such endeavor. Consequently, in drafting the story for Babylon 5, I made sure to compensate for any possible changes. For lack of a better term, there is a "trap door" built into the storyline for every character. Obviously, you don't want to lose anyone, but in every case any such change momentarily shifts the story about ten degrees to one side for a little bit, and then you're back on track again....

> Now to the beginning of the story. Over the last few weeks, we've been re-activating our cast, making the deals for the coming season. One aspect of this has been a series of conversations with Michael O'Hare. Having produced one full season, and having learned a lot, and having fine-tuned the "saga" along the way, it was our goal to expand the show, bring in some new characters, and take the show in some new directions, which will prove quite interesting, I think.... There is also the question, from an actor's point of view, about other opportunities, any possible concern about typecasting, the limitations

of a continuing role (and the role of the commander does have some definite "walls," giving more freedom in many ways to other characters). Now is the point where one needs to take a breath and assess one's future, because the deeper we get into the story, the more problematic it is to change things... As a result of these discussions, it has been agreed that we will have a separation, in the role of the commander. Let me emphasize this very clearly, so there is no chance of miscommunication: this is a mutual, amicable, and friendly separation.

This isn't a Tasha Yar situation.

Moreover, we will be handling this in such a way that, down the road, Sinclair could potentially return to the story. The character of Sinclair will achieve an important destiny, and the mystery of the Battle of the Line will be explained, both in the first episode of the new season. His story will still track. And the series will still track precisely as planned. I take pains to mention this because both Michael and I want it clear that we both believe in the show, and want this in no way to interfere with the series. He has asked me to convey for him his encouragement, his best wishes, and to emphasize that this is, again, an amicable and friendly separation...

This will also allow us to pursue some new directions avenues for the show that will help to expedite the overall story. Sinclair disappearing for an indeterminate period after the events of "Chrysalis" will allow us to tighten the screws of the story, and heighten the tension of things going on in the storyline.

If I can speak personally for a moment... those of you reading this on-line know that I've always talked straight with you. If I thought this in any way would interfere with the story, you'd hear about it from me loud and clear. When problems have arisen in the past, I've always spoken about them quite bluntly here (much to the chagrin of some people). This is okay. We're all still very much friends. I speak frequently to Michael, and consider him a friend, just as he considers me a friend.

This was a hard decision, but we both knew that it was the right decision, for very different reasons. We both kinda came to the same place at the same time from different directions. We've got to do what's right for the show, and for each other, and in many ways, this does just that. So both we on the show, and Michael are served by this mutual and amicable separation. We will go our separate ways for now, with the possibility of meeting Sinclair again down the road a piece, as Gandalf disappeared for a time into Mordor, only to return when needed most... Once again, let me emphasize that the story continues on the path that has been set for it, everything you learn this season still obtains, the show remains solid, with all of the other *cast members coming back for a new season, and that the saga of Babylon 5 will continue to reveal itself exactly as planned. And I hope you will continue to stay with us for that journey.*

Sincerely,

Straczynski
Creator/Executive Producer
BABYLON 5

Finally, the *rec.arts.sf.written* newsgroup offers a place to post your short original science fiction, to read works by others users, and to discuss the whole works. It's a superb forum to fine tune your writing skills and ask for feedback.

Sex talk

- `alt.sex`
- `alt.sex.bestiality`
- `alt.sex.bestiality.barney`
- `alt.sex.bondage`
- `alt.sex.exhibitionism`
- `alt.sex.fetish.orientals`
- `alt.sex.movies`
- `alt.sex.sounds`
- `alt.sex.spanking`
- `alt.sex.stories`
- `alt.sex.stories.d`
- `alt.sex.wanted`
- `alt.sex.wizards`

It probably would be unfair to suggest that people on the Internet are obsessed with sex—mind, you won't find this extensive a list of newsgroups dealing with quantum mechanics or social sciences. If you want to make your sex life more erotic, exotic, painful, perverse, pleasurable, dangerous, or aerobic, one of these newsgroups certainly will be ready to offer you suggestions as to how to go about it.

The sexual discussions in the various *alt.sex* newsgroups vary from fairly serious,

clinical—and relatively unexciting—treatments of sex in *alt.sex.wizards* to very weird and near-orgasmic bits in *alt.sex.spanking* or *alt.sex.stories*. There's a mixture of both in the generic *alt.sex* newsgroup.

It seems important to note that it's your responsibility to decide how much of the *alt.sex* material you choose to believe. Unlikely sexual mythology is arguably an aspect of our culture, but there are things floating around in these newsgroups that would seem implausible to some species of single-cell organisms.

Some of the foregoing newsgroups probably deserve explanations. The *alt.sex* group deals with all matters prurient, from the exceedingly silly to the intensely deep. There's a decided leaning to the former, however. Fragments of other *alt.sex* newsgroups turn up in it regularly.

The *alt.sex.bestiality* newsgroup deals with the prospect of having sex with animals. That's real, four-footed, hairy, wet-nosed animals, by the way, not merely a partner who's a bit of a brute. Why do sheep farmers always wear wellies, you ask....

The *alt.sex.bestiality.barney* newsgroup is about having sex with animated purple dinosaurs. This is a really disgusting practice; wandering into the local benjo and finding some pervert having it off with a cartoon can ruin your whole evening. Mind, you can't catch anything nasty from an animation.

Those with a need to be tied up and whipped, or who long to inflict similar punishments upon their partners, will find likeminded souls in *alt.sex.bondage*. This newsgroup offers kinky stories and extensive discussions of bondage hardware. Mild suffering can be inflicted using things that you can find around the house—clothspins, rope, and such—but it seems that there are companies that actually manufacture and market dedicated bondage toys. One wonders what their stockholders' meetings must look like.

The *alt.sex.exhibitionism* newsgroup is for people who think they're built like gods and want everyone else to agree with them based on first-hand observation.

There are a number of *alt.sex.fetish* newsgroups; I couldn't quite bring myself to check out the ones dealing with amputees and diapers, among others. The *alt.sex.fetish.orientals* group offers discussions of the pleasures of the mysterious East. Sadly, if you spend enough time in this group, the East probably won't seem very mysterious any longer, which is something of a shame.

You can find a discussion of adult cinema and related forms of very bad acting in *alt.sex.movies*.

The *alt.sex.sounds* newsgroup is unique. It offers uuencoded digitized sound files of moans, grunts, and screaming orgasms. They all purport to be real, just like all orgasms purport to be real. You'll need a uudecoder and the appropriate sound hardware to play these things. Users of Microsoft Windows can attach them to system events,

replacing the canned bell sounds that come with the software. Make sure you don't exit an application when the boss is within hearing distance.

Check out the *alt.sex.spanking* newsgroup for everything that you've ever wanted to know about foreplay with a paddle. The topics in this group seem to blend into those in *alt.sex.bondage* to some extent.

The *alt.sex.stories* and *alt.sex.stories.d* newsgroups are for the posting of erotic fiction—at least, one hopes that most of this stuff is really fiction—and the discussion thereof, respectively. You can find more about these newsgroups in the "Erotic literature" section of this book. A spelling and grammar checker let loose on most of the postings in *alt.sex.stories* would overheat and burn out, but an evening spent with someone else's fantasies can be entertaining if you've run out of your own.

The *alt.sex.wanted* newsgroup is place to advertise for someone to perform that special, unspeakable act that you've been thinking about for years.

Finally, *alt.sex.wizards* is one of the least interesting sexual resources on the Internet. It's just crawling with people who seem to have read every sex manual ever printed and know the scientific names for every portion of the female genitalia. These souls take sex very seriously, which would seem to be a contradiction in terms of a sort.

There are a number of additional *alt.sex* newsgroups that I didn't visit; you might want to, if you're feeling daring. These include:

- *alt.sex.bondage.particle.physics*—I have no idea
- *alt.sex.fetish.fat*—Actually, it's *alt.sex.fetish.fa*, due to a spelling error
- *alt.sex.fetish.feet*—Probably needs no explanation
- *alt.sex.masturbation*—You can go blind reading this group.
- *alt.sex.voyeurism*—We're so far from our nearest neighbor that any serious voyeurism would require the Hubble telescope.
- *alt.sex.watersports*—I had to look this one up to find out what it meant. Go ahead… I dare you.

Whether you find the *alt.sex* newsgroups to be a passing curiosity or an ongoing source of entertainment and stimulation will to some extent be determined by how interested you are in hearing about other peoples' fantasies and sexual exploits. Much of what appears in these newsgroups is wildly improbable or more puerile than prurient. Reading enough of it might well put you off sex for a while; that which is wild and passionate beneath sweaty sheets or in the backseat of an Oldsmobile seems to lose its appeal when it's dissected and laid bare in the public forum of a newsgroup.

Society for Creative Anachronism

 rec.org.sca

The Society for Creative Anachronism is a diverse group. In a very general sense, its adherents seek to infuse the present with the best aspects of earlier times—for the most part the Middle Ages. As such, they busy themselves with the fabrication of armor, jousts, finding lyrics to old songs, and dealing with the twentieth century from a perspective that wouldn't have been out of place in the tenth.

One might well ask what a group of medieval souls is doing on the Internet. Oddly, they don't seem particularly out of place in their newsgroup.

The discussions in *rec.org.sca* range over a vast field of topics. You'll find aspects of medieval culture and society, the technology of the times, recipes for Middle Ages cuisine, very old points of trivia, and a great deal more. Far from being dilettantes about all this, most of the participants in *rec.org.sca* really know what they're on about.

One of the activities of the Society for Creative Anachronism is the staging of various feasts and other medieval events. To this end, there's a lot of practical discussion in *rec.org.sca* dealing with how to entertain large groups of people and how to come up with the appropriate hardware for things like jousting.

There's a fairly substantial pagan contingent in *rec.org.sca* and a fair bit of discussion about religion, especially as it pertains to medieval life and beliefs.

The *rec.org.sca* is among the most well-mannered and erudite newsgroups on the Net, with virtually no flaming or abuse. While it maintains a laudable sense of humor, the contemporary equivalent of that ubiquitous medieval character the village idiot is largely absent. The level of scholarship in this group is impressive.

Excerpt from `rec.org.sca`

Note: These are various postings about making armor, or having it made. Real knights don't do metalwork.

Greetings all

I am in the market for some SCA quality armor, especially shield and sword baskets. I have sent for catalogs from all the armorers advertising in TI but I'm sure a lot of people know some great hobby armorers who put out a catalog now and then. Any addresses would be welcome...

I'm making chainmail (16 gauge, .25 in); spinning the wire is no problem (thanks to a contraption involving a metal rod and a variable-speed drill), and I don't mind knitting it together. Cutting the links is a serious drag, though.

Oh and another thing, my good mate and mail maniac Juan Le Guard in Lochac went to a spring manufacturer there and got them to make him up several thousand annealed single turn steel springs. He made them make them out of a square wire.

What you get are lotsa mail links made with flat wire which look far better than the wound zinc coated wire most people normally make mail out of. Also you could then take the finished shirt and get the links hardened so they don't pull open on impact.

I can't recall the exact cost but it was about $100 for a few thousand. To make it cheaper you could buy a truly huge batch with some friends.

What is the best way to obtain cut links for mailmaking? Do I just need a manlier set of tin snips (how do I determine if they're adequate, short of using them until they wear out?), or am I better off buying the stuff pre-made (and what is the going rate, anyway?).

I use nail cutters, (not nail as in finger/toe), they didn't wear out for a long time and since I bought them at Sears I just took them back and got new ones. It's also an easier cut if you spread the coil a bit. Spreading also makes putting it together easier.

I use a set of 8:1 ratio compression aircraft tinsnips, the straight line model. I've cut a half mile of 14-gauge galvanized so far, and only tightened them up once. Going rate for precut and closed is $6 per pound. This is from the RamsHead armory last time I saw them...

I made a mail shirt using four-millimeter spring steel washers. Four millimeters was the wrong size, it looks absolutely gorgeous, but there isn't much elasticity in the suit. It's basically a short sleeved T shirt, and I'm not going to make it much larger as there isn't enough give in it to add long sleeves.

I've worn suits made from six-millimeter spring steel washers. They don't look as flashy as the four-millimeter stuff, but they are a lot more elastic and hence can be made with long sleeves and still be comfortable.

The spring steel washers are usually square section. It is possible to get round section washers as well, but they tend to be more expensive and difficult to find.

The spring steel the washers are made of is very strong, you don't have to repair the suit all the time as happens with some suits made of wire.

It took 50,000 four-millimeter washers to make my mail T shirt. I believe 50,000 six-millimeter washers should be enough for a long sleeved knee length mail shirt.

I recently heard someone talking about getting cut rings produced by a local company. Apparently they have automated machinery for making steel springs. The machinery can be adjusted to control the diameter of the spring as well as the length to as little as one loop — i.e., perfect rings for mail-making. It also leaves the ends cut nicely flat. Sounds like a great deal if you don't mind using some non-period technology to save a lot of work.

Song lyrics

```
ftp.uwp.edu:/pub/music/lyrics
ftp.sunet.se:/pub/music/lyrics
```

Compact discs by civilized musicians come with the song lyrics printed on the inside of the cover art. Not all musicians are this civilized, however. Actually, this probably is a meaningless observation; lyrics printed on anything small enough to fit in a jewel case typically can't be read without an electron microscope in any case.

The song lyric archive listed at the beginning of this section has an extensive library of lyrics to both contemporary and traditional songs. They're organized by performer for the former and by title for the latter. Many of the contemporary songs are collected into files corresponding to the albums that they were released on. As such, downloading the file *catfish.rising* would provide you with the lyrics to all the songs on Jethro Tull's *Catfish Rising* disc.

I have no idea how many songs are included at this archive; the complete list of titles is downloadable as a text file and comes to over 800 kilobytes as of this writing.

The primary archive for song lyrics is at *ftp.uwp.edu*; it's echoed at *ftp.sunet.se*. The latter typically is easier to get access to, but it resides in Sweden. If you're located in North America, you'll find that transferring files from it is relatively time-consuming.

Note that there is also a Gopher service that offers song lyrics. This is actually connected to the FTP site at *ftp.uwp.edu*. It's available periodically. As I write this, it seems to have entered a period of dormancy and will not respond to attempts to access it.

Spam

 `alt.spam`

It might seem as if Spam should be an acronym for something more interesting in this context—Sexual Pictures And Machines, perhaps, or Sticking Pins into AntiMatter. Actually, it means pretty much what it appears to mean. This is a newsgroup for the discussion of canned processed meat. Spam actually stands for spiced pork and ham. It's not even a proper acronym.

The *alt.spam* newsgroup is not particularly verbose, and few postings accumulate there. This probably isn't surprising; there isn't all that much to say about Spam. What does turn up in *alt.spam* usually is fairly peculiar.

> *I have a friend named Spam. He plays the tuba here at the University of Houston. Don't know if he eats it though; that would make him a cannibal.*

> *Please tell me that's a nickname! Hard to conceive (pardon the pun) of anyone's parents being that cruel...*

Occasionally *alt.spam* will include recipes and preparation tips to help you use Spam in ways that make it less likely to be mistaken for cat food. These are relatively infrequent and most often a bit hopeless. The best way to differentiate Spam from cat food is to attempt to feed both to a cat. The Spam will be the stuff the cat won't eat.

One posting offered the following incisive trivia about Spam:

> - Each year, 100 million pounds (45 million kg) of Spam are sold around the world.

> - Each second, 3.8 cans of the product are consumed by the more than 60 million Americans who eat the canned meat.

> - The average consumers of Spam are families with several children, especially in the southeastern U.S.

I'll bet you were wondering about those figures too.

Most of the postings in *alt.spam* are less culinary. The Church of Spam, for example, is an active force in this newsgroup.

> The Church of SPAM is here.
> For a free SPAMphlet, send a SASE to:
>
> Michael Martak
> Pontiff of SPAM
> One Canton Rd. #16
> North Quincy, MA 02171
>
> We advise you to make 100 photocopies each and hand 'em out. Thank yo'

The disturbing thought is that these characters appear to be real. The press of deadlines for this book, among other things, has prohibited me from sending away for a free SPAMphlet of my own. Perhaps it's all a dodge to acquire a tax shelter.

There are some scientific aspects of Spam as well.

> How does SPAM reproduce? The male gamete is clearly the spamatozoon, but what of the female? As a professional biologist, I find these questions fascinating.

One of dozens of weird little newsgroups, *alt.spam* is an agreeable diversion. It's the home of very little flaming and harsh language but more than the usual number of food fights. Many of its postings contain either facts about Spam thqt you'll really be happier not knowing if you've ever eaten Spam or new uses for Spam that defy conception.

Don't read it on a full stomach.

Star Trek

 `ftp.uu.net:/doc/literary/obi/Star.Trek.Parodies/`

 `ftp.uu.net:/doc/literary/obi/Star.Trek.Stories/`

 `CNS, Inc | ENTER THE CNS GOPHER | Entertainment | Star Trek-The Library`

 `rec.arts.startrek.info`

 `rec.arts.startrek.current`

 `alt.fan.q`

 `alt.wesley.crusher.die.die.die`

 `alt.startrek.creative`

It seems safe to note that the foregoing list of Internet resources pertaining to "Star Trek," probably is incomplete. Rare indeed is the net server that offers absolutely nothing of the voyages of the starship Enterprise. The more popular "Star Trek" files are to be found almost everywhere. These include episode guides, biographies of both the series characters and the actors who portray them, unauthorized "Star Trek" stories in their countless megabytes, "Star Trek" parodies, "Star Trek" pictures, "Star Trek" sounds, and the canonical "Star Trek" drinking game. The latter is not to be missed. It's excerpted later in this section.

If you have an hour to kill, try doing an Archie search for the word "Trek."

As I write this, the final episode of "Star Trek: The Next Generation" has yet to air. As you read this, the mysterious replacement series for "The Next Generation" probably won't be quite so mysterious.

The "Star Trek" stories archive listed at the beginning of this section is a large and growing collection of stories involving the crew of one Enterprise or the other, as written by fans of "Star Trek." Not being bounded by the confines of even the synthetic reality of "Star Trek" as it appears on television, some of these can get pretty strange. They include tales that might well have been actual episodes, variations on tales that *were* actual episodes, and bizarre pastiches of science fiction, such as *The Hitchhiker's Guide to The Next Generation*.

The "Star Trek" parodies archive is a bit more focused, with none of its contents coming within several parsecs of serious writing. It includes documents with titles like *Star Trek: The Next Generation—The Wrath of the Tribbles*, *Star Trek: The Next Generation—The Confused People of Megus-2 Who Just Need a Little Moral Guidance*, and *Star Trek: The*

Next Supermarket. They're all stored as numbered files. There's a list of the actual titles in the archive as well.

The "Star Trek" library at the CNS gopher is singularly enjoyable. It offers a wealth of files under the following broad categories:

Frequently Asked Questions about "Star Trek"
"Star Trek" (TOS) Sounds
"Star Trek" Library
"Star Trek" Parodies
"Star Trek" Reviews
"Star Trek" Stories

If you browse through the "Star Trek" library, you'll find guides to all the episodes, lists of the actors who have appeared in "Star Trek" in one capacity or another, episode reviews, "Trek" gossip, and a number of less mainstream documents. For example, there's a Klingon vocabulary. You also will find the most complete "Star Trek" drinking game ever compiled. The idea behind the game is to drink whenever someone in the show does something idiosyncratic. This might well seem like a worry-free way to get hammered before the first commercial, and so it is.

The "Star Trek" newsgroups listed at the beginning of this section are far from exhaustive either. The *rec.arts.startrek.info* and *rec.arts.startrek.current* currently are the most productive places to find information about current episodes and topics of interest to fans of "Star Trek." The *alt.fan.q* newsgroup is one of a number of newsgroups dedicated to interest in a particular character. The *alt.wesley.crusher.die.die.die* newsgroup is another... sort of. Clearly, it's not usually populated by anything resembling a fan of the Enterprise's youngest one-time ensign.

Finally, the *alt.startrek.creative* newsgroup is inhabited by the authors of some of the "Star Trek" parodies and original stories mentioned earlier.

Excerpt from The Canonical Drinking Game

Note: This is a small fraction of the entire drinking game list.

Instructions: Watch the show, and whenever a condition is met, take the appropriate number of drinks. The definition of "drink" should be decided before game play starts. Usually, a good mouthful will suffice.

```
Category : Condition                                 : Number of Drinks
=====================================================================
General  : "Open hailing frequencies"                : 1
Quotes   : "Medical emergency"                       : 1
         : "Hell", "Damn" and other swearing.        : 1
```

	: "It's not like anything I've ever seen	:
	: before"	: 1
	: "Impossible"	: 1
	: "Impossible" while watching the	:
	: "impossible"	: 2
	: "The Klingon Home Planet" or other	:
	: reference without actually giving it	:
	: a name	: 2

General	: A female crewmember has flawless	:
	: makeup after	:
Actions	: she's been put through the ringer	: 1
	: First names while sexual tension	:
	: present	: 2
	: The same matte painting of an alien	:
	: planet is used after each	:
	: commercial break	: 1
	: The matte painting has a moving	:
	: ground vehicle	: 2
	: Transporter Room 3 is used	: 1
	: Someone reads a book	: 1
	: Mention of dilithium crystals	: 1
	: Someone adopts a persona (Dixon	:
	: Hill, Sherlock Holmes, etc.)	: 1 ea.
	: A new alien has latex on its forehead	: 1
	: A new alien also has differently	:
	: shaped hands	: 1
	: A new alien doesn't have latex on its	:
	: forehead	: 2
	: An "Old Earth Saying" is brought up	: 1
	: They fade to commercial playing the	:
	: "ominous horns"	: 1
	: Klingon is spoken	: 1
	: English is spoken by Klingons when	:
	: they are alone and have no reason	:
	: to speak English	: 2
	: Someone uses the episode's title in a	:
	: sentence	: 2
	: The saucer section separates	: Whole Beverage
	: TNG contradicts a fact stated in TOS	: 2
	: A poker game is shown	: 1
	: A guest appearance is made by	:
	: someone from TOS	: 3
	: Someone mentions Jack Crusher	: 2
	: A star returns from the dead	: Whole Beverage
	: Ancient alien technology screws	:
	: things up	: 1

Picard Actions	Action	Value
	Straightens his uniform	2
	Straightens his uniform before giving a speech	3
	Drinks	2
	Drinks tea	3
	Drinks tea identified as Earl Grey	4
	Wears chest-revealing bedwear	2
	Is possessed	4
	Tries to avoid Lwuxana Troi	1
	Demonstrates knowledge of a foreign language	1
	Swears/hurls an insult in a foreign language	2
	Quotes Shakespeare, etc.	2
	Cries	Whole Beverage

Data Actions	Action	Value
	Uses his strength	1
	Uses his strength and shows up Worf	2
	Innards are revealed	1
	Innards are revealed other than his head	2
	Is cut off mid-sentence	1
	Is cut off during a list of synonyms	2
	Stops himself during an inappropriate speech	2
	Has to have "An Old Earth Saying" explained	2
	Gives a list of synonyms for the term he did not understand	1
	Is able to interpret/use alien technology in no time	1
	Uses a new colloquialism	1
	Uses a contraction	Whole Beverage
	Affects a human mannerism (e.g. Sherlock Data)	2
	Corrects somebody's grammar	1
	Brent Spiner breaks character for comic effect	1
	Gives an "approximation" out to several decimal places	1
	Does that little head twitch	1
	Gets kissed, etc.	3
	Is told that he's more human than he thinks	2

Tantra

 quartz.rutgers.edu:/pub/sex/kama.sutra

 ftp.spies.com-/Library/Article/Sex/massage.txt

 Rutgers Quartz Text Archive (quartz.rutgers.edu) | Sex | kama.sutra

 Wiretap Online Library (wiretap.spies.com) | Articles | Sex | Yoni Massage How-To

Tantra is a Sanskrit word meaning "weaving." The etymology is a bit convoluted. The complete body of works that comprise the Tantra embrace a wide variety of topics couched as dialogues between Shiva and his Shakti. Shakti is a Sanskrit word that can mean either "wife" or "vagina."

The Tantra would never have been published if it had been written in the nineties.

Perhaps the most famous of the works associated with the Tantra is *Love Teachings of Kama Sutra* by Vatasyayana. Kama Sutra embodies a bit more Sanskrit etymology. *Kama* is a Hindu god of erotic love, and *sutra* is a collection of teachings about an aspect of life.

The word *sutra* means "thread," along the lines of a cord binding a collection of ideas. Consider the meaning of the word *tantra*. Think of the structure of the Internet.

The Kama Sutra can be regarded as anything from a rather poetic discourse on how to have a really good time in bed right on up to a very spiritual perception of sex as a path to higher enlightenment. The Tantra implies that it's both.

You can find a translation of selected portions of the Kama Sutra—sadly without the original illustrations—at various FTP sites. Among these are *quartz.rutgers.edu*. It's in a file called *pub/sex/kama.sutra*.

A second fragment of the Tantra to appear on the Internet is a very detailed discussion of *yoni* massage. *Yoni* is another Sanskrit word. It means "sacred place," a euphemism for "vagina." This document is a treatise on how to arouse a woman and assist her in enjoying the greatest physical pleasure. It's called *massage.txt* and can be found at *ftp.spies.com*.

An Excerpt from Kama Sutra

*Indrani draws up both her knees
until they nuzzle the curves of her breasts
her feet find her lover's armpits.
Small girls love this posture,
but becoming a goddess takes a lot of practice.*

*She cups and lifts her buttocks with her palms,
spreads wide her thighs,
and digs in her heels beside her hips,
while you caress her breasts:
this is "Utphallaka" (The Flower in Bloom).*

Tasteless

 `alt.tasteless`

 `Wiretap Online Library | Fringes of Reason | Gross and Disgusting | Alt.Tasteless 26 Best of 1992`

Some Internet resources require considerable elaboration to expand on the meanings of their cryptic titles. One of the agreeable aspects of the *alt.tasteless* newsgroup and its associated gopher resource is that the name largely says it all. If you'd like to read the most tasteless postings that you can imagine, and no doubt many you cannot, this is unquestionably the newsgroup to subscribe to.

Almost nothing in *alt.tasteless* could be quoted in this book, and the publisher of *Planet Internet* made it clear when I signed the contract for it that they were prepared to be pretty broadminded about its contents. If one were to edit out all the four-letter words, sexual perversions, rude bodily functions, and cruelty to animals in *alt.tasteless*, there would be nothing left but e-mail addresses. Even those are frequently a bit vulgar.

Most of the postings in *alt.tasteless* are outrageously funny, but only if you're alone. You wouldn't want to be caught laughing at any of this where someone could see you. If you happen across *alt.tasteless* in the company of anyone that you hope to undertake a civil conversation with later, be sure to shake your head disapprovingly, make contemptuous noises, and wonder aloud how anyone could be that twisted.

Just make sure that you mail it all to yourself so that you can have a proper read of it later.

At its simplest level, posting to *alt.tasteless* is an exercise in being as base and warped as a human being can get without spontaneously combusting. Many of the postings are short narratives about really coarse experiences; in other circumstances, a few examples of the craft probably would serve to illustrate the nature of *alt.tasteless*, but I think we'll pass in this case. Some postings are quotes or excerpts of tasteless reporting by the popular press. Some are just bits of mindless cruelty to new subscribers, people looking for *rec.pets.cats*, and everyone who accesses the Internet through America Online.

Cats seem to be a particularly common subject in *alt.tasteless*— usually centering around imaginative ways to dispatch them. If it were any other helpless creature being so maligned, I'd certainly take umbrage.

There are a few things to keep in mind about *alt.tasteless* should you dare venture into its darkened corridors:

- Lurk in *alt.tasteless* for a while before you post anything, or be prepared to be flamed.
- Don't agree with anything that's said.
- Avoid *alt.tasteless* if you have just eaten.

If you can get an e-mail address with something vulgar in it, you'll be accepted immediately.

Television Nielsen ratings

CNS, Inc | ENTER THE CNS GOPHER | Entertainment | Nielsen TV Ratings

If you've occasionally wondered what everyone else thinks of your favorite television programs or whether your favorite television programs are not long for this world, you'll find a measure of insight in the weekly Nielsen ratings. Updated every week, this list rates the top 20 shows and illustrates the viewer "share" of a still larger group. As of this writing, the ratings are based on 942,000 American households, representing 94.2 million television sets in the United States.

These are the numbers that networks use to decide the continued longevity of their programs. They also are influential in helping the people who make those irritating commercials decide who to inflict them on.

The excerpt in this section is the ratings list for the week in which I wrote this entry. I should note that I didn't actually watch any of these programs. If you didn't watch them either, you might begin to wonder just who did. There are an awful lot of couch the land by the look of things.

You might well consider that the average commercial spot in a highly rated prime-time network program can run well into six figures. If you do watch commercial television, you can utterly defeat this vast expenditure of funds through the ruthless application of a "mute" button or the fast forward function of a VCR. This is the sort of power that wars were fought over a few centuries back.

Imagine 16 million television sets tuned to "Roseanne"; it damages the imagination.

Excerpt from the Weekly Nielsen Ratings at the CNS Gopher

Note: This list is the first nineteen entries. The list typically runs considerably longer.

1. (1) "Home Improvement," ABC, 22.9, 21.6 million homes
2. (5) "Three Friends Of Mine," ABC, 18.2, 17.1 million homes
3. (3) "Seinfeld," NBC, 17.8, 16.8 million homes
4. (7) "Frasier," NBC, 17.3, 16.3 million homes
5. (4) "Roseanne," ABC, 17.0, 16.0 million homes
6. (13) "Thunder Alley," ABC, 16.3, 15.4 million homes
7. "Hearts Afire," CBS, 16.0, 15.1 million homes
8. (X) "Home Improvement," ABC, 15.8, 14.9 million homes
9. (8) "Coach," ABC, 15.7, 14.8 million homes
10. (11) "Murphy Brown," CBS, 15.2, 14.3 million homes
11. (18) "Primetime Live," ABC, 14.8, 13.9 million homes
12 (14) "20 - 20," ABC, 14.8, 13.9 million homes
13. (16) "Northern Exposure," CBS, 14.6, 13.8 million homes
14. (25) "Fresh Prince Of Bel Air," NBC, 13.6, 12.8 million homes
15. (12) "Children Of The Dark" "CBS Sunday Movie," 13.4, 12.6 million homes
16. (21) "NYPD Blue," ABC, 13.4, 12.6 million homes

17. (9) "Murder, She Wrote," CBS, 13.3, 12.5 million homes
18. (42) "Law and Order," NBC, 13.2, 12.4 million homes
19. (21) "Rescue: 911," CBS, 13.0, 12.2 million homes

Tennyson

 ftp.std.com:/obi/Tennyson

Alfred Lord Tennyson is a dead poet of some note. Unlike most of the dead poets that we all become encumbered with in high school, Tennyson's work is genuinely absorbing. Much of his writing is mythological and somewhat romantic. He wrote several long poems about the Arthurian legends, of which the best known is arguably *The Lady of Shalott*.

Tennyson was named poet laureate in 1850 and was a favorite of Queen Victoria. He was immensely popular throughout Britain in his day. In an age when 15 minutes of fame seems more than all but the most notorious can aspire to, it's hard to imagine people getting worked up about poetry. Keep in mind that television sets were hard to come by at the time.

Our contemporary view of poetry often seems to include with it those works suited only to the exceedingly pedantic and to devotees of some of the unmentionable *alt.sex* newsgroups. A hundred years after it was written, Tennyson's work still speaks with a timeless eloquence that little that followed it quite manages. You can sample some of it at the FTP site mentioned at the beginning of this section.

As an aside, you can find Tennyson's *The Lady of Shalott* set to music on Loreena McKennitt's album *The Visit*; one imagines that Alfred would have approved. See the section on "Compact discs" elsewhere in this book.

 ### Excerpt from *The Lady of Shalott*

There she weaves by night and day
A magic web with colours gay.
She has heard a whisper say,
A curse is on her if she stay
   To look down to Camelot.

She knows not what the curse may be,
And so she weaveth steadily,
And little other care hath she,
   The Lady of Shalott.

And moving through a mirror clear
That hangs before her all the year,
Shadows of the world appear.
There she sees the highway near
    Winding down to Camelot;

And sometimes through the mirror blue
The knights come riding two and two.
She hath no loyal Knight and true,
    The Lady of Shalott.

But in her web she still delights
To weave the mirror's magic sights,
For often through the silent nights
A funeral, with plumes and lights
    And music, went to Camelot;

Or when the Moon was overhead,
Came two young lovers lately wed.
"I am half sick of shadows," said
    The Lady of Shalott.

A bow-shot from her bower-eaves,
He rode between the barley sheaves,
The sun came dazzling thro' the leaves,
And flamed upon the brazen greaves
    Of bold Sir Lancelot.

Texas slang

 Wiretap Online Library ¦ Humor ¦ Everything Else ¦ Crude Texican Lexicon

The Crude Texican Lexicon is a fascinating document with enough vulgarity and generally amusing harsh language in it to make most old ladies faint clean away. Purporting to be a collection of colorful expressions popular in Texas, it can be used to make people think that you're rustic and inbred. It's especially handy if you'd like to leave a boring party without specifically offending your hosts.

Almost none of the entries in *The Crude Texican Lexicon* will be suitable for use in polite company. Actually, almost none of them were suitable for use in the excerpt for this section, either. *The Crude Texican Lexicon* runs to several tens of kilobytes. The following items were the only ones which didn't involve whores, animal by-products, or unusual sexual practices.

Excerpt from Crude Texican Lexicon

"That'd gag a maggot!"
1. Refers to something terminally disgusting.

stump-broke

1. Unquestionably obedient. A "stump-broke" mule is a mule which has been trained to back up to, and stand before a stump for purposes of passive sexual intercourse.

"What's wrong with my nose? I'll tell you what's wrong with my nose. I asked Gunther if he had his girlfriend stump-broke yet, and he hit me on it, that's what."

mullygrubbing

1. Sulking, petulant behavior.

"So your sister Darlene runned off with a albino motorcycle gang president. Mullygrubbin' around the house ain't gonna help. Don't you worry, Tyshonda, we'll find you somebody just as good!"

Roebuckers

1. Prosthetic dentures.

A Blue Tick-Plot cross bitch

1. A female cross-bred raccoon-hunting hound.

Sucks... like a bucket of ticks.

1. Something, or someone, that "sucks" is of little value.

"This job sucks like a bucket of ticks."

Back when snakes used to walk.

1. Once upon a time, long ago.

Travel advisory

 University of California- San Diego, Infopath | US State Department Travel Advisories

If you've always dreamt about taking an exotic holiday to someplace that no one else had ever heard of or if your employer has just booked tickets for you to a similar spot, check out the resources at the Gopher site listed at the beginning of this section before you leave. An exhaustive list of destinations, the State Department travel advisories will tell you about things like the crime rate that you can expect when you get where you're going, what you can't bring into the country with you, how stable the local government is, what sort of medical facilities are available, and how to contact an American embassy or consulate.

The world is a somewhat peculiar place, and many countries have laws and customs that you might consider somewhat bizarre. Nonetheless, they're the laws of the places that you might be visiting, and it's worth knowing about them before the local constabulary has to explain them to you.

For example, as I write this, most North Americans have become aware that vandalism is severely frowned upon in Singapore. If you decide to visit Singapore nonetheless—even if you have no vandalous intentions at all—you also should be aware that possession of chewing gum is illegal, for example. It's illegal to bring Vicks inhalers or Sudafed into Japan, and the Japanese legal system is somewhat unkind to travelers caught with them. It's illegal to take radar detectors into some parts of Canada, as they contravene local taxation ordinances. Bringing undeclared foreign currency into Cuba can cause you to become a guest of Fidel for two to five years. The work week in the United Arab Emirates is Saturday through Wednesday.

There are even entries for places that you probably wouldn't visit even if the tickets were free, such as Bosnia. The entry for Bosnia is relatively short. In effect, it says that you shouldn't go there and that, if you do, you probably should plan to become dead somewhere during your journey.

Travel agents only want your money, but the government has a vested interest in seeing to it that you come home safely so that you can keep paying taxes. The State Department travel advisories are well researched and updated regularly. Don't leave home without them.

From Russia with GlasNet

As of this writing, you can catch a glimpse of what life's like in the former Soviet Union through the GlasNet gopher server. Privately created and managed, GlasNet is a nonprofit network for Russian computer users to contact the more familiar network services in the west, such as CompuServe, the Internet, and America Online (God help 'em). It runs on two Sun workstations donated by Sun Microsystems.

GlasNet was one of the communications media used to inform people across Russia about the events of the August 1991 coup in Moscow and of the siege of the Russian Parliament in September 1993.

The GlasNet gopher server offers an electronic brochure in English describing GlasNet, its structures and facilities and what it costs. It includes the e-mail addresses of GlasNet in Russia and other people around the world associated with it, should you want to learn more about this resource.

GlasNet accounts are available outside the former Soviet Union. While the fees for the system are charged in rubles for local users, an American office exists to accept payment in U.S. dollars. GlasNet maintains a somewhat inscrutable system for converting between dollars and rubles, allowing for the chaotic inflation in Russia at the moment.

The GlasNet pamphlet also discusses things like obtaining an adapter to connect a Hayes-compatible modem to a former Soviet Union telephone jack and how to manage the connection with a pair of wire cutters and some alligator clips if that's all that's available.

Trivia

 rec.games.trivia

What's the average mean weight of a Texas armadillo? Where does Alfred Hitchcock turn up in *Psycho*? Where was the Battle of Hastings fought? Which American president appears on the $1000 bill? What's the tensile strength of a typical house cat? How many toes does a three-toed sloth have?

These are the sorts of questions that drive people mad. Knowing the answers won't change the direction of the universe, but it will keep you from bending all the paper clips on your desk into medieval weaponry for mice.

The *rec.games.trivia* newsgroup appears to have been started to discuss trivia games, but it long ago degenerated into a place to discuss trivia questions. You can post messages asking for the answers to trivia questions that have you stumped, or you can post questions of your own and see how long it takes for someone to correctly answer them.

Be warned, however, the questions in *rec.games.trivia* are frequently pretty deep. Most of them are removed by several light-years from the questions found in trivia board games. Plan to think if you post in this group.

By the way, a three-toed sloth has twelve toes—three on each foot.

The Undiscovered Country

 `wiretap.spies.com:/Library/Zines/Undiscov`

Weird little 'zines are one of the notable features of the Internet. This one is one of the weirdest. *The Undiscovered Country* is a journal of poetry and short fiction—and a fair amount of undirected rambling—originating in Los Angeles. It frequently is somewhat boorish and sophomoric, almost universally pornographic, but an amusing read in small quantities nonetheless.

A typical issue of *The Undiscovered Country* might include titles like "Extensive Pretentious Interlude," "Pornography Masquerading as Literature," "A Sniper's Poem," "Post Modern Housewife," and "Stoner Adventures V." Propriety forbids me from quoting anything that appeared under these titles; some things are best found out for one's self.

Perhaps the closing message of one issue of *The Undiscovered Country* expresses the situation best:

> *Thanks for reading this issue of *The Undiscovered Country*. If you didn't think it was *all* outright shit, please forward copies to friends or print it out and tape it to your least used extremity. We take submissions at cblanc@pomona.claremont.edu, and would love to hear feedback as well. Thank you again and join us in our fight against rational thought and the dominant paradigm.*

```
        invocation:     There seems to be so little left to say.
                        &'&'&'&'&'&'&'&'&'&'&'&'&'&'&
                        &`                          '&
                        &`   the undiscovered       '&
                        &`              country     '&
                        &`                          '&
                        &`  29MAR93    v1: .        '&
                        &`             is: ....     '&
                        &'&'&'&'&'&'&'&'&'&'&'&'&'&'&
                (c) copyright 1993 sdi, inc
                  s.r. prozak & l.b. noire
                                                              !
                                                            spo
                                                         nsored&
                                                      created&wri
              *==+==+==*                             tten&edited&pro
              *sdi,inc.*                            motedexhaustivelyby
              *==+==+==*                           spinozarayprozak&labete
                                                 noire,foundatcblanc@pomona.
                                                claremont.edu&rm09216@nyssa.swt
                                               .edu&groupsontheusenet&dedicatedtot
                                              thestudyofliteraturelife&humanunkind..

:-----/-----/-----/-----/-----/-----/-----/-----/-----/-----/----/-----:
:the undiscovered contents:                                            :
:.        brief villification of theory & functionality                :
:..       musings in solitude after a primal clash of wills            :
:...      random poetic ramblings section                              :
:....     stoner adventures, vol. v                                    :
:.....    virulent interlude of emotional attrition                    :
:......   the lust of the flesh, the shine of the skin                 :
:.......  interpolation & contributor biographornication               :
:-----/-----/-----/-----/-----/-----/-----/-----/-----/-----/----/-----:
```

Weather

 NOAA Environmental Information Services Gopher | Weather Information and Images/

Being able to predict the weather reliably can be a very useful facility. The NOAA Gopher really won't make you capable of doing this any more than it does for television weathermen and other ostensible professionals who attempt it for a living; however, it will provide you with the same raw information that they have access to, allowing you to draw erroneous conclusions of your own, rather than relying on someone else's mistakes.

As will be apparent if you study the materials offered by NOAA, the problem with weather prediction is that there's rather a lot of weather, and weather is a somewhat large thing. While it's possible to say that it will rain tomorrow in the American midwest, for example, and be pretty certain that this will take place, it's very much more difficult to know whether your house will be included in the area to be rained upon. Weather goes where it pleases, and it gets there on feet the size of a continent.

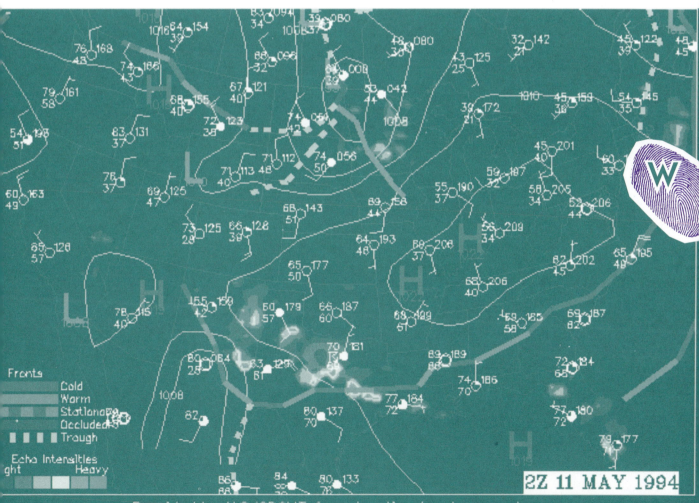

There's a wealth of meteorological information offered by the NOAA Gopher. The section listed at the beginning of this section will provide you with a current weather map for North America in the form of a GIF file called WEATHER.GIF, as well as a text weather forecast for the next 24 hours. There are much more involved documents and pictures on hand as well.

Wicca

nic.funet.fi:/pub/doc/occult/wicca

In its simplest sense, Wicca is the worship of a fertility goddess and whatever ritual surrounds her. This is a seriously inadequate description, however, owing to the nature of Wicca, or perhaps to the nature of the Goddess. Unlike more well-organized religions, Wicca lacks a written-down bible, any clearly defined dogma, priests, a pope, churches, prayers, hand gestures, beads, relics, reliquaries, knee pads, confessionals, collection plates, and tax shelters. On the assumption that your relationship with the Goddess should be between you and her, Wicca is to a large extent what you want it to be.

Wicca is associated with witches and witchcraft; you might want to see the section on "Pagans" elsewhere in this book for more about the distinction between witches who follow Wicca and witches who follow the yellow brick road and turn princes into frogs.

The FTP site listed at the beginning of this section offers a wealth of documents related to Wicca. Some of these writings are singularly interesting and well worth downloading all the way from Finland, especially as it doesn't cost anything to do so. Included are writings about the nature of Wicca, descriptions of various rituals and meditations, bits of historical perception, and various introductory and descriptive pieces about fertility magick in general.

One of the things that you'll find common to many of these files is a header that enjoins anyone reading them not to believe everything there. While it's likely that whoever wrote these documents was writing the truth as it pertained to him or her at the time, the personal nature of Wicca makes such generalizations somewhat suspect. Seriously inadequate descriptions might be all that really can be said of it without fear of contradiction.

Wine

 `rec.crafts.winemaking`

Homemade wine can be every bit as good as the finest vintages of France, or it can taste like it's been run through a goat. Being offered a glass of the house pressings can be one of the great terrors of western civilization. Wine kits have a lot to answer for.

The expression "great wine in just thirty days," as displayed prominently on the sides of these kits, is unquestionably a contradiction in terms.

Of course, you can make really superb wine. It takes patience and some understanding of the craft involved in doing so, however. While simple in theory, the art of making good wine is subtle and rich with tradition and nuance. There also is a lot of common sense involved, such as never drinking the batches that turn out to be green.

The *rec.crafts.winemaking* newsgroup is a gathering of amateur winemakers. For the most part, you'll find it to be a forum in which to trade recipes, bits of wine esoterica, and other aspects of the craft of making wine. It's a great place to seek after unusual recipes. Wine can be made from all sorts of things besides grapes; wines made from dandelions, oranges, blueberries, and such have remarkable and truly exotic tastes. Some of them also have a sufficient alcohol content to curl your toenails.

 Excerpt from `rec.crafts.winemaking`

Since February, I've made several red wines from a number of different "brands" — European, Select-Vineyard, Select-Ultra — and a couple of others. A beginner, I've followed the directions as laid out in each kit. The first two kits were three-week kits (sugar additive); the rest were four-week kits with all ingredients enclosed; for one of these, oak chips were added. The results have not been to my satisfaction, although a Brouilly and a Burgundy were "palatable".

I'm hopeful that, with time, these will be more to my liking, considering that they are young but I have doubts. I like a very dry, earthy wine and results thus far reflect wines that are sweet, fruity, thin or have no body. Am I searching the elusive "pie in the sky" or is it that I have just not found the right "brand"? Any suggestions?

You are not going to get Mondavi-grade wines using a kit. One kit that I have tried with good success is the Vintners Reserve. It sounds

similar to the kit with everything including the oak. Many of us are making wines from fresh grapes. A guy in our wine club has 500 to 1000 pounds of grapes shipped in each fall. Others are using frozen grapes or grape juice.

Your starting product will be the determining factor in your end product, good grapes-good wine.

I know that doesn't help much. Don't expect great (good maybe) results with kits.

You will have a hard time getting "earthy" from your kits (I assume you are talking about the characteristics of *pinot noir*). The best grapes do not make it into the concentrates. Although the grapes in concentrates may be as good as most of us can get even when we get fresh fruit.

To improve concentrate wines, don't use sugar. The use of sugar to increase the specific gravity of the must will result in the correct alcohol content, but a thin wine. Dilute the concentrate with only enough water to reach the SG you want. Also avoid fining agents if possible. Usually, you will find that concentrate wines clear easily by themselves.

Ignore the directions on the kit about making the wine in 3-4 weeks. After fermentation, rack the wine into a carboy and bulk age for several months (like 6 months) with one racking a week or so before bottling to help remove sediment.

You may not get the perfect wine from concentrates, but you can make a good one by taking your time.

Oh yea, one more thing. You should measure and adjust your acidity. Many concentrate kits ignore this. There is no way they can always supply a balanced juice to you. It will be up to you to adjust the acidity for proper balance.

Wiretap Online Library

 Internet Wiretap | Wiretap Online Library

The Wiretap Online Library is a vast repository of text documents. It offers everything from the Declaration of Independence to 50 ways to fail an exam in style. Easily accessible through Gopher, the Wiretap Online Library allows you to browse through its resources in menu-driven comfort. Its first menu level offers the following broad classifications as of this writing:

Articles
Assorted Documents
Civic & Historical
Classics
Cyberspace
Fringes of Reason
Humor
Mass Media
Miscellaneous
Music
Questionables
Religion
Technical Information
Zines

Each of these topics leads to numerous submenus. For example, Humor eventually worked its way down to this menu:

A Visit From St Nicholas.
Adventures of Micro Farad and Milli Amp.
Answering Machine Messages.
Anti-Smurf Poetry.
Barbequeue "Legal" Invitation/Summons.
Bush Quotes.
Canonical DOIT List.
Climbing Letters to the Editor.
Confess That You Are a Rabbit.
Cows (Huge Mar 1992).
Cows (Jan 1988).
Cows (Nov 1988).
Crude Texican Lexicon.
Dick & Jane Instigate a Popular Revolution.
Excuses.
Failing An Exam In Style (50 Ways).
Found Humor (it occurs in nature).
Hedgehog flavored potato chips.

How to Write Real Good.
Idaho Does Not Exist.
Impure Mathematics.
Institutions of Higher Learning.
Oxymorons.
People that you meet in the bathroom.
Pickup Lines from net.singles.
Practical Jokes.
Quayle Quotes.
Roommate Confusion.
SAT Preparation Exam.
Signatures from 1987 Usenet.
Telecom Quotes.
The Bonehead Quotes File.
The Donut File.
The Last Full Deck List.
Too Easy To Create Conspiracies.

Browsing everything on the list will take several hours and will make your mouth ache after a while. For example, here's one of the files it offers, "How to Write Real Good":

HOW TO WRITE GOOD
by Frank L. Visco

My several years in the word game have learnt me several rules:

1. Avoid alliteration. Always.
2. Prepositions are not words to end sentences with.
3. Avoid cliches like the plague. (They're old hat.)
4. Employ the vernacular.
5. Eschew ampersands & abbreviations, etc.
6. Parenthetical remarks (however relevant) are unnecessary.
7. It is wrong to ever split an infinitive.
8. Contractions aren't necessary.
9. Foreign words and phrases are not apropos.
10. One should never generalize.
11. Eliminate quotations. As Ralph Waldo Emerson once said: "I hate quotations. Tell me what you know."
12. Comparisons are as bad as cliches.
13. Don't be redundant; don't use more words than necessary; it's highly superfluous.
14. Profanity sucks.
15. Be more or less specific.
16. Understatement is always best.
17. Exaggeration is a billion times worse than understatement.
18. One-word sentences? Eliminate.
19. Analogies in writing are like feathers on a snake.

20. The passive voice is to be avoided.
21. Go around the barn at high noon to avoid colloquialisms.
22. Even if a mixed metaphor sings, it should be derailed.
23. Who needs rhetorical questions?

Don't miss the lists of cows.

Each of the initial menu items at Wiretap offers a similar scope of topics, often with many more files. Most of them are somewhat less frivolous than this one.

The Wiretap Online Library can be regarded as both a serious resource and a well-executed, richly varied little time waster. Don't approach it without at least an hour to kill.

Zen

 `alt.zen`

Zen is a Buddhist teaching that seeks to find enlightenment through inner awareness. That's probably a serious oversimplification, but Zen seems to lean toward very simple explanations for things. Complexities are to be found between the words.

Perhaps the most engaging aspect of Zen is that you can spend your life studying it or you can acquire little fragments of it and enjoy them for what they are. Zen gives you something in relation to whatever you put into it—or into yourself.

In its simplest sense, Zen is very easy to understand. The problem is that one rarely encounters a discussion of Zen in its simplest sense. In the West, Zen often turns up as someone's idea of the next great self-help program, complete with seminars, videos, and four-color brochures. Having an attention span shorter than the life cycle of a rat on a pile driver, many Western adherents of the Zen of the month would clearly prefer it as a short television insert, to be absorbed over breakfast.

There's also a nasty side to Zen as it appears in North America. Several recent exposes have disclosed the existence of Zen cults, groups in which the meditative techniques of Zen are used to lure people into long-term submission and economic servitude. As with most cults, some of this can sound unreal and a bit bone-chilling to the rest of us.

The *alt.zen* group is very...well, very Zenlike. It's a comfortable fusion of casual observations about Zen and a universe viewed through perceptions inspired by Zen. None of it will change your life or grant you sudden, blinding enlightenment, but you'll probably enjoy reading the postings.

There are also a number of less spiritual elements of *alt.zen*. You'll frequently find postings about Buddhist monasteries that offer meditation services—numerous ones exist in the United States. Finally, as I write this there's quite a bit in *alt.zen* about Zen cults.

It seems fair to note that, while Zen is often perceived as being serious and reserved, the *alt.zen* newsgroup is frequently enlivened by Zenlike observations of less weighty matters. For example, as I write this there's a thread progressing through *alt.zen* concerning the Zen of limericks, and why they're funny. In traditional Zen meditation, such thoughts would probably earn one a clip 'round the ears from a Zen master. Or not.

Zima
alt.zima

Colorless, almost alcohol free, largely tasteless and hyped by an advertising machine that could probably have sold icebergs at the sinking of the Titanic, Zima is the perfect beverage for the nineties. Ten years ago it would have been sold as hair conditioner.

Zima has the distinction of being the only alcohol that Murphy won't drink. Murphy is a 150-pound labrador retriever that learned to bite through beer cans at an early age; you can find him in the section of this book that discusses dogs. Murphy would suck cold sake through a 40' garden hose given half a chance, but he left the Zima where it was. Honesty bids me to note that he only had a chance to sample Zima because none of the human beings around him could finish the stuff.

The *alt.zima* newsgroup is a forum for compatriots of Murphy who feel that Zima should be left in a steel dog dish until one of the local cats falls in and drowns. I suppose that, in theory, someone could come by and champion Zima, responding to its hoards of detractors, but thus far few champions have appeared on the horizon.

If you've never had the opportunity to sample Zima, be sure to drop by *alt.zima* for several dozen good reasons to stay that way.

Excerpt from `alt.zima`

How does Zima taste? Zhitty!

> If Zima is a marketing "nightmare" then I need some bad dreams! Like it or not, that "nightmare" is selling like crazy all over this country. Look for two "copycat" clear malts to be on the shelves by year's end. People don't compete with you if your products aren't selling. You don't see anybody copying "OK" from Coca-Cola do you? I'd say it's marketing genius.
>
> Zo, Zou Zeed Zome Zad Zeems, Zmagine ZeveryZody Zalking Zike Zis....
>
> Zit Zould Zuck! Zo Zake Zour Zhitty Zrink Zand Zhove Zit Zhere Zhe Zun
>
> Zon't Zhine.

It's not marketing genius that sells Zima, it's the simple fact that feminine men need something to drink to. I'll stick with beer and SoCo.

Most of the men I know who drink Zima zertainly zeem to be quite manly.

Zey'd have to be, to zurvive the zickly tazte of zat zhit.

Proof that the American people can be sold *anything*, no matter how crappy it is. I had hoped that the "clear" craze was dying out, but apparently not. When someone tells me they like the way Zima tastes, I figure they're too stupid to realize that they're another victim of corporate advertising.

Zines

 alt.zines

Zines are a singular fixture of the Internet. Magazines without dead trees to reside upon for the most part, zines are unpredictable, periodically fascinating, and usually so far off the wall as to place them in an adjacent parallel universe. Zines are often published only in an electronic form and propagate over the Internet. Freed from the constraints of having to appeal to a wide enough audience to make large-scale paper publishing financially viable and relieved of the drudgery of abiding with advertisers, parent companies, and stockholders, the authors and publishers of zines can say what they like about whatever they feel deserves mention.

If *People* magazine were a zine, it would have burnt its own corporate offices to the ground years ago.

Several zines have been discussed in detail in this book. However, there are more zines about the Net than most of us can imagine, with new ones springing up like hallucinogenic mushrooms even as you read this. The *alt.zines* newsgroup offers a gathering place for zine publishers and readers of these eclectic little journals.

There are a lot of announcements of new zines or new issues of zines in *alt.zines*. For example, this seems like a likely candidate for a zine bestseller:

I am about to go to press with issue #1 of my zine, Brain Distortion. If there are any Punk/Indie/Gothic/techno people out there that would like to give a report on their scene, then please e-mail.

Punk Rock submission will get printed, 100% sure. But anything else (techno/ambient/Gothic/indie/alternative) will be looked over, with a good chance of getting printed.

A few zines are somewhat private affairs, with the editorial staff and all the contributors occupying the same bodies. Many others will be happy to publish your ravings as well as their own. Here's a typical call for submissions:

The Morpo Review is seeking submissions of poetry and short, unhinged essays and short stories for future issues.

What kind of work do we want? How about sonnets to Captain Kangaroo, free-verse ruminations comparing plastic lawn ornaments to Love Boat or nearly anything with cows in it. No, not cute, Smurfy little "ha ha" ditties — back reality into a corner and snarl! Some good examples are "Oatmeal" by Galway Kinnell, "A Supermarket In California" by Allen Ginsberg, or the 6th section of Wallace Stevens' "Six Significant Landscapes."

But, hey, if this makes little or no sense, just send us good stuff; if we like it, we'll print it, even if it's nothing close to the above description of what we want (life's like that at times). Just send us good stuff, get published, and impress your peers and neighbors.

So send us your unhinged poetry, prose and essay contemplations to:
morpo-submissions@morpo.creighton.edu

Your submission will be acknowledged and reviewed for inclusion in a future issue, which will be made available to World Wide Web readers, e-mail subscribers, Gopher users, anonymous FTP'ers, BBS users and others.

If you would like to subscribe to The Morpo Review, just drop us a note at:
morpo-request@morpo.creighton.edu
and include the line:
subscribe morpo

Appendix

Making the Internet connection

Should you be fortunate enough to have Internet access through your business or school, you can ignore this appendix entirely and get straight on to looking for erotic art on the world's largest computer network. For a growing number of Internet users, however, getting connected to the Net is itself something of a learning experience. A year ago, you'd probably have been lucky to have had one option for Internet connectivity. As you read this, you might find yourself confronted with half a dozen. More will be coming.

There are a number of things to take into account when you choose a path to the Internet—don't make the mistake of grabbing the first one that presents itself. Differing access facilities might present you with wildly varying degrees of functionality and substantial price variations. As a very simple example, I can access the Internet through a local Internet provider at a cost of $3 Canadian an hour or through CompuServe at a cost of something over $12 Canadian an hour. The local Internet provider is not only cheaper but provides much more complete access to the facilities of the Net.

CompuServe is much easier to locate, of course. Internet access is being provided by many of the large online services. As I will discuss in this appendix, these forms of Net connectivity are easy to acquire and quick to learn, but they might not be the best way to get online.

Honesty bids me to suggest that accessing the Internet through some of the big online services might not see you as warmly received by current citizens of the Net as you might want. For example, the recent influx of America Online members into the Net has prompted the formation of a new Usenet newsgroup, called *alt.aol-sucks*. Very little of its contents can be said to be civil. This is by no means in keeping with the egalitarian spirit and tolerance of the Internet, but it seems to be the way things are at the moment.

Much of the hostility of long-time Internet users to immigrants from America Online and other large dial-up services is due at least in part to how Internet access is being provided by some of these networks. Treated as just another special interest group, users of America Online and Delphi can access the Internet without knowing anything much about it. By contrast, most dedicated Internet providers will provide you with at least a bit of Net-specific indoctrination before turning you loose.

This appendix will discuss the details of several approaches to dial-up access to the Internet. This probably deserves some clarification—it will of necessity be somewhat platform- and system-specific. It also will be software-specific in some cases, and some of the software to be discussed here will no doubt have become a bit smarter and more capable by the time you read this.

You should keep in mind that you can change the way that you access the Internet after you've had a while to work with it. Having said this, there might be a penalty of sorts in doing so: your e-mail address will probably change, with the attendant confusion for anyone who wants to send you mail.

Dedicated Internet providers

I access the Internet through a dedicated Internet provider for the most part. It's a company called *UUnorth*. The function of UUnorth is to sell access to their hardwired connection to the Internet through dial-up modem lines. The access that is provided by UUnorth is typical of what a dedicated Internet provider will do for you. Specifically, UUnorth allows me to connect to the Internet in several ways. I can do so using their menu-driven text-based interface, which is called "Access Point," or I can talk directly to the Net using software running on my computer. Let's deal with Access Point first as it's considerably simpler and is typical of the sort of entry-level Internet access you're likely to get through an independent Internet provider.

Access Point deals with the resources of the Internet through text menus like the ones illustrated in Fig. A-1a through A-1f. If you've read the Introduction to this book, many of the features of these menus will be familiar.

```
ID: alchemy                          Date: Aug 11, 94 Time: 12:13
Menu: Main Menu

    ? - Help on Main Menu
    c - Primary Configuration
    d - Download Files
    u - Upload Files
    t - Talk & Chat
    m - The Mail box - send and receive mail
    a - Accounting information
    f - File browser & archives
    z - Zen and the Art of the Internet (Hypertxt)
    b - information Booth
    i - Internet facilities - telnet ftp etc
    n - USENET News Facilities
    q - Quit from AccessPoint


Elapsed: 00:05
Enter command keyletter or CR to back up:



VT100  ONLINE  57600 8N1  [ALT-Z]-Menu  FDX 8 LF X ♪ ♫ CP LG ↑ PR  00:00:22
```
A-1a

```
ID: alchemy                                    Date: Aug 11, 94 Time: 12:13
Menu: Internet facilities

        ? - Help on Internet Facilities
        l - remote Login (rlogin)
        w - World Wide Web hypertext browser
        f - transfer files by FTP
        o - internet whOis lookup
        a - Anonymous FTP mechanism (easy to use)
        t - Telnet to another site
        c - Chat with another user across the Internet
        i - fInger another site or user
        r - Internet Relay Chat
        g - Gopher (browse the Internet)
        e - archiE (seach for FTP file location)
        q - Quit from AccessPoint


Elapsed: 00:24
Enter command keyletter or CR to back up:
```

A-1b `VT100    ONLINE   57600 8N1   [ALT-Z]-Menu   FDX 8 LF X ♪ ♫ CP LG ↑ PR   00:00:40`

```
                                              Table of Contents (p1 of 2)

                        THE UUNORTH WWW SERVER

        This page is a broad listing of materials available via WWW and other
        services.

                        _____

                * Announcements
                * News and Weather
                * Since you asked...


                * Guide to Internet resources
                * Finding things on the Internet
                * Finding people on the Internet
                * The Internet Public Library
                * The Internet Reference Library
                        _____

Arr keys: Up and Down to move. Right to follow a link; Left to go back.
    S)earch P)rint M)ain menu O)ptions G)o Q)uit [delete]=history list
Type a command or ? for help:_____    Press space for next page
```

A-1c `VT100    ONLINE   57600 8N1   [ALT-Z]-Menu   FDX 8 LF X ♪ ♫ CP LG ↑ PR   00:00:55`

```
                        Internet Gopher Information Client v1.11

                             Other Gopher and Information Servers

        -->  1.  All the Gopher Servers in the World/
             2.  Search All the Gopher Servers in the World <?>
             3.  Search titles in Gopherspace using veronica/
             4.  Africa/
             5.  Asia/
             6.  Europe/
             7.  International Organizations/
             8.  Middle East/
             9.  North America/
            10.  Pacific/
            11.  Russia/
            12.  South America/
            13.  Terminal Based Information/
            14.  WAIS Based Information/
            15.  Gopher Server Registration.







Press ? for Help, q to Quit, u to go up a menu              Page: 1/1
```

A-1d `VT100    ONLINE   57600 8N1   [ALT-Z]-Menu   FDX 8 LF X ♪ ♫ CP LG ↑ PR   00:01:40`

```
        Group Selection (33)                      h=help
     1    27  alt.magick.sex
     2   624  rec.arts.books
     3   521  rec.video.satellite
     4  7294  alt.magick
     5  1020  alt.pagan
     6  5440  alt.binaries.pictures.misc
     7   237  alt.tv.babylon-5
     8   156  alt.tv.red-dwarf
     9    14  alt.graffiti
    10    63  alt.books.reviews
    11   262  alt.binaries.pictures.utilities
    12     1  alt.tla
    13  4188  alt.video.laserdisc
    14  3189  alt.sex.stories
    15  1086  alt.binaries.pictures
    16        alt.binaries.sounds

   <n>=set current to n, TAB=next unread, /=search pattern, c)atchup,
   g)oto, j=line down, k=line up, h)elp, m)ove, q)uit, r=toggle all/unread,
   s)ubscribe, S)ub pattern, u)nsubscribe, U)nsub pattern, y)ank in/out

VT100   ONLINE  57600 8N1  [ALT-Z]-Menu  FDX 8 LF X ♪ ♫ CP LG ↑ PR  00:00:36
```

A-1e

```
Fri, 05 Aug 1994 02:23:03        alt.magick.sex          Thread    9 of   14
Lines 20                   Re: Dreams with strong sexual content   No responses
ivorydove1@aol.com         IVORYDOVE1 at America Online, Inc. (1-800-827-6364)

In article <1994Jun5.010015.6996@news.cs.indiana.edu>, "amy lynn
young-leith" <alyoung@cherry.ucs.indiana.edu> writes:

I too have dreams with strong sexual content. Some of the dreams i've had
are of male acquaintences and people i know. The wierdest i think was of a
dream i had where i had to "save the world" by having sex with an alien
(who was a very goodlooking guy). Why i was chosen, i don't know. I really
didn't mind but in the dream i was suppose to not want to. Very strange!
I also have repeated dreams of flying.....and oh what a feeling, it's
really undescribable. They usually start out with me doing gymnastics. i
then procede to fly into the air for long periods of time, after a
tumbling run. if i feel myself falling i can usually move my arms in large
circles and stay up longer....this don't always work.   I also have dreams
where i know i'm dreaming....for example: I'm running from someone who is

   <n>=set current to n, TAB=next unread, /=search pattern, ^K)ill/select,
       a)uthor search, B)ody search, c)atchup, f)ollowup, K=mark read,
       !=pipe, m)ail, o=print, q)uit, r)eply mail, s)ave, t)ag, w=post
                                                        --More--(78%) [1467/1880]
VT100   ONLINE  57600 8N1  [ALT-Z]-Menu  FDX 8 LF X ♪ ♫ CP LG ↑ PR  00:01:26
```

A-1f

    In its most elemental sense, an Internet session consists of you telling the software that is connecting you to the Net what facilities you want to access and the software in turn mediating between you and the Net. This points up a fundamental consideration of dial-up access to the Net. Communication over the Net itself is relatively fast. Communication over a phone line typically is very much slower, even if you're using a high-speed modem. To display pages of menus or other information, software running on a remote computer must send the pages over the line to your modem.

    In the case of Access Point's text-based menus, a complete page will consist of no more than 4000 characters—the number of characters of an 80 by 25 character screen—and will typically require far fewer. These sorts of data blocks can be moved around by a high-speed modem in less time than it takes most liberal politicians to devise a plausible explanation for a fact-finding tour to the Bahamas. This means that Access Point's menus can be snappy and responsive and not require that you undertake a protracted session of head scratching and paper clip torture every time that you want to look at a different screen.

Text-based interfaces like this one work through the use of a terminal protocol. This means that there's a way for Access Point to send commands along with the text of its pages to do things like relocate the text cursor, turn on highlighting and inverse text, and so on. For example, Fig. A-2 illustrates the posting list of a newsgroup. Notice that the currently selected item in the list has been highlighted.

```
alt.magick.sex (14T 27A 0K 0H R)                              h=help
     1  +    How wierd are you? The Kook Report!         Ed Erst
     2  +    Massage Salon in Seattle. WA                Lord of L
     3  +    Sex Magick                                  Lord of L
     4  +    CAW CHAT LIST                               Lord of L
     5  +    Kundalini yoga                              Lord of L
     6  + 5  Namaste                                     Lord of L
     7  + 6  What If...                                  Pendragon
     8  + 4  SANTA CRUZ CAW NEST MEETING!!!!             Lee Levine
     9  +    Dreams with strong sexual content           IVORYDOVE1
    10  +    student love                                IVORYDOVE1
    11  +    CAW in Davis, CA                            Keith Relf
    12  +    PENIS FOR SALE                              JEERYME
    13  + 2  Intro to Tantra                             JHEIDER
    14  +    PENIS FOR SALE. Need more info.             ronb@cc.usu.edu


   <n>=set current to n, TAB=next unread, /=search pattern, ^K)ill/select,
   a)uthor search, c)atchup, j=line down, k=line up, K=mark read, l)ist thread,
   !=pipe, m)ail, o=print, q)uit, r=toggle all/unread, s)ave, t)ag, w=post

                            *** End of Articles ***
VT100   ONLINE  57600 8N1  [ALT-Z]-Menu  FDX 8 LF X ƒ ♪ CP LG ↑ PR  00:01:08
```

A-2

To work with a text-based interface like Access Point, it's necessary to have a terminal software package running on your computer that will emulate one of the terminal types supported by the remote computer of your Internet provider. There are several commonly used terminal emulations, including VT100, VT52 and ANSI.

Terminal emulations probably deserve a moment's discussion. While you will most likely access the Internet through a personal computer running software to make it look like a terminal—a terminal "emulation"—there are actually dedicated hardware boxes that do, nothing but access a larger computer. These appear in travel agents offices, among other places. Each of these brands of terminals defines a protocol of commands for things like moving the text cursor around, turning highlighting on and off, and so on. The model numbers of the terminals—such as VT100, a terminal made by DEC—have come to be synonymous with the definition of how they perform these functions.

Terminal emulation software typically emulates a number of popular terminals. This means that, if a computer running a VT100 terminal emulator encounters the commands supported by a real VT100 terminal, it will imitate the response of the real terminal.

The most widely used terminal emulation in the Unix environment that dominates the Internet is VT100. While most Internet providers will allow you to interact with them using other terminal emulations, you'll run into problems when you start using Telnet to get to other systems on the Net. Many facilities on Telnet don't offer a wide variety of terminal types.

Fortunately, anything that emulates a terminal on a personal computer is almost certain to support VT100. The second most common terminal emulation type in PC circles is an ANSI terminal. For historical reasons, this is a very bad choice of terminal emulation modes to use on the Internet. The VT100 terminal standard was designed by a single manufacturer and is unambiguous. The ANSI standard is not as well defined, and it's not at all unlikely that you'll find that your computer and the computer of your Internet provider don't speak the same dialect of ANSI.

Thus far, I've discussed terminal emulation software. You might well be wondering where you'd find a terminal emulator. Chances are you need not look for one. Terminal emulation is a basic feature of all telecommunications packages. If you have software to drive your modem—packages such as Procomm, QModem, Telix, or even the dreaded Windows Terminal application—you have a terminal emulator. I use QModem. Figures A-3a and A-3b illustrate the terminal emulation settings for QModem and the Windows Terminal application.

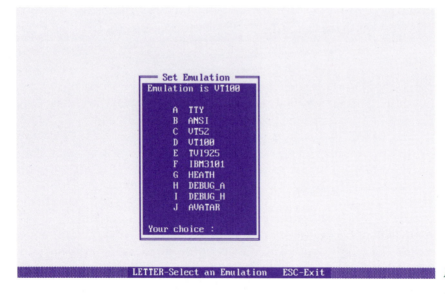

A-3a

A-3b

[Terminal Emulation dialog: TTY (Generic); DEC VT-100 (ANSI) selected; DEC VT-52; OK; Cancel]

It's very important to make sure that your terminal emulation and that of your text-based Internet provider match, lest you find mysterious symbols and bits of text all over your screen.

Access Point is very easy to use and is very fast. It's just not very pretty. It—and text-based interfaces to the Internet like it—represent the quickest way to deal with the Internet over a dial-up connection. It will be of some help if you can type; this software has no interest at all in a mouse. It's also worth mentioning that, as Internet access through an Internet provider is typically billed by the minute, this sort of interface will tie up the least amount of time moving menu pages and such around and should be the least expensive to use.

Access Point is partially an assembly of extant applications to do things like manage mail and newsgroups, connect you to FTP sites, and so on. This has two important consequences. The first is that, because the various bits of Access Point were written by disparate parties, they don't integrate all that well. Commands that move around the screen in the Pine mail reader, for example, don't work in the World Wide Web browser that Access Point incorporates. This isn't particularly crippling; it just takes some getting used to.

The other consequence of a system like Access Point is that it runs on a Unix machine and was written by people who like a Unix environment. Unix-based software has its own set of commands for things like moving a cursor around a screen. They're typically different from those one might employ on a PC system. You can get around this problem by programming macros into some of the keys of your keyboard in your terminal software, such that the keys will emit the control codes that Unix software would expect. This isn't as awkward or as technical as it sounds, and once done, the interface to a system like Access Point will be very much less funky.

Other text-based Internet access packages might require less of this sort of thing, depending on which applications they've chosen to perform the basic functions of an Internet provider.

You can communicate with a simple Internet provider like Access Point using very modest hardware and software. A modem capable of at least 9600 baud will be pretty well essential. A faster modem still will make the system much more responsive. At Alchemy Mindworks, we use Intel and Zoom modems. You'll need a suitable communications package to run on your computer, such as the ones discussed earlier in this section. Even old, glacially slow PCs can run a terminal package.

Windows Internet and WinSock

As with many dedicated dial-up Internet providers, UUnorth offers a second way to connect to the Net. It will allow your computer to do all the work, sorting out the low-level messages and protocols of the Internet with software running on your system. This might sound intensely complicated, and it probably would be if you had to write the software. Fortunately, there's a lot of very good PC software available to perform these tasks for you. I'm going to look at an elegant way to access the Internet from within Microsoft Windows.

Long-time Internet users will no doubt look at Windows and mutter something like "If I'd wanted a prefontal lobotomy, I'd have bought a chainsaw and given myself one." Despite the obviously consumer-oriented, user-obsequious nature of Windows, it does make a good platform to deal with the Net from. For one thing, it can do multiple things at once.

Keep in mind that, while you might well ultimately use the Windows software to be discussed in this section, it's unlikely that you'll start off with it if you're new to the Internet or new to dial-up Net access. For one thing, while these applications do turn up outside the Net from time to time on public access bulletin boards, for the most part, you'll really need access to the Internet to find them. You'll also benefit by having had some experience with the basic functions of the Net before you plunge into all this.

Unless you know someone who can provide you with this software and get it up and running for you, plan to begin with one of the less-complex approaches to Internet access—such as a text-based interface like the one discussed in the previous section—before you start bashing away at Windows.

Figures A-4a through A-4d illustrate my computer running Cello, one of a suite of public domain and shareware applications to interact with the Internet in a very user-friendly manner. Cello is a World Wide Web browser.

Cello probably looks about as unlike the text-based Access Point menus in the preceding section as it could get. However, it's effectively performing the same function as the text Word Wide Web browser that was illustrated back in Fig. A-2. In this case, however, it's possible to select items from the pages of the World Wide Web by clicking on the icons of Cello, rather than by moving a cursor around a text page. Graphical items will display as graphics if you like.

Windows-based Internet access involves two layers of software and a variety of applications. The first thing that you'll require is a Windows "socket" manager, an application that will connect to the Internet through an access provider like UUnorth and allow other

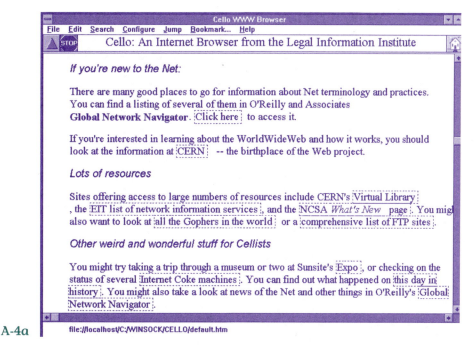

A-4a

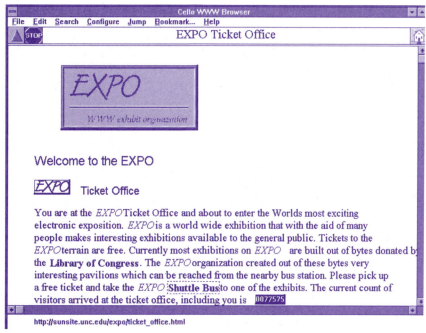

A-4b

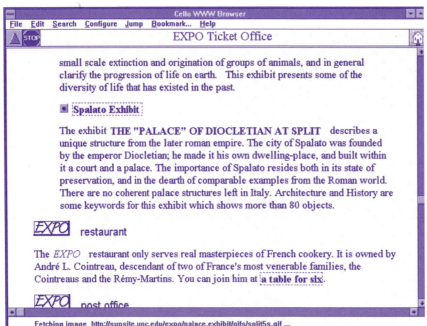

A-4c

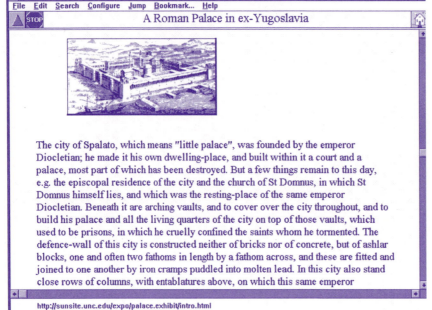

A-4d

Windows software to communicate over your modem. The software that does this is called Trumpet WinSock. This is a shareware package that was written by Peter Tattam from Tasmania. It costs $20 US to register and is easily worth it. When you tell Trumpet WinSock to connect you to your Internet provider, it will dial the appropriate telephone number and perform all of the handshaking required to establish the connection. It can also be set up to enter your password for you, such that, when it has completed its obeisances and groveling, you'll be ready to deal with the Net.

Actually, this is almost true. While it's not explicitly documented anywhere, you must remember to hit the Esc key on your keyboard once Trumpet WinSock has completed a connection.

Setting up Trumpet WinSock is a pig of no small dimensions. It will require that you enter a number of mysterious Internet addresses into its setup dialog and modify its "script" file—it's list of commands that directs the process of logging you into the remote computer of your Internet provider. Your Internet provider should be able to help you with this. They might even provide you with a predefined script. While a bit of an ordeal, this is something that you need to do only once.

Once you have Trumpet WinSock working properly, you can run any of a number of Windows applications to handle various functions of the Internet. They'll communicate through Trumpet WinSock. There are Windows applications to read your mail, interface with Usenet newsgroups, do FTP transfers, perform Archie searches, and browse Gopher and the World Wide Web. I'll deal with some of these applications here, but the really attractive aspect of assembling your own suite of software to connect to the Net is that you can select tools that you can get along with. There are multiple packages available to handle many of these functions, and you're free to choose among them.

As I write this, many of these applications are fairly new; some are still being released as betas. They're all available as shareware or as public domain software over the Internet. Some specific sites at which they can be obtained will be listed later in this section.

One of the advantages to using multiple Windows applications to access various functions over the Internet is that it's possible to have multiple things being done at once, rather than having to wait for one task to be completed before starting another. For example, I frequently set Archie to work finding things, then go browse the newsgroups until something turns up.

The following, then, is the software I run under Windows to work with the Internet.

Gopher

Gopher can be handled using a program called Windows Gopher from the Computer Services Centre of the University of Hong Kong. This appears to be a public domain entity, as no shareware beg notices are to be found in it. While not particularly flashy—and claiming to be still "under development"—Windows Gopher is an excellent, stable Gopher client. It will present Gopher pages in pretty much the format that you'd expect them to be in, except that they'll live in a window. You can move around by double clicking on the items you're interested in.

By default, Windows Gopher wants to start with the Gopher server at the University of Hong Kong. You can deal with this in several ways. Simply selecting the Other Gophers and Information Servers item from the main page of the University of Hong Kong Gopher server will get you to the main page of the University of Minnesota Gopher, which is typically where most Gopher users will want to begin. Alternately, you can configure the software to start up by looking for any Gopher server that you like. The usual place to start is *gopher.micro.umn.edu*, the main Gopher at the University of Minnesota.

Figure A-5 illustrates Windows Gopher at work.

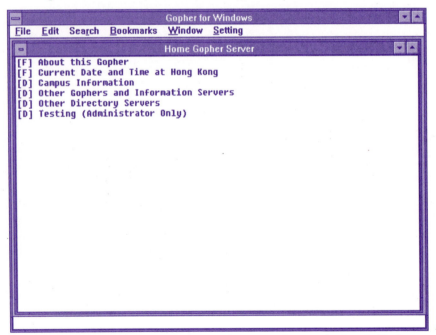

A-5

It's interesting to compare Windows Gopher with the Cello Internet browser that I'll look at in a moment. The two applications have analogous functions, and Cello can also be used as a Gopher client. The former is nowhere near as flashy. It doesn't sprout icons or graphics under any circumstances, and all its controls are standard gray

Windows objects; however, it's fast and dead easy to use. Cello, for all its attractive graphics and intuitive operation, is something of a cow.

Anonymous FTP

I handle anonymous FTP transfers with an application called WinFTP. This is another package that has been released into the public domain with no shareware fees attached. It's simple, pretty stable, and only slightly funky. It's illustrated in Fig. A-6.

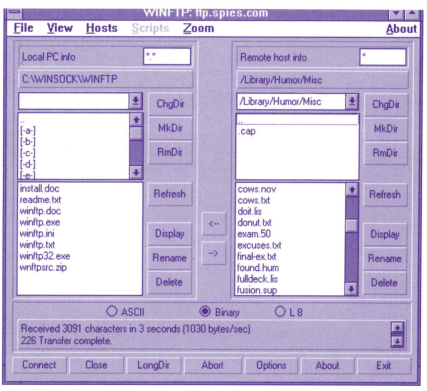

A-6

The basic structure of WinFTP is fairly easy to understand. The left side of its window is your computer and the right side is the computer of the FTP server that you've logged into by clicking on the Connect button at the bottom of the window, you can log into a new FTP server. The two arrow buttons between these virtual machines are for moving files around. Select a file on the remote FTP and click on the left arrow to have it moved to your computer.

By default, double clicking on a remote file will cause it to be sent to your machine and viewed. What in fact happens is that the file will be passed to one of a number of predetermined applications based on its type. If you double click on a text file, it will be passed to Windows Notepad. This doesn't prove to work very well in some cases, as the

Windows Notepad doesn't display Unix-style text files properly. This is, admittedly, a minor hiccup.

In fairness, WinFTP is not without its rough edges, but it's a surprisingly workable little tool for chasing after files. It will also remember the FTP sites you've visited through its auspices, allowing you to select them from a list in its Connect dialog should you want to return to them at a later date.

Archie

The Archie function is invaluable for finding things on the Internet. For example, you might use Archie to locate the files that contain the applications being discussed in this section if you find you can't get access to the FTP sites listed here. There's something of a problem with this if you lack Archie itself, of course; using Archie to find Archie is somewhat tricky.

The Archie client that I use is called WSARCHIE, which was written by David Woakes. It appears to be in the public domain as of this writing. The copy I use has a version number of 0.6, which was released on July 12, 1994. Despite this, it's pretty stable. It's illustrated in Fig. A-7.

A-7

The WSARCHIE application is extremely simple to use. Type the text string that you'd like to search for into the "Search For" field.

Select an Archie server to run the search with from the Archie Server combo box. Click on Search and go for a Coke. Actually, better than all that caffeine and phosphoric acid, just run another Windows application and let WSARCHIE get on with things in the background. Check it periodically to see what it has turned up.

Mail

There are several mail readers available, but the one that I've settled on is PC Eudora by Qualcomm, which was written by Jeff Beckley and Jeff Gehlhaar. It's a workable balance between a mail reader that just reads mail and one that also makes toast, locates invisible collapsed pulsars, and calculates the exact trajectory for shooting geese such that the decapitated birds will fall squarely on the head of a passing pedestrian. Eudora is illustrated in Fig. A-8.

A-8

The first time that you run Eudora, it will fetch all of your pending mail and store it on your hard drive in a file called IN.MBX. Subsequent invocations of Eudora will cause it to fetch any new mail that accrues. It will also keep track of outgoing mail, allow you to compose replies as you read, and so on.

Unlike mail readers built into an online text-based interface, Eudora will allow you to look at your mail offline. It has flexible options for managing mail; composing, routing, and redirecting mail can be handled with simple menu items.

World Wide Web

The Cello Internet browser was created by the Legal Information Institute. It appears to be a public domain entity as of this writing. It can be used to access Internet resources other than World Wide Web; you can get to Gopher servers, FTPs, and so on through it.

Unlike many of the Windows Internet applications that I've discussed thus far, Cello really takes advantage of the facilities of Windows. It's exceedingly graphic. It uses clickable icons to indicate options as you work through its pages. It can download and display the GIF images included with Mosaic documents. It's breathtakingly easy to work with. Be warned, however—especially if you have it fetch images for every page that includes them—Cello is often pretty slow over a dial-up connection.

Figure A-4, which was shown earlier in this appendix, illustrates some views of Cello at work.

Because of its graphic nature, Cello is somewhat more demanding of hardware than the other software that's been discussed in this section. You'll need a fast modem to make the delays between pages workable; 14,400 baud is a beginning, and 38,400 wouldn't go to waste. A Windows screen driver capable of at least 256 colors is pretty well essential if you'd like the graphics in Mosaic pages to look recognizable.

In theory, Cello will replace a number of other applications that are discussed in this section. It makes a workable Gopher browser, for example. In practice, you'll probably find that this isn't the case. After you've been dazzled by the graphics and general user friendliness of Cello for a while, you might prefer the speed and stripped down convenience of something like Windows Gopher.

Newsgroups

There are several news readers available to run under Windows, but the most flexible of the lot is Trumpet, which was written by the author of Trumpet WinSock. Flexible and easy to work with, it will allow you to subscribe to your favorite newsgroups and browse their postings. It's illustrated in Figures A-9a through A-9c.

One of the singular aspects of Trumpet is that, while it's fairly dripping with features, you can ignore most of them as you first get started using it. The only thing that you really need to know is how to bring up the Subscribe dialog. Beyond this, everything is handled by clicking on the items that you want to browse; it's all pretty intuitive.

The Subscribe dialog of Trumpet is particularly easy to work with; it will search for newsgroup names with selected text strings in them, making it easy to locate the group that you're interested in.

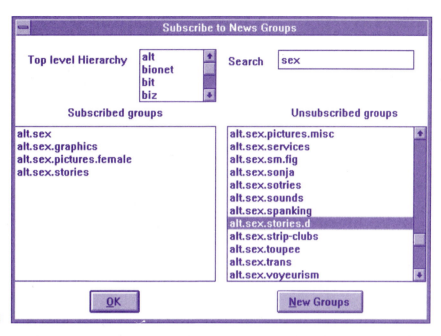

A-9a

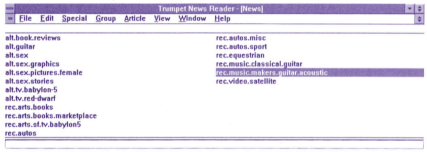

A-9b

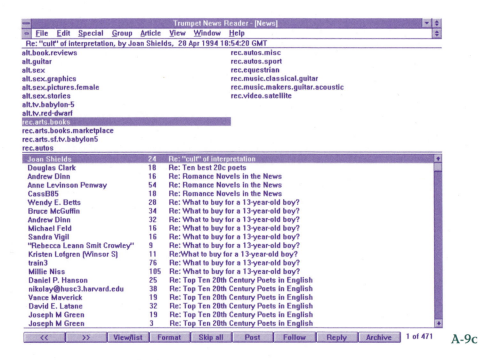

A-9c

Where to find the software

The following are FTP sites that offered the software that was discussed in this section at the time of this writing. There are certainly many others. Note that the file names listed here might well have changed by the time that you read this; newer versions of some of these applications will probably have been released, and the version numbers in the file names will as such have increased.

The PC Eudora application is distributed as a self-extracting EXE archive. The remaining files are ZIP archives.

- PC Eudora—EUDORA14.EXE—
  gatekeeper.dec.com:/micro/msdos/win3/winsock/eudora14.exe
- Cello—CELLO.ZIP—
  gatekeeper.dec.com:/micro/msdos/win3/winsock/cello.zip
- Trumpet—WTWSK10A.ZIP—
  tasman.cc.utas.edu.au:/pc/trumpet/wintrump/wtwsk10a.zip
- Trumpet WinSock—TWSK10A.ZIP—
  tasman.cc.utas.edu.au:/pc/trumpet/wintrump/twsk10a.zip
- WSArchie—WSARCH06.ZIP—
  monu6.cc.monash.edu.au:/pub/win3/winsock/wsarch06.zip
- WinFTP—WINFTP.ZIP—
  monu6.cc.monash.edu.au:/pub/win3/winsock/winftp.zip
- WGopher—WGOPHER.ZIP—
  monu6.cc.monash.edu.au:/pub/win3/winsock/wgopher.zip

If you do decide to keep those applications that are distributed as shareware, please be sure to register them.

Some Internet providers

The following is a somewhat abbreviated list of independent Internet access providers. These companies offer widely varying services and equally widely varying prices. Some of them offer access through various sorts of long distance calling plans for users outside of their local calling areas. As the facilities of these services are constantly changing, you should contact the one nearest you for complete information. In the list, a "+" stands for the international access code.

You can download a more detailed list of Internet providers as *pdial* from the FTP site at *ftp.netcom.com:/pub/info-deli/public-access/*.

a2i communications
Modem: 408-293-9010 (v.32, v.32 bis)
   or 408-293-9020 (PEP) 'guest'
Phone: 408-293-8078 voice mail

RainDrop Laboratories
Modem: 503-293-1772 (2400)
   503-293-2059 (v.32, v.32 bis) 'apply'

Anomaly—Rhode Island's Gateway To The Internet
Modem: 401-331-3706 (v.32)
   or 401-455-0347 (PEP)
Phone: 401-273-4669

Ariadne - Greek Academic and Research Network
Modem: +301 65-48-800 (1200-9600 bps)
Phone: +301 65-13-392
Fax: +301 6532910

Communications Accessibles Montreal
Modem: 514-281-5601 (v.32 bis, HST)
   514-738-3664 (PEP), 514-923-2103
   (ZyXeL 19.2K) 514-466-0592 (v.32)
Phone: 514-923-2102

CAPCON Library Network
Modem: contact for number
Phone: 202-331-5771
Fax: 202-797-7719

Cooperative Library Agency for Systems and Services
Modem: contact for number
Phone: 800-488-4559
Fax: 408-453-5379

Community News Service
Modem: 719-520-1700 id 'new', passwd 'newuser'
Phone: 719-579-9120

CONCERT-CONNECT
Modem: contact for number
Phone: 919-248-1999

connect.com.au pty ltd
Modem: contact for number
Phone: +61 3 5282239
Fax: +61 3 5285887

CTS Network Services (CTSNET)
Modem: 619-593-6400 HST,
   619-593-7300 V.32bis,
   619-593-9500 PEP 'help'
Phone: 619-593-9597
Fax: 619-444-9247

CR Laboratories Dialup Internet Access
Modem: 415-389-UNIX
Phone: 415-381-2800

Colorado SuperNet, Inc.
Modem: contact for number
Phone: 303-273-3471
Fax: 303-273-3475

The Cyberspace Station
Modem: 619-634-1376 'guest'
Phone: n/a

Demon Internet Systems (DIS)
Modem: +44 (0)81 343 4848
Phone: +44 (0)81 349 0063

DIAL n' CERF or DIAL n' CERF AYC
Modem: contact for number
Phone: 800-876-2373 or 619-455-3900

DIAL n' CERF USA
Modem: contact for number
Phone: 800-876-2373 or 619-455-3900

The Direct Connection
Modem: +44 (0)81 317 2222
Phone: +44 (0)81 317 0100
Fax: +44 (0)81 317 0100

Eskimo North
Modem: 206-367-3837 300-2400 bps,
   206-362-6731 for 9600/14.4k,
   206-742-1150 World Blazer
Phone: 206-367-7457

Express Access—Online Communications Service
Modem: 301-220-0462, 410-766-1855,
   908-937-9481 'new'
Phone: 800-546-2010, 301-220-2020

'genesis', MCSNet
Modem: (312) 248-0900 V.32, 0970 V.32bis,
   6295 (PEP), follow prompts
Phone: (312) 248-UNIX

Grebyn Corporation
Modem: 703-281-7997, 'apply'
Phone: 703-281-2194

Halcyon
Modem: 206-382-6245 'new', 8N1
Phone: 206-955-1050

Institute for Global Communications/IGC Networks (PeaceNet, EcoNet, ConflictNet, LaborNet, HomeoNet)
Modem: 415-322-0284 (N-8-1), 'new'
Phone: 415-442-0220

HoloNet
Modem: 510-704-1058
Phone: 510-704-0160

UK PC User Group
Modem: +44 (0)81 863 6646
Phone: +44 (0)81 863 6646

The IDS World Network
Modem: 401-884-9002, 401-785-1067
Phone: 401-884-7856

The John von Neumann Computer Network—Tiger Mail & Dialin' Terminal
Modem: contact for number
Phone: 800-35-TIGER, 609-258-2400

The John von Neumann Computer Network—Dialin' Tiger
Modem: contact for number
Phone: 800-35-TIGER, 609-258-2400

Maestro
Modem: (212) 240-9700 'newuser'
Phone: 212-240-9600

Texas Metronet
Modem: 214-705-2902 9600bps,
  214-705-2917 2400bps, 'info/info' or
  'signup/signup' 'signup/signup'
Phone: 214-401-2800
Fax: 214-401-2802 (8am-5pm CST weekdays)

Merit Network, Inc.—MichNet project
Modem: contact for number
Phone: 313-764-9430

MindVOX
Modem: 212-989-4141 'mindvox' 'guest'
Phone: 212-989-2418

The Portal System
Modem: 408-973-8091 high-speed,
  408-725-0561 2400bps; 'info'
Phone: 408-973-9111

PREPnet
Modem: contact for numbers
Phone: 412-268-7870
Fax: 412-268-7875

PUCnet Computer Connections
Modem: 403-484-5640 (v.32 bis) 'guest'
Phone: 403-448-1901
Fax: 403-484-7103

NeoSoft's Sugar Land Unix
Modem: 713-684-5900
Phone: 713-438-4964

Telerama Public Access Internet
Modem: 412-481-5302 'new' (2400)
Phone: 412-481-3505

The Meta Network
Modem: contact for numbers
Phone: 703-243-6622

UUnorth
Modem: contact for numbers
Phone: 416-225-8649
Fax: 416-225-0525

Vnet Internet Access, Inc.
Modem: 704-347-8839 'new'
Phone: 704-374-0779

The Whole Earth 'Lectronic Link
Modem: 415-332-6106 'newuser'
Phone: 415-332-4335

APK-Public Access UNI*Site
Modem: 216-481-9436 (2400),
  216-481-9425 (V.32bis, SuperPEP)
Phone: 216-481-9428

The World
Modem: 617-739-9753 'new'
Phone: 617-739-0202

Wyvern Technologies, Inc.
Modem: (804) 627-1828 Norfolk,
  (804) 886-0662 (Peninsula)
Phone: 804-622-4289
Fax: 804-622-7158

CompuServe*

CompuServe is unique among the large dial-up networks with Internet access in that not only can the Internet be accessed from CompuServe—at least to some extent—but CompuServe can also be accessed from the Internet. The latter is handled by Telnet to the address *compuserve.com*. This will present you with the same prompts that would be displayed upon logging directly into CompuServe with a modem.

You must have a valid CompuServe account to get past the login prompts.

Telnet to CompuServe is useful if you're using the Net and suddenly want to check your CompuServe mail, for example. It's also handy if you have local access to the Internet but long distance access to CompuServe. However, keep in mind that, if you're paying for Internet access by the hour, you'll be paying both the connect charges from your Internet provider and those from CompuServe if you access CompuServe over the Net.

As of this writing, CompuServe only provides very limited access to the Internet. Rumbles from Ohio suggest that this will change to some extent in the immediate future, if it has not already done so by the time you read this.

The most elemental Internet function that CompuServe provides is electronic mail. It has had a mail gateway going since 1989, although the syntax for moving mail over it is a bit daunting. My CompuServe account number is 70451,2734, so sending mail to me on CompuServe from the Internet would require that it be sent to:

70451.2734@compuserve.com

You can also send mail from CompuServe to users of the Internet. Here's how I'd address a message to myself on the Internet if I was using the CompuServe mail system:

INTERNET:alchemy@accesspt.north.net

As I write this, CompuServe is developing a graphical-user-interface-based Usenet newsgroup reader. This is reportedly pretty sophisticated, providing a mouse-driven interface to Usenet.

There are a number of ways that you can use the mail facilities of CompuServe's Internet gateway to access many popular Internet facilities, such as Archie and FTP. These are by no means convenient and, in comparison with some of the other approaches to using the facilities of the Internet, are barely workable. You can do Archie searches from within CompuServe by sending mail to an Archie server. Here's a list of popular ones:

- archie.rutgers.edu
- ans.net
- archie.sura.net

* See publisher's note on page 291.

- archie.unl.edu
- archie.mcgill.ca
- archie.au
- archie.funet.fi
- archie.doc.ic.ac.uk

For example, you might address a message to INTERNET:*archie.rutgers.edu*. The body of the request message can contain the following commands, among others:

- path—This should be your Internet mail address through CompuServe (for example, 70451,2734@compuserve.com).
- help—This will cause the current set of instructions for using an Archie server through CompuServe to be sent to you.
- prog—A search of the Archie database will performed with each expression after this command. Any matches that are found will be returned to you as electronic mail. See the help page for more information about forming complex expressions. The searches are case sensitive.

The process of accessing FTP sites through CompuServe mail is somewhat beyond the scope of this appendix. There's a complete discussion of it to be found in the file FTPLIB.ZIP in library six of GO INETFORUM on CompuServe.

At present, CompuServe users have very limited workable access to the Internet. This situation is changing gradually, and CompuServe's approach to adding Internet access seems to be measured and well thought out. However, keep in mind that it might never offer you the same level of access to the Net that a dedicated Internet provider can today, and it will probably always cost a great deal more to use. As I write this, 9600-baud CompuServe access costs $9.60 US per hour, plus a communication surcharge, plus whatever long distance charges you have to incur if you don't have a locally available CompuServe access number.

You can contact CompuServe at 1-800-621-1253 or 1-614-529-1349.

America Online

The Internet access provided by America Online is midway between that of CompuServe and the facilities of Delphi, which will be discussed in a moment. Having said this, Delphi's user interface is unworkably awkward, while the menu-driven comfort of America Online will make it accessible to anyone with a mouse and two or more working brain cells. If you must access the Net through one of the large dial-up networks, rather than through an independent Internet provider, there's a lot to be said for America Online.

There are also a few things to be said against it, however. The basic connect charges for America Online are $3.50 US per hour as of this writing, which makes it more expensive than most independent access providers but cheaper than, say, CompuServe, If you're outside the continental United States, America Online will add $12 US an hour to this, making it one of the most expensive ways to access the Net short of buying your own phone company.

The second catch in using America Online to access the Net is that 9600-baud connections to America Online are only just becoming available in some areas and are not available at all in others. This will make some activities on the Internet uncomfortably slow and others, such as downloading large graphics, effectively impractical.

Unlike the other large dial-up services that are discussed in this appendix, America Online uses a dedicated user interface package exclusively to provide access to its system. This means that you'll never encounter a command-line prompt. There are no commands or key words to remember. Online help is available at all times. You can click your way through any service you like. Those elements of the Internet that are provided by America Online are about as easy to deal with as one could imagine.

This section will illustrate the Windows version of the America Online software. It's also available for DOS and Macintosh platforms.

To access the Internet with America Online, sign onto the system with the America Online software and hit Ctrl–K. Type INTERNET in the prompt dialog, as shown in Fig. A-10.

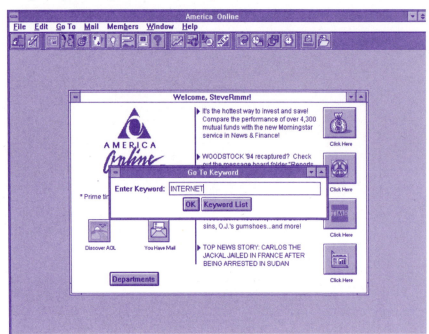

A-10

The main Internet dialog is shown in Fig. A-11. This illustrates the facilities of the America Online Internet gateway at the moment. It will provide you with access to Internet e-mail, Usenet newsgroups, Gopher, and mailing lists. Notably absent are things like anonymous FTP transfers, the World Wide Web, Finger, and Telnet. If you click on the button marked Expert Connection, a dialog will appear informing you that some of these facilities are planned for the future.

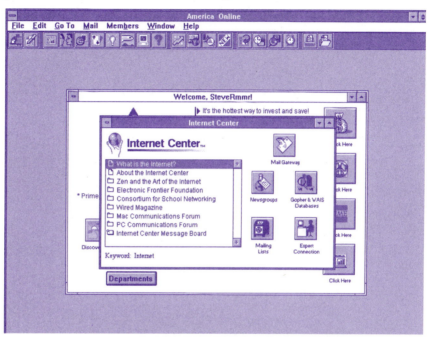

A-11

The Usenet interface of America Online is potentially its most contentious, and I was surprised to find that it doesn't restrict one's access to newsgroups as much as might be expected. For example, it won't attempt to prevent you from subscribing to *alt.aol-sucks*, a newsgroup devoted to flaming America Online, or to extreme groups like *alt.sex.bondage*. It does have a fairly lengthy initial text file warning new Internet users that some of the language of Usenet might be a bit harsher than that which they've been used to in the warm, safe confines of America Online itself. I'm told that much of what appears in Usenet postings would be censored if it were to be mailed between America Online users.

The main Newsgroups dialog of America Online will allow you to subscribe to any newsgroups that you like. It has search facilities to locate newsgroups; these proved to be workable but less than ideally intuitive in many cases. A printed list of newsgroups would probably be an asset.

Figures A-12a through A-12d illustrate the process of subscribing to a newsgroup, selecting a message and reading it. I feel moved to add that this all happened without the appearance of a dialog warning me that the dipstick of my conscience must surely be coming up practically dry as a result of what I was about to perpetrate.

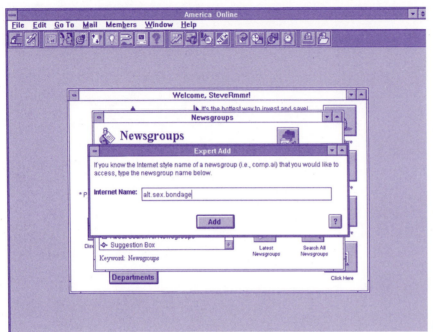

A-12a

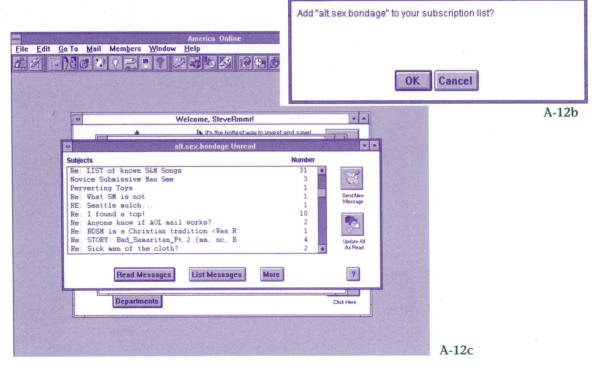

A-12b

A-12c

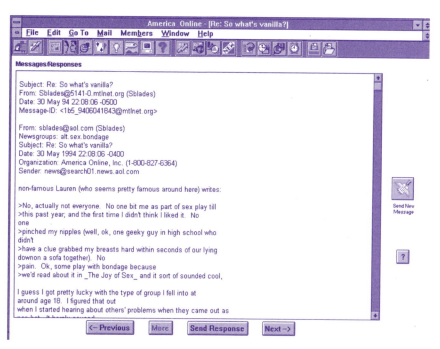

A-12d

The Internet e-mail facilities that are provided by America Online are easy to master and about what you'd expect. You can compose electronic mail messages using a convenient Windows-style editor and maintain an address book of frequently used Internet addresses. The mail editor looks like Fig. A-13.

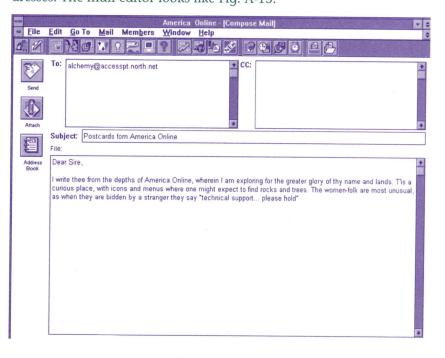

A-13

The Gopher access provided by America Online is engagingly cute—little furry rodent icons appear in the predictable locations. Its classifications of the list of Gopher servers is somewhat arbitrary, and I found it more difficult to locate specific Gophers using America Online than would be the case for simpler, less-graphic Gopher access packages. Figures A-14a through A-14d illustrate the sequence of dialogs involved in accessing a Gopher.

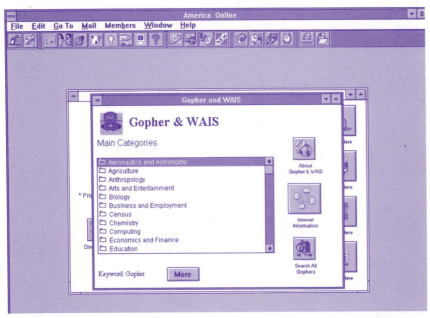

A-14a

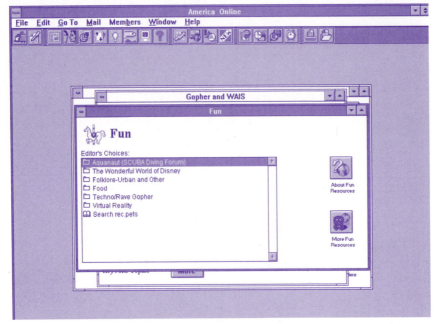

A-14b

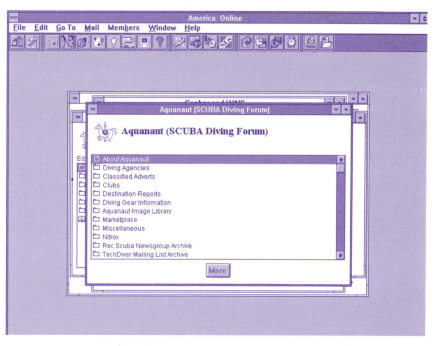

A-14c

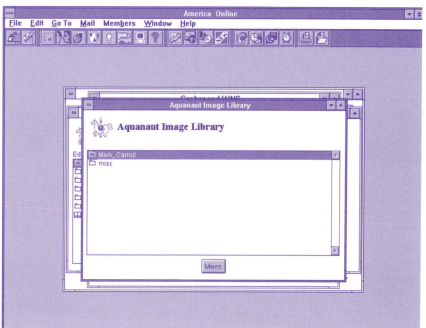

A-14d

If you're currently a member of America Online, the Internet services that it provides will serve as a comfortable introduction to the facilities of the Net. Few things could be easier to use, and unlike in the real world of the Internet, America Online provides technical support if you encounter something that you don't understand.

The somewhat high cost of America Online, coupled with relatively slow access to its Internet facilities, will probably make this a less than ideal path for serious Internet access. The potential for serious Net surfing and other forms of cyberspace exploration have largely been filtered out of America Online in the interest of user friendliness. However, if all the peculiar terms and discussion of access methods surrounding the Internet have left you feeling like you've been beamed up by aliens, you'll probably find America Online a comfortable place to spend a few hours.

You can order the free America Online software by calling 1-800-827-6364.

Delphi

The Delphi online service is presumably named after the Greek oracle of Apollo at Delphi. The oracle was said to be the center of the earth in classical times. It was probably destroyed in 396 A.D. by invading Goths.

The usual method for divination at the Delphic oracle was for the Pythia, young priestesses in a state of ecstasy, to moan whatever was on their minds at the time and have the results translated by the oracle's priests. While this probably seems a bit unreliable—and to be sure, the oracle at Delphi did provide some singularly bad advice from time to time—it's probably no less flaky than weather forecasting or Time/CNN polls.

I'm pretty certain there are no horny young priestesses at Delphi in Boston.

The Delphi service offers many of the same things that turn up on CompuServe, albeit on a much smaller scale. Clearly, someone decided to bolt Internet access onto it recently, and as such for a slight additional charge, you can have the basic Net resources that are discussed in this book. However, while Delphi does permit you access to the Net, it does so in a form that will probably keep you from doing much with it.

To begin with, Delphi isn't cheap. It will cost you something approaching $2 US per hour for connect time, depending on which billing plan you choose. This wouldn't be too bad, except that Delphi insists on billing you in blocks, that is, making you pay for a fixed number of hours per month whether you actually use them or not. If you pay for 20 hours but only use 10, the effective cost per hour will have doubled. There's a $3 US per month surcharge for Internet access, with a 10MB per month limit on the amount of data you can move through Delphi's Internet gateway. While this might seem like a lot of information, it's not difficult to exceed it if you'll be making extensive use of the Net.

Unless you're local to Delphi's offices in Boston, you'll also be confronted with an additional surcharge for connect time. This will vary enormously depending on which long distance system you use to access Delphi; it was $9 US an hour for Tymnet in my case.

The Delphi Internet interface is singularly primitive. Everything's handled by text menus. Commands must be typed in many cases, rather than moving a cursor around your screen and hitting Enter. Working through newsgroups is particularly tedious. While clearly designed to be operable with absolutely any terminal hardware on the planet—you won't even need terminal emulation to interact with the Net through Delphi, as there's no cursor positioning required—Delphi's constantly recurring menus are very time-consuming.

Here's what's involved in browsing a newsgroup. To begin with, this is the main menu of the Delphi Internet interface:

About the Internet	FTP-File Transfer Protocol
Conference	Gopher
Databases (Files)	IRC-Internet Relay Chat
EMail	Telnet
Forum (Messages)	Utilities (finger, traceroute, ping)
Guides (Books)	Usenet Newsgroups
Register/Cancel	
Who's Here	Help
Workspace	Exit

Internet SIG>Enter your selection: USENET

Having typed USENET at the prompt, the following menu appeared:

USENET Menu:
About Usenet Discussion Groups
Usenet (Delphi Newsreader)
NN Newsreader (Usenet)
Instructions for the NN Newsreader
Exit
USENET>Enter your selection: USENET

Having typed USENET again, the system seemed convinced that I did actually want to look at a newsgroup. Here is the first of three pages of the main menu for the Usenet interface:

Type HELP for a list of commands
Usenet Discussion Groups
Page 1 of 3
  1 PERSONAL FAVORITES   Menu
  2 Access Any Newsgroup (by typing its name)   Usenet

```
 3  DELPHI Newsreader Help                                    Text
 4  READ BEFORE POSTING TO ANY NEWSGROUP!!!!                  Text
 5  New User Topics and FAQS (NEW USERS, START HERE!)         Menu
 6  How to Create Signature, edit Personal Favorites          Text
 7  How to Create New Newsgroups (FAQs)                       Menu
 8  Usenet FAQs (Frequently Asked Questions files)            Menu
 9  Usenet by gopher (works better in gopher GRAB BAG menu)   Menu
10  DELPHI Command Summary                                    Menu
11                                                            Text
12       ==============NEWSGROUP LISTS ============           Text
13  Search for (but not connect to) Newsgroups, Mailing Lists Menu
14  Newsgroup Lists (Delphi lists: 8/03/94, others: 08/01/94) Menu
15                                                            Text
16       ============SELECTED NEWSGROUPS==========            Text
17  Best of Internet—DON'T POST!See FAQ (alt.best.of.internet) Usenet
18  Comet Shoemaker-Levy 9 (alt.sl9)                          Usenet
19  Commercial Online Services (alt.online-service)           Usenet
Enter Item Number, MORE, ?, or EXIT: 2
Please enter a Usenet discussion topic, such as alt.online-service.
Topic: rec.arts.books
```

I entered *rec.arts.books*. To its credit, Delphi doesn't seem to be particularly censorious about the newsgroups it will carry. You can subscribe to *alt.sex.bondage* if you like. Delphi responded with:

```
1958 messages have been posted in the last 14 days; You've read none of
them.
Select which messages: Unread, All, Date or ?> [unread] date
Show messages posted in last ___ days: [5] rec.arts.books
Page 1 of 11 [216 messages in 207 discussion threads]
  1  rec.arts.BOOKS !!!!!!!!!!!!!!!!!!!!!!!!!!!!!!
  2  Asimov's _Foundation_ (11 msgs)
  3  Help Compile Palindrome List (13 msgs)
  4  Top Ten 20th Century Poets in English (33 msgs)
  5  Top Ten 20th Century Poems in English (8 msgs)
  6  Henry Rollins (8 msgs)
  7  Winterson's novels - (2 msgs)
  8  Fave Sci Fi books? (10 msgs)
  9  STANISLAW LEM (19 msgs)
 10  Jurgen (8 msgs)
 11  America's Greates Living Writer (2 msgs)
 12  Latin Platitudes (2 msgs)
 13  Lonesome Dove (3 msgs)
 14  Please suggest a book - Go ahead, make my day. (10 msgs)
 15  New Flashman Novel (3 msgs)
 16  Where to find old magazines?
 17  New Reviews at IBIC WWW Server (Barnes, McBain, Atkinson)
 18  Iris Murdoch's _The Message to the Planet_ (5 msgs)
 19  Asimov's _Foundation_READ/NEXT
```

Typing a number from the list called up the posting in question. Following up on a posting was particularly clumsy.

Delphi does offer a reasonably full range of Internet resources, including newsgroups, electronic mail, Gopher, and so on. Missing are things like the World Wide Web, which really couldn't be run using Delphi's limited interface. It has complete electronic mail facilities, although you'll have to know how to work them if you want to send mail between Delphi and the Net. To send mail from Delphi to an Internet user, you would address the mail like this:

    internet"alchemy@accesspt.north.net"

The bit in the quote marks is my Internet mail address. To send mail from the Internet to someone using Delphi, you would address the mail to:

    STEVERIMMER@delphi.com

The name before the @ symbol is the Delphi "user name" of the person to whom you want to send mail. I should note that I didn't keep my account at Delphi, and as such this user name isn't valid.

Should you currently be a member of Delphi, the Delphi Internet facilities might serve as a worthwhile way to taste the Net for a while. You could use them to download the list of independent Internet providers discussed earlier in this section, for example. If you start finding the Net pretty claustrophobic, however, the problem is not in the Internet itself. It's in Delphi.

If you're looking for a way to access the Internet, Delphi should probably be somewhere near the bottom of your list of options. It's workable, but gray and lifeless. As the oracle at Delphi is said to have uttered:

    Go, tell the king—the carven hall is felled,
    Apollo has no cell, prophetic bay
    Nor talking spring, the cadenced well is stilled.

You can contact Delphi by voice at 1-800-695-4005 or 1-617-491-3393. You can sign up for Delphi online by calling 1-800-695-4002. Note that when you call Delphi itself with a modem, you must type a lower case "o" and wait for five seconds, something the introductory information isn't wont to tell you.

Publisher's note:

CompuServe recently announced that its members can now access "thousands" of Usenet newsgroups. These newsgroups can be accessed either through ASCII menus (via terminal emulation mode, which all major communications programs support) or through the CompuServe Information Manager (CIM) graphical user interface software, available from CompuServe, software retailers, or some bookstores. Newsgroups are part of CompuServe's extended services, so there's an additional fee to access them. For the latest information on CompuServe's Internet offerings, CompuServe members should key in GO INETFORUM.

Address index

e-mail
President@Whitehouse.Gov, 78

Finger
adam@mtv.com, 96-97

copy@oddjob.uchicago.edu, 21, 124-126

hotlist@mtv.com, 96-97

taylor@netcom.com, 146

FTP
bigbang-ether.berkeley.edu:/ftp/pub/Library/Monty_Python, 174

casbah.acns.nwu.edu:/pub/acoustic-guitar, 23-24

cathouse.org:/pub/cathouse/, 15, 66

colonsay.dcs.ed.ac.uk:/pub/jhb/silly/cokemachine, 87-89

cs.dartmouth.edu:/pub/bagpipes, 44

cs.dartmouth.edu:/pub/lute/, 165-167

csn.org:/pub/misc/glossary.acronyms, 25-26

dixie.aiss.uiuc.edu:/pub/cathouse/humor/british.humor, 62

dixie.aiss.uiuc.edu:/pub/cathouse/humor/murphys.laws/, 178

dixie.aiss.uiuc.edu:/pub/cathouse/humor/politcally.correct, 197-198

dixie.aiss.uiuc.edu:/pub/cathouse/humor/sex/a.girls.guide.to.condoms, 93

f.ms.uky.edu:/pub3/mailing.lists/japan/japanno.Z, 149

f.ms.uky.edu:/pub3/mailing.lists/japan/japanyes.reply.Z, 149

f.ms.uky.edu:/pub3/mailing.lists/japan/japanyes.Z, 149

****ftp.eff.org:/pub/EFF*, 113-115

ftp.loc.gov:/pub/exhibit.images/deadsea.scrolls.exhibit, 99-100

ftp.neosoft.com:/pub/rec.food.recipes/site, 133

ftp.netcom.com:/pub/Guides/, 146

ftp.netcom.com:/pub/info-deli/public-access/, 277

ftp.netcom.com:/pub/jvasquez/dirty.limericks, 163-164

ftp.nevada.edu:/pub/guitar, 23-24

ftp.quartz.rutgers.edu:/pub/humor/limericks, 163-164

ftp.spies.com, 18

ftp.spies.com:/Library/, 59-61

ftp.spies.com:/Library/Article/Aero/airport.lis, 26

ftp.spies.com:/Library/Article/Food/newcoke.txt, 83-85

ftp.spies.com:/Library/Article/Language/esperant.eng, 123

ftp.spies.com:/Library/Article/Language/grammar.jap, 149

ftp.spies.com:/Library/Article/Sex/massage.txt, 233

ftp.spies.com:/Library/Documents/arcana.doc, 35-36

ftp.spies.com:/Library/Fringe/Conspiry/, 93

ftp.spies.com:/Library/Fringe/Pharm/, 109-110

ftp.spies.com:/Library/Fringe/Ufo, 132

ftp.spies.com:/Library/Music/Disc, 105

ftp.spies.com:/Library/Untech/tbbom13.txt, 51

ftp.spies.com:/Library/Untech/alcohol.mak, 29

ftp.std.com:/obi/Ambrose.Bierce/
The.Devils.Dictionary.Z, 103-104

ftp.std.com:/obi/Tennyson, 237-238

ftp.sunet.se:/pub/music/lyrics, 225

ftp.tcp.com:/pub/anime/Images,
33-34

ftp.uu.net:/doc/literary/obi/
Anglo-Saxon, 31-33

ftp.uu.net:/doc/literary/obi/Star.Trek.
Parodies, 228

ftp.uu.net:/doc/literary/obi/Star.Trek.
Stories, 228

ftp.uu.net:/networking/news/config/,
9

ftp.uwp.edu, 15

ftp.uwp.edu:/pub/music/lyrics, 225

gatekeeper.dec.com:/pub/recipes,
133

gdead.berkeley.edu:/pub/gdead, 136

maelstrom-ether.berkeley.edu:/ftp/
pub/Library/Monty_Python, 174

monsoon-ether.berkeley.edu:/ftp/
pub/Library/Monty_Python, 174

mthvax.cs.miami.edu:/pub/
homebrew/, 143-144

mtv.com:/pub/sleaze, 96-97

nic.funet.fi:/pub/culture/beer/,
143-144

nic.funet.fi:/pub/doc/literary/etext/
carroll, 158-159

nic.funet.fi:/pub/doc/literary/etext/
fannyhill.txt.gz, 131

nic.funet.fi:/pub/doc/occult/Wicca,
248

ocf.Berkeley.EDU:/typhoon/usr/local/
ftp/pub/Library/Recreation/, 108

quartz.rutgers.edu:/pub/computer/
fortune/, 201-204

quartz.rutgers.edu:/pub/sex/
kama.sutra, 233-234

quartz.rutgers.edu:/pub/tv+movies/
letterman, 157

ramses.cs.cornell.edu:/Clinton/, 79

ramses.cs.cornell.edu:/pub/elster/
perot/clinton.humor, 16

rtfm.mit.edu:/pub/usenet/
news.answers/cats-faq/, 69-70

rtfm.mit.edu:/pub/usenet/
news.answers/dogs-faq/, 107-108

rtfm.mit.edu:/pub/usenet/
news.answers/pets-birds-faq/, 52-53

rugcis.rug.nl:/origami/, 182-183

slopoke.mlb.semi.harris.com:/pub/
magick/magick/Crowley, 95-96

techno.staford.edu:/pub/raves, 205

toaster.ee.ubc.ca:/pub/red-dwarf,
206-208

tsunami-ether.berkeley.edu:/ftp/
pub/Library/Monty_Python, 174

ucslex.sdsu.edu:/pub/doc/etext/
japan-than-can-say-no.txt, 149

wiretap.spies.com:/Library/Article/
Food/oculis.rcp, 181-182

wiretap.spies.com:/Library/Zines/
Undiscov, 245

Gopher

Albert Einstein College of Medicine |
Internet Resources | Miscellaneous |
Search the Food Recipes Databank,
134

CNS, Inc., 162

CNS, Inc |
ENTER THE CNS GOPHER |
Entertainment | Nielsen TV ratings,
235-237

CNS, Inc |
ENTER THE CNS GOPHER |
Entertainment |
StarTrek-The Library, 228

CNS, Inc |
ENTER THE CNS GOPHER |
Entertainment |
Concerts on the Road, 91-92

cs.dartmouth.edu | Lute Files,
165-167

Dartmouth Colleg cs:dartmouth.edu
| Bagpipe Archives, 44

Electronic Frontier Foundation, 113-115

Electronic newsstand, 116

GlasNet server, 242

Gopher.micro.umn.edu, 270

Internet Wiretap Online Library | Articles | Food and Drink, 134

Internet Wiretap Online Library | Electronic Books | CIA World Factbook, 75

MTV | sleaze, 96-97

National Chung Cheung University | miscellanies | Japanese Anim Picture, 33-34

NOAA Environmental Information Services Gopher | Weather Information and Images, 247

Rutgers Quartz Text Archive (quartz.rutgers.edu) | Sex | kama.sutra, 233

University of California Berkeley, 136

University of California-SanDiego Infopath | US State Department Travel Advisories, 240

Wiretap Online Library, 20, 251-253

Wiretap Online Library | Articles | Aeronautics and Space | Airport 3-Letter Abbreviations, 21, 26

Wiretap Online Library | Articles | Language | Esperanto English Dictionary, 123

Wiretap Online Library | Articles | Sex, 119-121

Wiretap Online Library | Electronic Books at Wiretap, 59-61

Wiretap Online Library | Fringes of Reason | Gross and Disgusting | Alt.Tasteless, 234

Wiretap Online Library | Humor | Everything Else | Crude Texican Lexicon, 238

Wiretap Online Library | Questionables | How To Make Alcohol, 29

Wiretap Online Library | Questionables | :of The Big Book of Mischief v1.3, 51

Wiretap (wiretap.spies.com) | Articles | Sex | Yoni Massage How-To, 233

wiretap.spies.com:/Library/Zines/Watcher, 213-215

wiretap.spies.com | WOL | Articles | Food and Drink | LaszloNibble:TheNewCoke, 82

Yellow Silk Magazine, 119-121

mailing list address

bagpipes@cs.dartmouth.edu, 15, 44

esperanto@rand.org, 123

homebrew@hpfcmi.fc.hp.com, 143-144

lute@cs.dartmouth.edu, 165-167

New CD Releases, 89

origami-l@nstn.ns.ca, 182-183

newsgroup

alt.activism, 128-130

alt.alien.visitors, 132

alt.alt.alt.alt.alt newsgroup, 74

alt.answers, 97

alt.aol-sucks, 259

alt.archery, 37-40

alt.beer, 47-50

alt.binaries.pictures.erotica, 122

alt.binaries.pictures.erotica.blondes, 122

alt.binaries.pictures.erotica.d, 122

alt.binaries.pictures.erotica.female, 122

alt.binaries.pictures.erotica.male, 122

alt.binaries.pictures.erotica.orientals, 122

alt.bonsai, 57-59

alt.comedy.british, 62

ADDRESS INDEX

alt.cult-movies.rocky-horror, 208
alt.destroy.the.earth, 100-101
alt.devilbunnies, 9, 74, 101-102
alt.discordia, 105-106
alt.drugs, 109-110
alt.drugs.caffeine, 65
alt.evil, 126-127
alt.exotic-music, 9
alt.fan.g-gordon-liddy, 135-136
alt.fan.karla-homolka, 9
alt.fan.letterman, 157
alt.fan.q, 228
alt.feminism, 128-130
alt.flame, 8, 90-91
alt.food, 133
alt.food.cocacola, 82-85
alt.food.mcdonalds, 172-173
alt.guitar.bass, 46
alt.illuminati, 10, 145-146
alt.magick, 169-172
alt.magick.sex, 169-172
alt.music.a-capella, 9, 23
alt.music.enya, 9, 116
alt.pagan, 185-187
alt.pantyhose, 119-121
alt.pave.the.earth, 188-190
alt.peeves, 90-91
alt.personals, 190-193
alt.personals.misc, 190-193
alt.privacy.clipper, 80-82
alt.pub.coffeehouse.amethyst, 85-87
alt.radio.pirate, 196-197
alt.rave, 205
alt.religion.christian, 128-130
alt.satanism, 213-215
alt.sex, 9, 119-121
alt.sex.bestiality, 220-223

alt.sex.bestiality.barney, 220-223
alt.sex.bondage, 9, 220-223, 283
alt.sex.bondage.particle.physics, 222
alt.sex.exhibitionism, 220-223
alt.sex.fetish.fat, 222
alt.sex.fetish.feet, 222
alt.sex.fetish.orientals, 220-223
alt.sex.masturbation, 222
alt.sex.movies, 9, 220-223
alt.sex.pictures, 9, 122
alt.sex.pictures.d, 122
alt.sex.pictures.female, 122
alt.sex.pictures.male, 122-123
alt.sex.sounds, 220-223
alt.sex.spanking, 220-223
alt.sex.stories, 119-121, 220-223
alt.sex.stories.d, 220-223
alt.sex.voyeurism, 222
alt.sex.wanted, 220-223
alt.sex.watersports, 222
alt.sex.wizards, 220-223
alt.skinheads, 128-130
alt.slack, 71-73, 74
alt.spam, 226-227
alt.startrek.creative, 228
alt.tasteless, 234-235
alt.tv.babylon-5, 43, 97, 218-220
alt.tv.prisoner, 199-200
alt.tv.red-dwarf, 206-208
alt.video.laserdisc, 155-157
alt.wesley.crusher.die.die.die, 228
alt.zen, 255
alt.zima, 256-257
alt.zines, 257-258
misc.forsale, 63-64
misc.health.alternative, 30-31
rec.antiques, 9, 34-35

rec.arts.animation, 33-34
rec.arts.anime, 33-34
rec.arts.anime.info, 33-34
rec.arts.anime.marketplace, 33-34
rec.arts.anime.stories, 33-34
rec.arts.bodyart, 56-57
rec.arts.erotica, 119-121
rec.arts.movies, 175-177
rec.arts.sf.announce, 217-220
rec.arts.sf.fandom, 217-220
rec.arts.sf.marketplace, 217-220
rec.arts.sf.misc, 217-220
rec.arts.sf.movies, 217-220
rec.arts.sf.reviews, 217-220
rec.arts.sf.science, 217-220
rec.arts.sf.starwars, 217-220
rec.arts.sf.tv, 217-220
rec.arts.sf.written, 217-220
rec.arts.startrek.current, 228
rec.arts.startrek.info, 228
rec.audio, 40-41
rec.audio.high-end, 40-41
rec.autos, 65-66
rec.bicycles.marketplace, 50
rec.crafts.brewing, 143-144
rec.crafts.misc, 95
rec.crafts.winemaking, 249-250
rec.equestrian, 117-118
rec.folklore.herbs, 142-143
rec.food.cooking, 133
rec.food.drink, 133
rec.food.historic, 133
rec.food.recipes, 133
rec.food.restaurants, 133
rec.food.sourdough, 133
rec.food.veg, 133
rec.games.trivia, 243

rec.guns, 137-140
rec.heraldry, 141
rec.juggling, 153-154
rec.music.bluenote, 152
rec.music.cd, 89
rec.music.celtic, 70
rec.music.classical, 76-78
rec.music.early, 111-113
rec.music.gdead, 136
rec.music.makers.acoustic, 23-24
rec.music.makers.bass, 46
rec.music.makers.guitar, 23-24
rec.music.makers.tab, 23-24
rec.org.sca, 223-225
rec.pets.cats, 69-70
rec.pets.dogs, 107-108
rec.photo, 194-195
rec.skydiving, 154
rec.travel.air, 26-28
rec.video.satellite, 215-216
talk.bizarre, 53-55
talk.politics.guns, 137-140
talk.rumors, 209

mailing lists subscription address

bagpipes-request@cs.dartmouth.edu, 15, 44
esperanto-request@rand.org, 123
homebrew-request@hpfcmi.fc.hp.com, 143-144
listproc@mot.com, 157
lute-request@cs.dartmouth.edu, 165-167
new-releases-request@cs.uwp.edu, 89
origami-l-request@nstn.ns.ca, 182-183

Telnet sites
books.com, 59
cdconnection.com, 89
compuserve.com, 280
locis.loc.gov, 160-161

Subject index

A

a2i communications, 277
a capella music, *alt.music.a-capella*, 23
AccessPoint, 260-265, **260**, **261**, **262**, **263**, **264**, **265**
access systems for Internet, 5-6
acoustic guitar music, 23-24
  casbah.acns.nwu.edu:/pub/acoustic-guitar, 23
  ftp.nevada.edu:/pub/guitar, 23
  rec.music.makers.acoustic, 23
  rec.music.makers.guitar, 23
  rec.music.makers.tab, 23
acronyms, 25-26
adult content (*see* erotica)
AIDS-WAR.TXT, Conspiracies FTP site, 94
airlines, 26-28
  ftp.spies.com:/Library/Article/Aero/airport.lis, 26
  rec.travel.air, 26-28
  Wiretap Online Library ¦ Articles ¦ Aeronautics & Space ¦ Airport 3-Letter Abbreviations, 26
Alchemy Mindworks, 1, 22, 265
alcohol making, 29-30
  ftp.spies.com:/Library/Untech/alcohol.mak, 29
  Wiretap Online Library ¦ Questionables ¦ How To Make Alcohol, 29
alt newsgroups, 8
Altan, musical group, 70
alternative medicine, *misc.health.alternative*, 30-31
America Online, 97, 259, 281-288, **282**, **283**, **284**, **285**, **286**, **287**
Anomaly, 277
anonymous FTP (*see* FTP sites)
anarchy
  Big Book of Mischief, 51
  extremists and activists, 128-130
  guns, 137-140
Anderson, Ian, 24
Anglo-Saxon literature, 31-33
  ftp.uu.net:/doc/literary/obi/Anglo-Saxon, 31-33

animals
  birds, 52-53
  cats, 69-70
  dogs, 107-108
  equestrians, 117-118
animation, 33-34
  ftp.tcp.com:/pub/anime/Images, 33-34
  National Chung Cheung University ¦ miscellanies ¦ Japanese Anim Picture, 33-34
  rec.arts.animation, 33-34
  rec.arts.anime, 33-34
  rec.arts.anime.info, 33-34
  rec.arts.anime.marketplace, 33-34
  rec.arts.anime.stories, 33-34
antiques, *rec.antiques*, 34-35
APK-Public Access UNI*Site, 279
ARC archive standard, 18
arcana arcanorum, 35-36
  ftp.spies.com:/Library/Documents/arcana.doc, 35-36
archery, *alt.archery*, 37-40
Archie, 11, 19
  CompuServe, 280-281
  Windows Internet and WinSock, 269, 272-273, **272**, 276
  WSARCHIE, 272
archived files, FTP sites, 18-19
  ARC archive standard, 18
  executable software, compatibility with your system, 19
  filenames and unarchiving, 19
  GZIP archive standard, 19
  SIT archive standard, 18
  TAR.Z archive standard, 19
  ZIP archive standard, 18
Ariadne, 277
art
  animation, 33-34
  body piercing, 56-57
  crafts, 95
  erotic pictures, 122-123
  japanimation, 34
  origami, 182-183
  photography, 194-195
  science fiction, 217-220

Society for Creative Anachronism, 223-225
audio systems, 40-41
　rec.audio, 40-41
　rec.audio.high-end, 40-41
Australian and Overseas Telecommunications Corporation, 151
automotive interest, cars, 65-66

B

Babylon 5, 43, 97, 218-220
bagpipes, 44-45
　bagpipes-request@cs.dartmouth.edu, 44
　bagpipes@cs.dartmouth.edu, 44
　cs.dartmouth.edu:/pub/bagpipes, 44
　Dartmouth Colleg cs:dartmouth.edu ¦ Bagpipe Archives, 44
bandwidth as restriction to improper use, 4
Barlow, John, 113, 114-115
bass playing, 46
　alt.guitar.bass, 46
　rec.music.makers.bass, 46
beer, 47-50
　alt.beer, 47-50
　home brewing, 143-144
Beowulf, 31-33
bicycles, *rec.bicycles.marketplace*, 50
Bierce, Ambrose G., 103
Big Book of Mischief, 51
　ftp.spies.com:/Library/Untech/tbbom13.txt, 51
　Wiretap Online Library ¦ Questionables ¦ The Big Book of Mischief v1.3, 51
binary files (see also pictures), 10-11
　formats used, 11-12
　GIF format, 11
　JPEG format, 11
　text editor to edit uuencoded text, 11
　uudecoding for binary files/pictures, 10-11
bionet newsgroups, 8
birds, 52-53
　rtfm.mit.edu:/pub/usenet/news.answers/pets-birds-faq/, 52-53
bit newsgroups, 8
biz newsgroups, 8
bizarre newsgroup, *talk.bizarre*, 53-55
Blackadder, 62

body piercing, *rec.arts.bodyart*, 56-57
Bohemian Rhapsody, song, 23
bombs, Big Book of Mischief, 51
bonsai, *alt.bonsai*, 57-59
Book Stacks Unlimited, *books.com*, 19-20
BOOKFILE.TXT, Conspiracies FTP site, 94
books and literature
　Anglo-Saxon literature, 31-33
　Beowulf, 31-33
　Books at Wiretap, 59-61
　books, Telnet site, 59
　books.com, 59
　Carroll, Lewis, 158-159
　Dead Sea Scrolls, 99-100
　Devil's Dictionary, 103-104
　electronic newsstand, 116
　erotic literature, 119-121
　Fanny Hill, 131
　ftp.spies.com:/Library/, 59-61
　Library of Congress, 160-161
　Project Gutenberg, 61
　quotations, 201-204
　science fiction, 217-220
　Tennyson, 237-238
　Undiscovered Country, The, 245
　Wiretap Online Library, 251-253
　Wiretap Online Library ¦ Electronic Books at Wiretap, 59-61
　zines, 257-258
Books at Wiretap, 59-61
Boys of the Lough, musical group, 45
brewing (see distilling and brewing)
British comedy, 62
　alt.comedy.british, 62
　dixie.aiss.uiuc.edu:/pub/cathouse/humor/british.humor, 62
bulletin boards, 1
　newsgroups vs., 7
　organization, 1
　rules and regulations, 1
　system operators, 1, 4
buy and sell, 63-64
　Internet Mall, 147-148
　misc.forsale, 63-64

C

caffeine, *alt.drugs.caffeine*, 65
calendar, Events of the Day, 124-126
CAPCON Library Network, 277
Carroll, Lewis, 158-159
　nic.funet.fi/pub/doc/literary/etext/carroll, 158-159

cars newsgroup, *rec.autos*, 65-66
Carthy, Martin, 70
cathouse archives,
    cathouse.org:/pub/cathouse/,
    67-68
cats, 69-70
  rec.pets.cats, 69-70
  *rtfm.mit.edu:/pub/usenet/news.
    answers/cats-faq/*, 69-70
cd command (Unix), 16, 17
Cello, 267, **268**, **269**, 274
  Windows Internet and WinSock,
    276
Celtic music, *rec.music.celtic*, 70
Cherish the Ladies, musical group,
    70
Church of the SubGenius, *alt.slack*,
    71-73
CIA World Factbook, 75
  *Internet Wiretap Online Library ¦
    Electronic Books ¦
    CIA World Factbook*, 75
clari newsgroups, 8
Clarion Corporation, 8
classical music, *rec.music.classical*,
    76-78
classified advertising (see buy and
    sell; personal ads)
Cleland, John, 131
Clinton jokes, 79
Clipper, *alt.privacy.clipper*, 80-82
CNS, Inc. Gopher, 162
Coca-Cola, 82-85
  alt.food.cocacola, 82-85
  *ftp.spies.com/Library/Article/
    Food/newcoke.txt*, 82-85
  *wiretap.spies.com ¦ WOL ¦ Articles ¦
    Food&Drink ¦ LaszloNibble:
    TheNewCoke*, 82
coffee house,
  alt.pub.coffeehouse.amethyst,
    85-87
Coke servers, 87-89
  *colonsay.dcs.ed.ac.uk:/pub/jhb/
    silly/cokemachine*, 87-89
Colorado SuperNet Inc., 278
commercial online services, 259-260
  America Online, 97, 259, 281-288,
    282, **283**, **284**, **285**, **286**, **287**
  CompuServe, 1-3, 22, 259, 280-281
  cost of service, 259
  Delphi, 259, 288-291

Communications Accessibles
    Montreal, 277Community News
    Service, 278
comp newsgroups, 8
compact discs, 89
  199.35.15.2 (The CD Connection),
    89
  cdconnection.com, 89
  New CD Releases, 89
  new-releases-request@cs.uwp.edu, 89
  rec.music.cd, 89
complaints, 90-91
compressed files, FTP sites,
  (see archived files)
CompuServe, 1-3, 22, 259, 280-281
  commands, 3
  forums, 1-2
  messages, 3
  organization, 1-2
  prompts, 3
  rules and regulations, 1-2
CONCERT-CONNECT, 278
Concerts on the Road, 91-92
  *CNS,Inc. ¦
    ENTER THE CNS GOPHER ¦
    Entertainment ¦
    Concerts on the Road*, 91
condoms, 93
  *.dixie.aiss.uiuc.edu:/pub/cathouse/
    humor/sex/a.girls.guide.to.
    condoms*, 93
ConflictNet, 278
connect.com.au pty ltd, 278
connecting to Internet, 259-260
  AccessPoint, 260-265, **260**, **261**,
    262, **263**, **264**, **265**
  America Online, 281-288, **282**,
    283, **284**, **285**, **286**, **287**
  Cello, 267, **268**, **269**
  commercial online services,
    259-260, 259
  CompuServe, 280-281
  cost of service, 259
  DEC VT-100 terminals/terminal
    emulation, 263-265
  dedicated Internet providers,
    260-265
  Delphi, 288-291
  modems, 265
  providers list, 277-279
  terminal emulation,
    non-DEC VT-100 terminals,
    263-265

Unix vs. non-Unix machines, 265
UUnorth, 260, 266
Windows Internet and WinSock, 266-277
World Wide Web (WWW), 265
conspiracies, 93-94
  ftp.spies.com:/Library/Fringe/ Conspiry/, 93
conversational groups
  bizarre, 53-55
  coffee house, 85-87
  devilbunnies, 101-102
  discordia, 105-106
  pave the Earth, 188-190
  rumors, 209-211
  Spam, 226-227
  tasteless, 234-235
  Undiscovered Country, The, 245
Cooperative Library Agency for Systems and Services, 277
copyrighted materials, 12
cost of Internet service, 259
Coucher, Mimi, 93
CR Laboratories Dialup Internet Access, 278
crafts, 95
  origami, 182-183
  rec.crafts.misc, 95
crime, Big Book of Mischief, 51
Crowley FTP site, 95-96
  slopoke.mlb.semi.harris.com:/ pub/magick/magick/Crowley, 95-96
Crowley, Aleister, 95-96, 169-170
Crude Texican Lexicon, The, 238
CTS Network Services (CTSNET), 278
Curry, Adam, 96
cybersleaze, 96-97
  adam@mtv.com, 96-97
  hotlist@mtv.com, 96-97
  MTV | sleaze, 96-97
  mtv.com:/pub/sleaze, 96-97
Cyberspace Station, 278
Cynic's Word Book, The, 103

D

Dead Sea Scrolls, 99-100
  ftp.loc.gov:/pub/exhibit.images/ deadsea.scrolls.exhibit, 99
DEC VT-100 terminal emulation, 263-265
dedicated Internet providers, 260-265
  list, 277-279

Defense Department, U.S., 2
Delphi, 259, 288-291
Demon Internet Systems (DIS), 278
Destroy the Earth,
  alt.destroy.the.earth, 100-101
Devil's Dictionary, 103-104
  ftp.std.com:/obi/Ambrose.Bierce/ The.Devils.Dict.Z, 103
Devilbunnies, *alt.devilbunnies*, 101-102
DIAL n' CERF, 278
Dialin' Terminal, 278
Dialin' Tiger, 278
directories and subdirectories, FTP sites, 15-16, 17
  change directories, cd command, 17
  downloading files, 17
  fetching files to your computer, 17
  INDEX file, contents/description of files, 17
  paths through subdirectories, 17
  public (/pub) subdirectories, 17
  README file, contents/description of files, 17
  root directory, 17
Direct Connection, The, 278
discographies, 105
  ftp.spies.com:/Library/Music/Disc, 105
discordia, *alt.discordia*, 105-106
distilling and brewing
  alcohol making, 29-30
  beer, 47-50
  home brewing, 143-144
  wine, 249-250
divination, arcana arcanorum, 35-36
Dodgson, Charles Lutwidge (*see* Carroll, Lewis)
dogs, 107-108
  rec.pets.dogs, 107-108
  rtfm.mit.edu:/pub/usenet/ news.answers/dogs-faq/, 107-108
downloading files from FTP sites, 17
drinks FTP site, 108
  ocf.Berkeley.EDU:/typhoon/usr/ local/ftp/pub/Library/Recreation/, 108
drugs (see also health and medicine), 109-110
  alt.drugs, 109-110

ftp.spies.com:/Library/Fringe/Pharm/, 109-110

E

e-mail, 3, 8, 12-15
  addresses, 13
  America Online, 283, 285
  boldface, 13
  CompuServe, 280-281
  Delphi, 291
  Eudora, 273
  editing/generation software, 13
  italics, 13
  libelous communications, 14
  mailing list postings, 15
  Pine mail reader, 265
  Presidential e-mail, 78
  privacy of communications, 14
  shouting, uppercasing, 13
  speed of delivery/response, 13-14
  text special effects, 13
  underscoring, 13
  unreadable mail, foreign text formats, 15
  Windows Internet and WinSock, 269, 273, **273**
early music, *rec.music.early*, 111-113
EcoNet, 278
economic issues, CIA World Factbook, 75
Electronic Frontier Foundation, 113-115
  ftp.eff.org:/pub/EFF/, 113-115
electronic newsstand, 116
emulation, non-DEC VT-100 terminals, 263-265
encryption, Clipper, 80-82
end-of-file markers, FTP sites, 18
environment, CIA World Factbook, 75
Enya, *alt.music.enya*, 116
equestrians, *rec.equestrian*, 117-118
erotic pictures, 122-123
erotica (see also sex talk group)
  alt.binaries.pictures.erotica, 122
  alt.binaries.pictures.erotica.blondes, 122
  alt.binaries.pictures.erotica.d, 122
  alt.binaries.pictures.erotica.female, 122
  alt.binaries.pictures.erotica.male, 122
  alt.binaries.pictures.erotica.orientals, 122
  alt.pantyhose, 119-121
  alt.sex, 119-121
  alt.sex.pictures, 122
  alt.sex.pictures.d, 122
  alt.sex.pictures.female, 122
  alt.sex.pictures.male, 122-123
  alt.sex.stories, 119-121
  body piercing, 56-57
  condoms, 93
  Crowley, 95-96
  erotic literature, 119-121
  erotic pictures, 122-123
  Fanny Hill, 131
  Kama Sutra, 233-234
  limericks, 163-164
  magic, 169-172
  rec.arts.erotica, 119-121
  sex talk, 220-223
  tantra, 233-234
  tasteless, 234-235
  Undiscovered Country, The, 245
  Wiretap Online Library | Articles | Sex, 119-121
  Yellow Silk Magazine, 119-121
Eskimo North, 278
Esperanto, 123-124
  esperanto-request@rand.org, 123
  esperanto@rand.org, 123
  ftp.spies.com:/Library/Article/Language/esperant.english, 123
  Wiretap Online Library | Articles | Language | Esperanto English Dictionary, 123
espionage
  AIDS-WAR.TXT, Conspiracies FTP site, 94
  BOOKFILE.TXT, Conspiracies FTP site, 94
  Clipper, 80-82
  conspiracies, 93-94
  OPAL.TXT, Conspiracies FTP site, 94
  STARWARS.RUS, Conspiracies FTP site, 94
Eudora, 273
  Windows Internet and WinSock, 276
eunet newsgroups, 8
Events of the Day, 124-126
  copy@oddjob.uchicago.edu, 124-126
evil newsgroup, *alt.evil*, 126-127
executable software, compatibility with your system, 19

Express Access, 278
extremists and activists
  alt.activism, 128-130
  alt.feminism, 128-130
  alt.religion.christian, 128-130
  alt.skinheads, 128-130

F

Fairport Convention, musical group, 70
Fanny Hill, 131
  nic.funet.fi:/pub/doc/literary/etext/fannyhill.txt.gz, 131
FAQ (*see* frequently asked questions)
file formats for pictures, 11-12
file transfer protocol (*see* FTP sites)
file processing, FTP sites, 15
  archived, 18-19
  compressed (*see* archived files)
  end-of-file markers, 18
  executable software, compatibility with your system, 19
  text files, 18
Finger sites, 21-22
  America Online, 283
  cybersleaze, 96-97
  Events of the Day, 124-126
  Internet Mall, 147-148
  notation, 21
flames, flaming, 8, 90-91
  alt.flame newsgroup, 8
flying saucers, 132-133
  alt.alien.visitors, 132
  ftp.spies.com:/Library/Fringe/Ufo, 132
folklore
  cathouse archives, 67-68
  flying saucers, 132-133
  herbs, 142-143
  Society for Creative Anachronism, 223-225
food and drink, 133-134
  wine, 249-250
  Zima, 256-257
  Albert Einstein College of Medicine | Internet Resources | Miscellaneous | Search the Food Recipe Databank, 134
  alcohol making, 29-30
  alt.food, 133
  beer, 47-50
  Coca-Cola, 82-85
  Coke servers, 87-89
  drinks, 108

ftp.neosoft.com:/pub/rec.food.recipes/site, 133
gatekeeper.dec.com:/pub/recipes, 133
herbs, 142-143
home brewing, 143-144
Internet Wiretap Online Library | Articles | Food and Drink, 134
McDonald's, 172-173
pig roast, 181-182
rec.food.cooking, 133
rec.food.drink, 133
rec.food.historic, 133
rec.food.recipes, 133
rec.food.restaurants, 133
rec.food.sourdough, 133
rec.food.veg, 133
recipe collection, 133-134
Spam, 226-227
formats, file formats for pictures, 11-12
fortune-telling (*see* divination; occult)
forums, 1
Four Seasons, The, 76
freemasonry, illuminati, 145-146
frequently asked questions (FAQ), 7
FTP sites, 7, 9, 12, 15-19
  accessing FTP sites, problems with access, 18
  acoustic guitar music, 23-24
  acronyms, 25-26
  airlines, 26-28
  alcohol making, 29-30
  America Online, 283
  Anglo-Saxon literature, 31-33
  animation, 33
  arcana arcanorum, 35-36
  Archie, 19
  archived files, 18-19
  bagpipes, 44-45
  Big Book of Mischief, 51
  birds, 52-53
  Books at Wiretap, 59-61
  British comedy, 62
  case sensitivity of commands/filenames, 16, 17
  cathouse archives, 15-16, 67-68
  cathouse.org:/pub/cathouse/, 15-16, 67-68
  cats, 69-70
  cd command (Unix), 16, 17
  change directories, cd command, 17

Clinton jokes, 79
Coca-Cola, 82-85
Coke servers, 87-89
commands in Unix, 16-17
compressed files (see archived files)
CompuServe, 280-281
condoms, 93
conspiracies, 93-94
Crowley, 95-96
cybersleaze, 96-97
Dead Sea Scrolls, 99-100
Devil's Dictionary, 103-104
discographies, 105
disk structure of FTP sites, 17
dogs, 107-108
downloading files, 17
drinks, 108
drugs, 109-110
Electronic Frontier Foundation, 113-115
end-of-file markers, 18
Esperanto, 123-124
executable software, compatibility with your system, 19
Fanny Hill, 131
fetching files to your computer, 17
filenames, 16, 17
files, 15
text files, 18
flying saucers, 132-133
ftp.spies.com, 18
ftp.uu.net/networking/news/config/, 9
ftp.uwp.edu, 15
get command (Unix), 16, 17
Gopher server vs., 20-21
Grateful Dead, 136-137
home brewing, 143-144
INDEX file, contents/description of files, 17
Internet Mall, 147-148
Internet providers list, 277
Japan, 149-151
Letterman, 157
Lewis Carroll, 158-159
limericks, 163-164
ls command (Unix), 16
lute music, 165-167
Monty Python's Flying Circus, 174-175
Murphy's Laws, 178-179
notation used, 15
oculis exciditis porcus dimidius facti (see pig roast)

open command (Unix), 18
opening new connection to FTP sites, 18
origami, 182-183
page command (Unix), 16, 17
problems with page command use, 18
paths through subdirectories, 17
pig roast, 181-182
political correctness, 197-198
Project Gutenberg, 61
public (/pub) subdirectories, 17
quit command (Unix), 16, 18
quotations, 201-204
ramses.cs.cornell.edu, 16
raves, 205
README file, contents/description of files, 17
recipe collection, 133-134
Red Dwarf, 206-208
root directory, 17
song lyrics, 225-226
Star Trek, 228-231
subdirectories, 15-16, 17
tantra, 233-234
Tennyson, 237-238
terminating connection, 18
Undiscovered Country, The, 245
Unix operating system, 16-17
Wicca, 248
Windows Internet and WinSock, 269, 271-272, **271**, 276

G

G.Gordon Liddy, 135-136
Garcia, Jerry, 24
games, trivia, 243
gardening (see horticulture)
Gehlhaar, Jeff, 273
genesis MCSNet, 278
get command (Unix), 16, 17
GIF format, 11
Girl's Guide to Condoms, A, 93
GlasNet server, 242
Gopher sites, 12, 20-21
  access, access problems, 20
  airlines, 26-28
  alcohol making, 29-30
  America Online, 283, 286, **286**, **287**
  animation, 33
  bagpipes, 44-45
  Big Book of Mischief, 51
  Books at Wiretap, 59-61

CIA World Factbook, 75
CNS, Inc., 162
Coca-Cola , 82-85
Concerts on the Road, 91-92
cybersleaze, 96-97
database structure of Gopher, 20
Delphi, 291
Electronic Frontier Foundation, 113-115
electronic newsstand, 116
erotic literature, 119-121
Esperanto, 123-124
files, 21
food and drink, 134
FTP sites vs., 20-21
GlasNet server, 242
Grateful Dead, 136-137
lute music, 165-167
menu structure, 20, 21
Nielsen ratings, 235-237
notation used, 21
Project Gutenberg, 61
satanism, 213-215
searchable databases, ? notation, 21
searching for files with Gopher, 21
Star Trek, 228-231
tantra, 233-234
tasteless, 234-235
Texas slang, 238-239
travel advisory, 240-242
University of Hong Kong, 270
University of Minnesota origination site, 20, 270
weather, 247-248
Windows Internet and WinSock, 269, 270-271, **270**, 276
Wiretap Online Library, 20, 21, 251-253
Graham, Bill, 174
Graphic Workshop image file software, 12
graphical user interfaces (GUI), 5
Grateful Dead, 105, 113, 136-137
 gdead.berkeley.edu:/pub/gdead, 136
 rec.music.gdead, 136
 University of California Berkeley, 136
Grebyn Corporation, 278
guitar music
 acoustic, 23-24
 bass playing, 46
Gummere, Francis B., 32

guns, 137-140
 rec.guns, 137-140
 talk.politics.guns, 137-140
Gutenberg (see Project Gutenberg)
GZIP archive standard, 19

H

Halcyon, 278
Hart, Michael, 61
health and medicine
 AIDS-WAR.TXT, Conspiracies FTP site, 94
 alternative medicine, 30-31
 caffeine, 65
 condoms, 93
 drugs, 109-110
 herbs, 142-143
Heimbaugh, Jason R., 67
heraldry, rec.heraldry, 141
herbs, *rec.folklore.herbs*, 142-143
history
 Dead Sea Scrolls, 99-100
 drugs, 109-110
 Events of the Day, 124-126
 G.Gordon Liddy, 135-136
 heraldry, 141
 herbs, 142-143
 Japan, 149-151
 Society for Creative Anachronism, 223-225
Hofmann, Albert, 109
HoloNet, 278
home brewing
 homebrew-request@hpfcmi.fc.hp.com, 143-144
 homebrew@hpfcmi.fc.hp.com, 143-144
 mthvax.cs.miami.edu:/pub/homebrew/, 143-144
 nic.funet.fi:/pub/culture/beer/, 143-144
 rec.crafts.brewing, 143-144
HomeoNet, 278
Hoover, J. Edgar, 94
horticulture
 bonsai, 57-59
 herbs, 142-143
humor (see also political/political humor)
 British comedy, 62
 cathouse archives, 67-68
 Church of the SubGenius, 71-73
 limericks, 163-164

Monty Python's Flying Circus, 174-175
Murphy's Laws, 178-179
pave the Earth, 188-190
political correctness, 197-198
Red Dwarf, 206-208
rumors, 209-211
Texas slang, 238-239
Undiscovered Country, The, 245

I

IDS World Network, 278
IGC Networks, 278
illuminati, 145-146
INDEX file, contents/description of files in FTP sites, 17
info newsgroups, 8
Institute for Global Communications, 278
Intel, 265
interfaces, 5-6
  graphical user interfaces (GUI), 5
  text-based, 5
Internet
  accessing Internet, 5-6
  adult-only material, 12
  Archie, 11, 19
  archived files, 18-19
  bandwidth as restriction to improper use, 4
  binary files, 10-11
  Cello, 267, **268**, **269**, 274
  connecting to Internet (see connecting to Internet)
  copyrighted materials, 12
  dummy sites and Finger function, 21
  e-mail, 3, 8, 12-15
  enforcing good behavior, 4-5
  Finger function, 21-22
  flames, flaming, 8
  formats used for pictures, 11-12
  frequently asked questions (FAQ), 7
  FTP sites, 7, 9, 12, 15-19
  GIF format, pictures, 11
  Gopher server, 12, 20-21
  history and development, 1-3
  interfacing with Internet, 5-6
  JPEG format, pictures, 11
  libelous communications, 14
  limited access to newsgroups, 8-9
  lurkers, lurking, 9
  mailing list postings, 15

  National Science Foundation Network use, 3
  netiquette, 4-5
  newsgroups (*see* newsgroups)
  organization, 1-3
  pictures, 10-12
    copyrighted materials, 12
    GIF format, 11
    JPEG format, 11
  postings, 6-7
  privacy of communications, 14
  protocols, 3, 5
  rules and regulations, 1, 4-5, 12
  "subscribing" to newsgroups, 6
  Telnet systems, 19-20
  text editor to edit uuencoded text, 11
  threaded postings, 6-7
  U.S. Department of Defense development, 2
  Usenet (*see* newsgroups)
  uudecoding for binary files/pictures, 10-11
  World Wide Web (WWW), 265
Internet Mall, 147-148
  ftp.netcom.com:/pub/Guides/, 146
  taylor@netcom.com, 146
Ishihara, Shintaro, 150

J

Japan, 149-151
  f.ms.uky.edu:/pub3/mailing.lists/ japan/japanno.Z, 149
  f.ms.uky.edu:/pub3/mailing.lists/ japan/japanyes.reply.Z, 149
  f.ms.uky.edu:/pub3/mailing.lists/ japan/japanyes.Z, 149
  ftp.spies.com:/Library/Article/ Language/grammar.jap, 149
  ucslex.sdsu.edu:/pub/doc/etext/ japan-than-can-say-no.txt, 149
japanimation, 34
jazz, *rec.music.bluenote*, 152
Jennings, Andrew, 151
Jethro Tull, 225
John von Neumann Computer Network, 278
JPEG format, 11
juggling, *rec.juggling*, 153-154

K

Kama Sutra, 233-234
Kapor, Mitchell, 113
Kennedy, John F., 94
Kiernan, Kevin, 32

L

LaborNet, 278
language
  acronyms, 25-26
  Esperanto, 123-124
  Japan, 149-151
  quotations, 201-204
  Texas slang, 238-239
laser discs, *alt.video.laserdisc*, 155-157
law, Electronic Frontier Foundation, 113-115
Leclerc, Louis, 150
Letterman, 157
  alt.fan.letterman, 157
  listproc@mot.com, 157
  quartz.rutgers.edu:/pub/tv+movies/ letterman, 157
Lewis Carroll (*see* Carroll, Lewis)
libelous communications, 14
Library of Congress, *locis.loc.gov*, 160-161
limericks, 163-164
  ftp.netcom.com:/pub/jvasquez/ dirty.limericks, 163-164
  ftp.quartz.rutgers.edu:/pub/ humor/limericks, 163-164
literature (*see* books and literature)
Lotus Development Corporation, 113
ls command (Unix), 16
lurkers, lurking, 9
lute music, 165-167
  cs.dartmouth.edu ¦ Lute Files, 165-167
  cs.dartmouth.edu:/pub/lute/, 165-167
  lute-request@cs.dartmouth.edu, 165-167
  lute@cs.dartmouth.edu, 165-167

M

magazines
  electronic newsstand, 116
  Undiscovered Country, The, 245
  zines, 257-258
magic group (*see also* occult), 169-172
  alt.magick, 169-172
  alt.magick.sex, 169-172
mailing lists, 15
  adding your name, 15
  America Online, 283
  bagpipes, 44-45

compact discs (New CD Releases), 89
  Esperanto, 123-124
  home brewing, 143-144
  lute music, 165-167
  origami, 182-183
Mall (*see* Internet Mall)
McDonald's, *alt.food.mcdonalds*, 172-173
McGoohan, Patrick, 199
McKennitt, Loreena, 237
medicine (*see* health and medicine)
Merit Network Inc., 279
Meta Network, 279
MichNet, 279
MindVOX, 279
misc newsgroups, 8
Monty Python's Flying Circus, 62, 174-175
  bigbang-ether.berkeley.edu:, 174
  maelstrom-ether.berkeley.edu:, 174
  monsoon-ether.berkeley.edu:, 174
  tsunami-ether.berkeley.edu:, 174
modems, 265
Morita, Akio, 150
Morton, Skip, 69
Mother Jones, 162
movies, 175-177
  cathouse archives, 67-68
  laser discs, 155-157
  rec.arts.movies, 175-177
  Rocky Horror Picture Show, 208-209
  science fiction, 217-220
Murdoch, Rupert, 94
Murphy's Laws, 178-179
  dixie.aiss.uiuc.edu:/pub/cathouse/ humor/murphys.laws/, 178
music
  a capella music, 23
  acoustic guitar music, 23-24
  audio systems, 40-41
  bagpipes, 44-45
  bass playing, 46
  cathouse archives, 67-68
  Celtic music, 70
  classical music, 76-78
  compact discs, 89
  Concerts on the Road, 91-92
  cybersleaze, 96-97
  discographies, 105
  early music, 111-113
  Enya, 116

Grateful Dead, 136-137
jazz, 152
lute music, 165-167
pirate radio, 196-197
raves, 205
song lyrics, 225-226

N

National Science Foundation Network, 3
NeoSoft Sugar Land Unix, 279
netiquette, 4-5
news newsgroups, 8
newsgroups, 6-11
   a capella music, 23
   access to newsgroups, limited by Internet site, 8-9
   acoustic guitar music, 23-24, 23
   adult-only material, 12
   airlines , 26-28
   "alt" designation explained, 74
   alt newsgroups, 8
   alt.alt.alt.alt.alt, 74
   alt.answers, 97
   alt.devilbunnies, 9, 74
   alt.flame, 8, 90-91
   alt.slack, 74
   alternative medicine (*misc.health.alternative*), 30-31
   America Online, 283
   animation, 33-34
   antiques, 34-35
   archery, 37-40
   Archie, 11
   audio systems, 40-41
   Babylon 5, 43, 97
   bass playing, 46
   beer, 47-50
   bicycles, 50
   binary files, 10-11
   bionet newsgroups, 8
   bit newsgroups, 8
   biz newsgroups, 8
   bizarre, 53-55
   body piercing, 56-57
   bonsai, 57-59
   British comedy, 62
   bulletin boards vs. newsgroups, 7
   buy and sell, 63-64
   caffeine, 65
   cars, 65-66
   cats, 69-70
   Celtic music, 70
   changing nature of newsgroup organization, 9
   Church of the SubGenius, 71-73
   clari newsgroups, 8
   classical music, 76-78
   classification and organization, 8
   Clipper, 80
   Coca-Cola, 82-85
   coffee house, 85-87
   comp newsgroups, 8
   compact discs, 89
   complaints, 90-91
   copyrighted materials, 12
   crafts, 95
   Delphi, 289, 291
   Destroy the Earth, 100-101
   Devilbunnies, 101-102
   discordia, 105-106
   dogs, 107-108
   dotted hierarchical notation organization, 8
   drugs, 109-110
   e-mail for semi-private correspondence, 8, 12-15
   early music, 111-113
   Enya, 116
   equestrians, 117-118
   erotic literature, 119-121
   erotic pictures, 122-123
   eunet newsgroups, 8
   evil, 126-127
   extremists and activists, 128-130
   flames, flaming, 8, 90-91
   flying saucers, 132-133
   food and drink, 133-134
   formats used for pictures, 11-12
   frequently asked questions (FAQ), 7
   FTP sites (see also), 7, 9, 12, 15-19
   G.Gordon Liddy, 135-136
   GIF format for pictures, 11
   Gopher servers, 12
   Grateful Dead, 136-137
   guns, 137-140
   heraldry, 141
   herbs, 142-143
   home brewing, 143-144
   illuminati, 145-146
   info newsgroups, 8
   jazz, 152
   JPEG format for pictures, 11
   juggling, 153-154
   laser discs, 155-157

Letterman, 157
libelous communications, 14
lurkers, lurking, 9
magic, 169-172
mailing list postings, 15
McDonald's, 172-173
misc newsgroups, 8
movies, 175-177
news newsgroups, 8
pagans, 185-187
pave the Earth, 188-190
personal ads, 190-193
photography, 194-195
pictures, 10-12
pirate radio, 196-197
postings, 6-7
privacy of communications, 14
raves, 205
rec newsgroups, 8
rec.antiques, 9
Red Dwarf, 206-208
relcom newsgroups, 8
restricted, illegal access, 8-9
Rocky Horror Picture Show, 208-209
rules and regulations, 12
rumors, 209-211
satanism, 213-215
satellite television, 215-216
sci newsgroups, 8
science fiction, 217-220
sex talk, 220-223
skydiving, 154
soc newsgroups, 8
Society for Creative Anachronism, 223-225
Spam, 226-227
Star Trek, 228-231
"subscribing" to newsgroups, 6
talk newsgroups, 8
tasteless, 234-235
text editor to edit uuencoded text, 11
The Prisoner, 199-200
threaded postings, 6-7
trivia, 243
unreadable mail, foreign text formats, 15
Usenet definition, 6
uudecoding for binary files/pictures, 10-11
Windows Internet and WinSock, 269, 274, **275**, **276**

wine, 249-250
Zen, 255
Zima, 256-257
zines, 257-258
Nielsen ratings, 235-237
  CNS Inc ¦ ENTER THE CNS GOPHER ¦ Entertainment ¦ Nielsen TV ratings, 235
NiftyServe network, 15
Nursie, song, 24

O

101 Uses for a Dead Cat, 69
O'Leary, Christy, 45
occult
  arcana arcanorum, 35-36
  Crowley, 95-96
  Devil's Dictionary, 103-104
  evil newsgroup, 126-127
  illuminati, 145-146
  magic, 169-172
  pagan, 185-187
  satanism, 213-215
  Watcher, The, 213-215
  Wicca, 248
oculis exciditis porcus dimidius facti (*see* pig roast)
OPAL.TXT, Conspiracies FTP site, 94
open command (Unix), 18
origami, 182-183
  origami-l-request@nstn.ns.ca, 182-183
  origami-l@nstn.ns.ca, 182-183
  rugcis.rug.nl:/origami/, 182-183

P

pagans, *alt.pagan*, 185-187
page command (Unix), 16, 17
  problems with using page command, 18
parties, raves, 205
paths through subdirectories, FTP sites, 17
pave the Earth, *alt.pave.the.earth*, 188-190
PeaceNet, 278
personal ads, 190-193
  alt.personals, 190-193
  alt.personals.misc, 190-193
pets (*see* animals)
philosophy (*see* religion and philosophy)
photography, *rec.photo*, 194-195
pictures on Internet, 10-12

binary files, 10-11
content, adult graphics, 12
copyrighted materials, 12
formats used, 11-12
GIF format, 11
Graphic Workshop image file software, 12
JPEG formats, 11
rules and regulations, 12
text editor to edit uuencoded text, 11
uudecoding for binary files/pictures, 10-11
pig roast, 181-182
Pine mail reader, 265
pirate radio, *alt.radio.pirate*, 196-197
playing card Tarot (*see* arcana arcanorum)
poetry
Tennyson, 237-238
Undiscovered Country, The, 245
political correctness, 197-198
dixie.aiss.uiuc.edu:/pub/cathouse/humor/pol.correct, 197
political/political humor
AIDS-WAR.TXT, Conspiracies FTP site, 94
BOOKFILE.TXT, Conspiracies FTP site, 94
cathouse archives, 67-68
CIA World Factbook, 75
Clinton jokes, 79
conspiracies, 93-94
extremists and activists, 128-130
G.Gordon Liddy, 135-136
guns, 137-140
Japan, 149-151
OPAL.TXT, Conspiracies FTP site, 94
political correctness, 197-198
Presidential e-mail, 78
STARWARS.RUS, Conspiracies FTP site, 94
Portal System, 279
postings, 6-7
threaded, 6-7
PREPnet, 279
Presidential e-mail, 78
Prior, Maddy, 70
Prisoner, The, alt.tv.prisoner, 199-200
privacy of communications, 14
Clipper, 80-82
Problem Child, 109-110

Project Gutenberg, 61
Lewis Carroll, 158-159
protocols, 3, 5
public (/pub) subdirectories, 17
PUCnet Computer connections, 279

Q
Qualcomm, 273
Queen, musical group, 23
quit command (Unix), 16, 18
quotations, 201-204
quartz.rutgers.edu:/pub/computer/fortune/, 201

R
radio, pirate radio, 196-197
RainDrop Laboratories, 277
raves, 205
alt.rave, 205
techno.staford.edu:/pub/raves, 205
README file, contents/description of files in FTP sites, 17
rec newsgroups, 8
Red Dwarf, 62, 206-208
alt.tv.red-dwarf, 206-208
toaster.ee.ubc.ca:/pub/red-dwarf, 206-208
relcom newsgroups, 8
religion and philosophy
Church of the SubGenius, 71-73
Dead Sea Scrolls, 99-100
evil newsgroup, 126-127
extremists and activists, 128-130
illuminati, 145-146
magic, 169-172
pagan, 185-187
satanism, 213-215
Spam, 227
tantra, 233-234, 233
Watcher, The, 213-215
Wicca, 248
Zen, 255
Renbourn, John, 24
Rocky Horror Picture Show, 208-209
alt.cult-movies.rocky-horror, 208
root directory, FTP sites, 17
rules and regulations, 1, 4-5, 12
rumors, talk.rumors, 209-211
Russia, GlasNet server, 242

S
satanism, 213-215
alt.satanism, 213-215
wiretap.spies.com:/Library/Zines/Watcher, 213-215

satellite television, 215-216
  Babylon 5 newsgroup, 43, 97, 218-220
  rec.video.satellite, 215-216
sci newsgroups, 8
science
  flying saucers, 132-133
  science fiction, 217-220
  weather, 247-248
science fiction
  Babylon 5, 43, 97
  rec.arts.sf.announce, 217-220
  rec.arts.sf.fandom, 217-220
  rec.arts.sf.marketplace, 217-220
  rec.arts.sf.misc, 217-220
  rec.arts.sf.movies, 217-220
  rec.arts.sf.reviews, 217-220
  rec.arts.sf.science, 217-220
  rec.arts.sf.starwars, 217-220
  rec.arts.sf.tv, 217-220
  rec.arts.sf.written, 217-220
  Star Trek, 228-231
sex (*see* erotica)
sex talk groups
  alt.sex, 220-223
  alt.sex.bestiality, 220-223
  alt.sex.bestiality.barney, 220-223
  alt.sex.bondage, 220-223
  alt.sex.bondage.partilce.physics, 222
  alt.sex.exhibitionism, 220-223
  alt.sex.fetish.fat, 222
  alt.sex.fetish.feet, 222
  alt.sex.fetish.orientals, 220-223
  alt.sex.masturbation, 222
  alt.sex.movies, 220-223
  alt.sex.sounds, 220-223
  alt.sex.spanking, 220-223
  alt.sex.stories, 220-223
  alt.sex.stories.d, 220-223
  alt.sex.voyeurism, 222
  alt.sex.wanted, 220-223
  alt.sex.watersports, 222
  alt.sex.wizards, 220-223
Silly Wizard, musical group, 70
Simpson, O.J., 129
SIT archive standard, 18
skydiving, *rec.skydiving*, 154
soc newsgroups, 8
Society for Creative Anachronism, *rec.org.sca*, 223-225
song lyrics, 225-226
  ftp.sunet.se:/pub/music/lyrics, 225
  ftp.uwp.edu:/pub/music/lyrics, 225

Sony, 150
Spam, *alt.spam*, 226-227
spies (*see* espionage)
sports
  archery, 37-40
  bicycles, 50
  equestrians, 117-118
  guns, 137-140
  juggling, 153-154
  skydiving, 154
Star Trek, 228-231
  alt.fan.q, 228
  alt.startrek.creative, 228
  alt.wesley.crusher.die.die.die, 228
  CNS Inc ¦ ENTER THE CNS GOPHEREntert ¦ StarTrek-The Library, 228
  ftp.uu.net:/doc/literary/obi/Star.Trek.Parodies, 228
  ftp.uu.net:/doc/literary/obi/Star.Trek.Stories, 228
  rec.arts.startrek.current, 228
  rec.arts.startrek.info, 228
STARWARS.RUS, Conspiracies FTP site, 94
Steiny, Don, 109
Straczynski, Joe, 218
StuffIt archive standard, 18
subdirectories, FTP sites (*see* directories and subdirectories)
subscription sites for mailing lists
  bagpipes, 44-45
  Esperanto, 123-124
  home brewing, 143-144
  Letterman, 157
  lute music, 165-167
  origami, 182-183
system operators, 1, 4

T

talk (*see* conversational groups)
talk newsgroups, 8
tantra, 233-234
  ftp.spies.com:/Library/Article/Sex/massage.txt, 233
  quartz.rutgers.edu-pub/sex/kama.sutra, 233-234
  Rutgers Quartz Text Archive (*quartz.rutgers.edu*) ¦ Sex ¦ *kama.sutra*, 233
  Wiretap (*wiretap.spies.com*) ¦ Articles ¦ Sex ¦ *Yoni Massage How-To*, 233
tasteless, 234-235 *alt.tasteless*, 234-235

Wiretap Online Library | Fringes of Reason | Gross and Disgusting | Alt.Tasteless, 234
TAR.Z archive standard, 19
Tarot cards (*see arcana arcanorum*)
Telerama Public Access Internet, 279
television
  Babylon 5 newsgroup, 43, 97, 218-220
  British comedy, 62
  cathouse archives, 67-68
  cybersleaze, 96-97
  Letterman, 157
  Monty Python's Flying Circus, 174-175
  Nielsen ratings, 235-237
  Red Dwarf, 206-208
  satellite television, 215-216
  science fiction, 217-220
  Star Trek, 228-231
  The Prisoner, 199-200
Telnet sites, 19-20
  accessing, 19-20
  America Online, 283
  Book Stacks Unlimited, *books.com*, 19-20
  books, 59
  CompuServe, 280-281
  help/service with problems, 20
  Library of Congress, 160-161
  menu structure, 19-20
Tennyson, 237-238
  ftp.std.com:/obi/Tennyson, 237
terminal emulation, non-DEC VT-100 terminals, 263-265
terrorism, Big Book of Mischief, 51
Texas Metronet, 279
Texas slang, 238-239
  Wiretap Online Library | Humor | Everything Else | Crude Texican Lexicon, 238
text editor to edit uuencoded text, 11
text-based interfaces, 5
threaded postings, 6-7
Tiger Mail, 278
travel, 240-242
  airlines, 26-28
  GlasNet server, 242
  Japan, 149-151
  travel advisory, 240-242

University of California-San Diego Infopath | US State Department Travel Advisories, 240
trivia, rec.games.trivia, 243
Trumpet WinSock, 269
  Windows Internet and WinSock, 276

U

UK PC User Group, 278
Undiscovered Country, The, 245
  wiretap.spies.com:/Library/Zines/Undiscov, 245
United States Department of Defense, 2
University of Hong Kong, 270
University of Minnesota origination site of Gopher, 20, 270
Unix, 16-17, 265
  case sensitivity of commands/filenames, 16, 17
  cd command, 16, 17
  commands in Unix, 16-17
  end-of-file markers, 18
  filenames, 16, 17
  get command, 16, 17
  ls command, 16
  open command, 18
  page command, 16, 17
    problems with page command use, 18
  quit command, 16, 18
uudecoding for binary files/pictures, 10-11
UUnorth, 260, 266, 279

V

Vivaldi, Antonio, 76
Vnet Internet Access Inc., 279

W

Warlocks, 105
Watcher, The, 213-215
weather, 247-248
  NOAA Environmental Information Services Gopher, 247
Whole Earth 'Lectronic Link, 279
Wicca, *nic.funet.fi:/pub/doc/occult/Wicca*, 248
Wilson, Robert Anton, 10, 145
Windows Internet and WinSock, 266-277, **267, 268, 270, 271, 272, 273, 275, 276**
  anonymous FTP, 271-272, **271**
  Archie, 269, 272-273, **272**

Cello, 266, 276
e-mail, 269, 273, **273**
Eudora, 273, 276
FTP transfers, 269, 276
Gopher, 269, 270-271, **270**, 276
newsgroups, 269, 274, **275**, **276**
software, 276-277
Trumpet WinSock, 269, 276
World Wide Web (WWW), 269, 274
wine (see also distilling and brewing), 249-250
rec.crafts.winemaking, 249
Wired, 162
Wiretap Online Library, 20, 21, 251-253
Woakes, David, 272

World Wide Web (WWW), 265
America Online, 283
Cello reader, 267, **268**, **269**, 274
Delphi, 291
Windows Internet and WinSock, 269, 274
World, The, 279
WSARCHIE, 272
Wyvern Technologies Inc., 279

Z

Zamenhof, Lazarus, 123
Zappa, Frank, 105
Zen, *alt.zen*, 255
Zima, *alt.zima*, 256-257
zines, *alt.zines*, 257-258
ZIP archive standard, 18
Zoom, 265

About the author*

Steve Rimmer lives in rural central Ontario with his wife Megan, two dogs, and a variety of unusual cars. All his neighbors are cows. He is the president of Alchemy Mindworks Inc., which is a small software company that creates graphics applications. He has written over a dozen books about computer-related topics and several novels about witchcraft and pagan magic. His computer books include *Bitmapped Graphics* and *Windows Multimedia Programming*, published by Windcrest/McGraw-Hill. His most recent works of fiction include *The Order* and *Wyccad*, published by Jam Ink Books.

His hobbies include archery and playing Celtic music with a local band.

*mostly true